TO
Two Young Dissenters
JOHN AND MARY
This book is affectionately dedicated
BY THEIR FATHER

Contents

The Story of American Dissent

Chapter I: Introduction

ONE WHO has followed the post-war movements, such as Fundamentalism and the militant triumph of the Anti-Saloon League, must be aware that among the most powerful sources of moral and spiritual energy in this country are the great dissenting-revivalistic churches, the Baptists, the Methodists, and the Presbyterians. One familiar with American history must also be aware that a little more than a century and a half ago these denominations, which now compose forty per cent of all adult church members and two-thirds of all Protestants, were despised dissenting minorities in the powerful colonies of Massachusetts and Virginia. Today the most influential of these churches owns a handsome granite building directly opposite the Capitol and hard by the marble temple that houses the Supreme Court. From this point of vantage it maintained until recently one of the most effective politico-religious lobbies in the history of that happy hunting ground of the lobbyist, the national capital. Verily, the stone which the builders of our national life rejected is become the headstone of the corner. The Baptists and Methodists, who were beaten and banished in Massachusetts, buffeted and ridiculed in Virginia, have become great conservative churches which in the prohibition controversy arrogated to themselves the right to control the conscience of the nation. How are we to explain this profound transformation?

I

The belief of the ancient Greeks that history moves in cycles seems to find a certain superficial confirmation in the story of Christianity. Inspired by Jesus' gospel of the disinherited, despised and neglected groups organize to safeguard their ideals, cultivate spiritual fellowship, and practice mutual aid. Discipline becomes necessary for the attainment of their hopes and the defense of their faith against the heavy hand of the persecutor. In time they gain numbers and a foothold in the political and economic orders. They become respectable and rich and powerful. The pride of power and affluence impels them to soften the earlier harsher faith and even to deny the radical doctrines they preached in the days of their poverty and suffering. They become secularized and given to the flesh pots of Egypt. In opposition to them arises another group of the disinherited, and the same cycle is repeated again. Christianity has never succeeded as a religion of the rich and powerful. Its material success seems to entail the negation of its life-giving principles.

This cycle is a familiar phase of the history of western Christianity. The Quakers arose in protest against the inadequacies of institutionalized Christianity in seventeenth-century England and brought to their interpretation of the teachings of Jesus a naïve and uncritical realism which made them dangerous radicals. They were bitterly persecuted both in England and New England. During the last half of the seventeenth and the first quarter of the eighteenth century, they fought a great battle for religious liberty against the intolerant New England theocracies. By the end of the century the Quakers had won for themselves a position of wealth and power in the colonies and had become "respectable." [1]

[1] For typical examples see the sketches of the highly respected and wealthy

Francis Asbury, the founder of American Methodism, the last great religious movement among the disinherited in this country, became involved in 1809 in a controversy with the Quakers and dismissed them in these contemptuous terms: "The respectable society of people called Quakers—respectable. Ah! there is death in that word." Jesus encouraged the disinherited to "rejoice and be exceeding glad" when they were reviled and persecuted. Asbury gave this a negative and anti-social turn when he said, "Woe unto you when all men shall speak well of you." His prayer was, "O Lord, save thy now despised Methodist children from the praises of the people of this world." [2] The deity, for reasons best known to himself, has seen fit not to answer Asbury's prayer and the Methodist church is today the most powerful and militantly successful Protestant organization in this country. It has ceased to be the despised religion of the disinherited of a hundred and thirty years ago and has become rich and "respectable."

The Salvation Army is a sort of *fin de siècle* attempt to revive the religion of the disinherited in a modern world in which religion no longer occupies the center of the stage. One who listens to their street harangues will be struck with the fact that their appeal to the disinherited is still based upon the revivalistic theology of Whitefield, Edwards, and the backwoods preacher rather than the teachings of Jesus—an eloquent testimonial to the extent to which the Pauline gospel of the disinherited still dominates our culture. It has remained for the liberal intelligentsia of the dissenting-revivalistic churches to rediscover Jesus' message to the disinherited based upon love.

Throughout the long history of western Christianity there existed side by side and always in conflict the complacent, in-

Quakers, William Northey and Stephen Goodhue of Salem, Massachusetts, in *Diary of William Bentley*, 1905-1914, Vol. III, pp. 93 ff. and 419 ff.
[2] Francis Asbury, *Journal*, 1809, Vol. III, p. 265.

tolerant, and secularized religion of success and power in the form of great institutionalized churches and the radical, sectarian religion of the disinherited. They repelled each other and yet they implied and even demanded each other. The Catholic church, continuing the tradition of the Middle Ages, has often sought to make a place for the religion of the disinherited within her world-wide institutional life through the monastic orders. She has wisely capitalized the spirit of dissent by offering to its leaders her far-flung and marvelously efficient organization as a means for realizing their ideals, on condition of course that these ideals do not disrupt but rather supplement her basic principles. Dissent needs institutional organization to make itself effective and the corporate life of the church needs the spirit of dissent to keep it sane and vigorous.

The tragedy of American Protestantism is that the dissenting groups have triumphed so completely that the great dissenting-revivalistic churches of today are unable to reconcile their institutional life with the original spirit of dissent to which they owe their origin. The result is that through the sheer fact of their growth and success they have come to stultify themselves and their past. The logical result of the rise of dissent within these churches is heresy, schism, and the formation of another sect. Each church as it exhausts the early spiritual enthusiasm and moral earnestness that gave it birth, in the creation of an institutional life congenial to this early enthusiasm, finds to its dismay that the precious *élan vital* of the early days is gone. It is one thing to develop a spirit of dissent and reform in opposition to intolerant secularized establishments; it is something quite different to develop a healthful and life-giving spirit of dissent within the institutional life of the church itself, especially in a community where church and state are separated. The problem, of course, is vitally affected in American democracy by the fact that ultimate social issues are now no longer approached from the point of view of religion. The dissenting tradition in the broad historic sense has become thoroughly secularized. It is our economic and political radicals rather than religious leaders who give expression to modern dissent. The religious reformer who approaches social issues from the point of view of Jesus' gospel of the disinherited is faced with the fact that the groups he wishes to aid and the community he seeks to reform no longer state their ultimate issues in terms of religion. Religion may be ancillary to social reform; it can hardly expect to direct it.

II

In the pages that follow we shall be concerned with the various factors that gave rise to the dissenting groups on American soil, the rôle they played in the struggle for religious liberty and the reasons for the passing of the dissenting tradition among those churches of dissenting-revivalistic background. The thesis maintained in the present discussion is that dissent is a highly relative term. It is always conditioned by innumerable factors, economic, social, political, and geographic. Dissent is affected by the social and economic status of the group concerned, the general pattern of culture of which it is a part, and the religious institutions and laws from which it dissents. We shall be forced, therefore, to reject the thesis maintained in a recent scholarly work that American dissent is to be traced back to Wyclif and the Lollards.[3] The dissent of Wyclif and the Lollards was not identical with the forms of dissent which arose under the Stuarts, much of which reflected the influence of the Continent. The environment of dissent in colonial Massachusetts varied in many ways from that which gave rise to dissent in

[3] T. C. Hall, *The Religious Background of American Culture*, 1930.

colonial Virginia the middle of the eighteenth century. It may be true that the general ideas, such as emphasis on the Bible, separatism, the inner freedom, and integrity of individual religious experience, lay preaching, opposition to sacramentarianism, and democratic organization are to be found more or less in all these forms of dissent. The concrete content of any given form of dissent, however, is always determined primarily by the peculiar cultural conditions under which the given form arises. Since no two cultural patterns ever duplicate each other the forms of dissent are never identical. Strict cultural continuity and identity are necessary to the persistence and identity of dissent.

Professor Hall's thesis does not take into account the fact that fundamental changes in the cultural pattern may turn conservatives into liberals, dissenters into churchmen. John Cotton, John Winthrop, John Norton, and the rest came originally from dissenting groups in England. Thanks to forces at work in colonial New England, these men became the heads of an intolerant and persecuting established church intimately blended with the state. That is to say, they passed over from the dissenting to the churchly type. The persecuted became the persecutors. The conditions that made them dissenters in England disappeared and conditions arose in the Bay colony that rendered them bitterly hostile to all forms of dissent.

Where we have cultural conditions similar to those in the past we are apt to have forms of dissent similar to those that arose under these earlier conditions; but in each case the type of dissent concerned is to be described, analyzed, and interpreted in terms of the given cultural situation and not in terms of some arbitrary assumption of permanent and unchanged dissenting tradition. No other one factor contributed more to the triumph of the dissenting-revivalistic form of Protestantism in American life than the frontier. It provided a far-flung social setting congenial to the gospel of the disinherited. It produced a "frontierized" Protestantism. In Professor Hall's scholarly work there is but one reference to the frontier. His pages do not indicate that he had familiarized himself with the considerable body of literature that treats of the influence of the frontier upon the religious life of Americans. It is a fatal mistake to try to interpret American life from the European point of view.[4]

In rejecting Professor Hall's thesis it is not necessary to assume that cultural continuity and cultural dissemination were not in evidence. They were very much in evidence. Moderate dissenting attitudes acquired in England were carried over by such leaders as John Cotton and persisted, as we shall see, in modified form even under the theocracy. The dissenting attitudes of Baptists and Quakers were not entirely the product of the immediate facts of New England society. In part they had been shaped by previous experiences in the mother-country. The habit of dissent was often transferred from the English establishment to the colonial establishments, a fact strikingly illustrated in the case of Roger Williams. But American dissent was determined primarily by American conditions and not by the European cultural background.

III

Dissent is of course the general term for all groups who fought the colonial establishments. In this sense the handful of Congregationalists in Virginia and the Episcopalians in Massachusetts and Connecticut were dissenters, for they opposed

[4] For reviews of this book see W. W. Sweet, *Journal of Religion*, 1931, p. 299. Pennington, *The Living Church*, November 22, 1930, p. 124. C. H. Grattan, *The Nation*, September 17, 1930, p. 302.

the establishments of those colonies along with the Quakers and Baptists. But neither Congregationalists nor Anglicans were opposed to the philosophy of the establishments. The Anglicans in the Puritan colonies always insisted that they alone represented the true established church. This made it difficult for them to make common cause with the Baptists and Quakers, for, unlike these radical dissenters, they did not seek to abolish all establishments but merely sought to substitute one establishment for another. We are concerned in this study primarily with those dissenting groups most active in opposing all forms of religious establishments, namely, the Quakers, the Baptists, and the Presbyterians. The Methodists appeared in Virginia as an independent church just as the fight for religious liberty was ended. Their influence was more important in the Puritan colonies towards the end of the eighteenth and the beginning of the nineteenth centuries.

Various New England sects, such as Separatists, Rogerenes, Sandemanians, and Shakers, lacked the numbers and the influence to make themselves felt to any great extent. They were often quite ephemeral in character. The Universalist movement that accompanied the rise of the Unitarians and shared its theological liberalism bore many of the earmarks of traditional dissent. From the days of the Anabaptists and earlier the doctrine of universal salvation had always found a following, especially among the sects that were mystically inclined.[5] Even prominent Episcopalians and Congregationalists were often tainted with this doctrine. Some Baptist leaders were also affected. Hell seems to have been altogether too popular with those staunch followers of John Calvin, the Presbyterians, for them ever to entertain any sympathy for Universalism. It

[5] Richard Eddy, *Universalism in America: A History*, 1884, Chap. II.

was to them a theologically weak-kneed and morally imbecile creed. An orthodox Congregationalist clergyman alluded scornfully to the spread of the new-fangled creed that sought to abolish hell and added this consolatory remark, "But, brethren, we hope for better things." The Methodist and Presbyterian pioneer revivalists with their brimstone theology made short work of Universalism, as the Reverend Peter Cartwright gleefully related on more than one occasion.[6]

Universalism could claim another tie with dissent in that it soon felt the heavy hand of the persecutor. Universalism took on organized form when four men and eleven women left the first parish church of Gloucester, Massachusetts, in 1779, under the leadership of Reverend Murray. In 1782, property of three prominent members of this organization was seized and sold at auction to pay the ministerial tax in support of the establishment. The Universalists took the matter to the courts on the ground that the Bill of Rights in the Massachusetts constitution of 1780 freed them from all such unjust levies. The courts after the customary contradictory decisions in the effort to interpret that classical example of statesmanlike wisdom and clarity, Article Three of the constitution, finally decided in 1786 that the Universalists, together with all the other sects, were entitled to the use of the ministerial tax in support of their own ministers.[7] The Universalists were a small and peace-loving group and played no large part in the fight for religious liberty. The movement usually associated with Universalism, namely, Unitarianism, cannot by any stretch of the imagination be called true dissent, for in spite of its cold-blooded liberal theology it defended the establishment to the bitter end.

[6] See Peter Cartwright, *Autobiography*, 1857.
[7] Eddy, *op. cit.*, pp. 400 ff.

To characterize adequately the cultural significance of the great dissenting groups with which we shall be mainly concerned, namely, Quakers, Baptists, Presbyterians, and Methodists, would of course require a separate treatise.[8] In the struggle for religious liberty the Quakers were the pioneers. It was due mainly to their indomitable martyr-spirit and persistence that by the end of the first quarter of the eighteenth century a measure of tolerance was enjoyed by the dissenters in New England. By the middle of the eighteenth century the Quakers had lost their militant spirit and the fight for freedom was carried on mainly by the Baptists, who after the Great Awakening rapidly increased in numbers and influence. The activity of the Presbyterians in the cause of liberty was limited principally to Virginia, where they provided an excellent buffer group between the Anglican establishment and the radical Baptists. The contribution of the Methodists to the cause of religious liberty is almost negligible. Their dissent was primarily moral rather than political. Earlier affiliations with the Anglican establishment cooled all enthusiasm for radical political dissent.

[8] The reader will find the two chapters devoted to "The Churches of the Disinherited" in H. R. Niebuhr, *The Social Sources of Denominationalism*, 1929, exceedingly suggestive. W. W. Sweet, *The Religion of the American Frontier; The Baptists*, 1931, is valuable for source material. Ernst Troeltsch, *The Social Teachings of the Christian Churches*, 1931, Vol. II, pp. 691 f., may also be consulted. A cultural history of the great dissenting churches that have played such a tremendous rôle in American life is still an historical desideratum.

Chapter II
The Sociology of Dissent

DISSENT in the comprehensive sociological sense includes all forms of religious revolt against the established churches of western Christianity. The typical form of dissent is the sect and we are concerned chiefly in this study with the conflicts between the churchly and the sectarian types of Christianity. The sect, however, does not exhaust the forms of the dissenting tradition. Dissent also manifested itself in a mystical and spiritualistic indvidualism as well as in amorphous mass movements closely connected with widespread political or social unrest. Illustrations of this latter phase of dissent are early monasticism, which was a protest against a decadent culture, and the Anabaptist movement that accompanied the rise of the Reformation. Later the Pietism of the Germanic peoples with its mystical individualism exercised a profound influence upon English dissent, such as the Quakers and the Methodists. The sect is to be distinguished from these vague and unorganized movements of dissent by definiteness of sociological form and insistence upon the moral purity of its members.[1] The sect was not necessarily mystical and enthusiastic in character, while these movements frequently were. Whenever these

[1] Ernst Troeltsch, *The Social Teachings of the Christian Churches*, Vol. I, pp. 348 ff. On this chapter see especially *ibid.*, Vol. I, pp. 328 ff. and Vol. II, pp. 691 ff.

movements sought permanent form they naturally adopted the
sect-type of organization. When they did not succeed in achieving permanent sociological form they tended to be absorbed
by the church-type or else they disintegrated into ephemeral
groups of enthusiasts.

I

It is possible to distinguish two forms of the sect-type, the
medieval and the Protestant, the cultural correlatives of which
were Catholic and Protestant state churches. The dissent that
found expression through the sects of early Christianity and the
Middle Ages was primarily spiritual and moral in character.
The issue raised by the Donatists of the fifth century was not
one of theology or church polity but turned upon the question
of the moral and spiritual fitness of an apostate (traditor)
bishop to administer the sacraments. Similarly the sects of the
twelfth century, such as the Waldenses, were primarily moral
and spiritual protestants against the abuses of a decadent Catholicism. They did not reflect nor did they sympathize with the
Pauline-Augustinian theology of Luther and the reformers.
They made no attempt to develop an official theology. Theoretical ideas were incidental. What they sought was a return
to the purity and simplicity of the teachings and example of
Jesus. They stressed the reading of the Bible and lay preaching,
and rejected all the forms of the Catholic church. Their unpardonable sin was not that they were heretics but that they
were rebels.

The Protestant, in contradistinction to the medieval sects,
had to deal with theology. Luther and the reformers found
their source of authority in an inspired Book, and hence creed
or an authoritative theological interpretation of the Book assumed a place of importance quite different from that of creed

in Catholicism. When dissent arose in opposition to the state-churches of Geneva, Germany, or England, the issues involved inevitably took on a theological form. Servetus, by attacking the doctrine of the Trinity, menaced the life of the Genevan state and was burned at the stake. Theological differences in England from the days of Elizabeth and the establishment easily became synonymous with treason. One has but to read the accounts of the Antinomian controversy raised by Ann Hutchinson or follow John Clarke's story of the trial of himself and his two Baptist companions by the General Court of Massachusetts to see how completely theology dominated all matters of dissent in the Bay colony. Differences between Presbyterian, Baptist, and Methodist are today still theological rather than moral and all forms of dissent within these communions are doctrinal in character. Theology is the congenital curse of Protestantism.

There is a very close kinship between sect-type and church-type in Protestant countries. This makes it all the more important that we demarcate as clearly as possible the sociological traits of the sect-type with special reference to Protestantism. The difficulties and obscurities involved have been accentuated, especially in the Protestant world, by the bitter controversies aroused by the sects and the consequent distorted notions as to the meaning of the term "sect." This term is usually taken either in an opprobrious or in an apologetic sense. To the representative of the churchly type the sect lay outside the corporate life of the church and was viewed as an unwarranted distortion of Christianity. Hence the sects were persecuted as anti-social. The state refused to grant them privileges and rights at all commensurate with those enjoyed by the state church. On the other hand, it is the habit of the modern liberal to look upon the sects with their direct appeal to the teachings of Jesus, their aloofness from the contaminating influences of the world, their demand for tolerance, their opposition to dogma and authoritarianism, and their purer ethics, as the true representatives of the primitive Christian ideal. Excuses are made for their lack of culture, their asceticism, their social and economic radicalism, and their chiliastic extravagances.[2]

II

To evaluate the sect in the strictly sociological sense we must divorce the term from its various theological and ecclesiastical connotations. A sect is not necessarily small, though a majority of the sects happen to be small in membership. A great church, such as the Baptist, is, sociologically speaking, still a sect though it numbers millions. A sect is not necessarily a group of schismatics that have split off from a larger organization, though sects often originate in schism. The persecution to which the sects are often subjected is not necessarily a hall-mark of the sect. *A sect, sociologically speaking, is any religious group which makes no claim to universality and the bond of union between whose members is free and voluntary in character.* The logical implications of particularism and voluntarism are *separatism* and an *ascetic ethics*. The sect is actuated by the ideal of a pure church and hence its emphasis of separatism. A church for the sect is not an external source of grace but a visible company of saints. Sects fall into various groups according to the tests of saintliness. For one group it may be God's predestinating grace that fixes the number of the saints; for another, the "Inner Light," as in the case of the Quakers and Pietists. The theological and metaphysical principles of the sects vary and are

[2] K. Mueller, *Kirchengeschichte*, Vol. I, pp. 207 f. and Vol. II, pp. 85 f., represents the churchly point of view. L. Keller, *Die Reformation und die Aelteren Reformpartien*, represents the liberal point of view. See Troeltsch, *op. cit.*, Vol. I, pp. 431 f.

usually important sociologically only as they condition the form and character of the group.[3]

The religion of the state, as opposed to that of the sect, develops along with the state, shares its authoritativeness, and is thoroughly identified with the cultural pattern. The sect, on the other hand, lacks this authoritativeness, stands aloof and often opposed to the secular order or seeks to introduce radical changes. The religion of the state is identified with the ruling classes while the religion of the sects usually spreads among the disinherited, often resulting in popular movements. The state-church is the patron of the arts and the guardian of morals. Sectarian religion is personal and insists upon the freedom and integrity of the individual, often resulting in moral anarchy and the belittling of art. The sect usually arises as a protest against the inadequacies of established religion, hence it is always characterized by the spirit of criticism and dissent. Both the established and the dissenting forms of religion spring from persistent human needs and are, therefore, permanent manifestations of the religious interest.

III

What sociological traits do these two types of Christianity tend to assume? The sectarian tradition tends to encourage a lay Christianity as opposed to a hierarchy. The emphasis is not upon sacrament and cultus but upon immediate religious and moral experiences. The more or less radical stress of equality and brotherhood based upon love often encourages radical ideas as to property and marriage. The sects, true to the teachings of Jesus, are marked by more or less indifference to

[3] Weber, *Grundriss der Sozialökonomik*, Vol. III, pp. 812 f.

the state, as seen in the refusal to bear arms, to take an oath, or to acknowledge civic rights. There is a tendency, also found in the early Christian tradition, to simplify the religious and moral life by cultivating poverty and freedom from the cares of this world's goods. This, when supplemented by antagonism to the vices of the upper classes, easily leads to an ascetic ethics. All forms of dogma and church authority are distrusted. There is constant harking back to the Bible and the *ipsissima verba* of Jesus, with the result that the Bible is turned into a religious fetish. The words of the Book become literal religious verities and no regard is paid to the cultural and historical setting in which the words were spoken. The great organic and unifying philosophy of the churchly type, which views the church as the mystical embodiment of the living Christ reaching back in unbroken cultural continuity to the earliest times, is lost upon the sectarian type. In its stead is placed a conception of Christ as the divine Lord of the individual conscience ruling directly through the revealed law of his Word.

The sectarian, as opposed to the churchly type, is at a distinct disadvantage when faced with the problem of organizing and controlling large masses. The essentially subjective and individualistic note renders any extensive institutionalization and socialization of sectarian ideals difficult. The sectarian tradition has found expression through small groups where the ties are intimate and personal rather than external and institutional. Under such conditions there is constant need for renewal of the ideal. Where the enthusiasm ebbs the cultural forms and traditions are lacking to hold the group together. Revivalism is the crude and costly sectarian method of renewing the group life. The price always being paid by the sects for continuity, stability, and growth is a negation of their basic ideas through institutionalization. The amazing growth of sectarian groups, such as the Baptists and Methodists, with the resulting institutionalization, has raised the question as to whether they have not lost all contacts with the early sectarian tradition and passed over into the churchly type. Their outward cultural forms stultify their inner traditional spirit and purpose.

Leaders of the sectarian tradition, belonging as they do to small and for the most part poverty-stricken groups, frequently have little first-hand knowledge of the complexities of the economic and political orders. They lack the wisdom and the insight as well as the sense of social responsibility that is usually associated with religious leadership identified with the churchly type. Actuated by a warm and sincere desire for social better-ment, and visualizing social ills in the clear white light of the individualistic and oversimplified ethics of Jesus, the leaders of the sectarian type fall easy victims to an impractical moral and religious ideology, through the radical application of which to the complicated social order they hope to reform the world. The result is that with the very best of intentions they often champion fatuous reforms and destructive radicalism. A study of the attitudes of early leaders of the Anabaptists, Quakers, Baptists, and Methodists will show that they were often char-acterized by a zeal that was without knowledge. The leader of the churchly group, while often lacking the courage, the depth of conviction, and the vivid sense of social ills of the sectarian leader, is apt to possess a larger social vision and a sobering sense of the responsibilities involved.

With all its inherent weaknesses, however, the sectarian type constitutes an essential element in the history of western Christian culture. It is a logical and inevitable development of phases of the teachings of Jesus. The churchly type met the needs for some sort of permanent objectification of the values of historic Christianity, spanning the generations and assuring cultural continuity. In the churchly type men are born into the church and their organic connection is symbolized by time-honored ordinances, such as baptism. For the dissenting sects a man is not born into the church; he voluntarily unites with it after he has been converted. Hence the radical sects, almost without exception, have failed to see any significance in ordinances, such as infant baptism, implying this continuity. They insist upon adult baptism. The Baptist church may legitimately claim to be the best representative of the sectarian tradition, for of all Protestant bodies it retains more of the cultural traits of the sect as sketched above.

IV

It is in the realm of the ideal perhaps that we find the most striking differences between the sectarian and churchly types. The churchly type seeks to attain the ideal by dominating society. This involves, of course, the socializing and secularizing of Christianity, the lowering of the moral ideal, and an inevitable drift towards this-worldliness as opposed to other-worldliness. The sects, being small groups, lacking both the desire and the machinery for the conquest of society, find their chief interests in inner perfection and the intimate personal contacts of a brotherhood of love and are inclined to abandon all hope of dominating the world. Yet they presuppose the world in a negative way, for the ideal is attained in opposition to the world. Without the wicked world their ideal would be meaningless. They need the world as a place to which they can banish apostates. Their purer and more spiritual ethics wins over the world but in the very process of winning the world the sect destroys the situation of sect versus world presupposed in the sectarian ideal. The very success of the sect thus tends to destroy it. The sect, from its very nature, cannot include society as a whole in its ideal without ceasing to be a sect.

The other world plays a much larger part in the ideal of the sect than of the state-church. The sect has rejected the world and hence must depend upon the other world for the rounding out of its ideal. Its ideal, if more spiritual, is perforce more remote and impractical. The sect has the greatest difficulty in establishing any organic relationship between this world and the world of the completed ideal. For the churchly type continuity of culture and a partial realization of the ideal in cultural forms assures an organic relationship to society lacking in the sect. Millennial hopes have always appealed to the sects because theirs is a religion of the disinherited. The ranks of the sects are filled with those habituated through the sheer hopelessness of the social situation to look to some divine cataclysm to right all wrongs and usher in the ideal. It is no accident that the unspeakable disaster of the World War served to revive the discussion of chiliastic hopes, especially among denominations with sectarian backgrounds. It was the chiliastic interest that first prompted the Philadelphia conference of 1919. Orthodoxy soon took precedence over eschatology and the transition was made to Fundamentalism.[4]

The sectarian ideal is usually radical and hence utopian in character, for any ideal is utopian that tends to disrupt the prevailing pattern of life. The radical application of Plato's *Republic* or Harrington's *Oceana* or Augustine's *City of God* (426 A.D.) to contemporary society would have resulted disastrously. On the other hand, this cannot be said of ideologies such as the Sermon on the Mount or the Declaration of Independence. An ideology, like an utopia, transcends reality and,

[4] S. G. Cole, *History of Fundamentalism*, 1931, pp. 233 f.

strictly speaking, is incompatible with it. But conduct inspired by an ideology so far from disrupting society often benefits it. For an ideology bears an organic relation to existing society lacking in the case of the utopia. It is close enough to reality so that actions it inspires may make for social good although what is accomplished is never the realization of the abstract ideal. The beneficial effects of the Sermon on the Mount in western culture can never be measured, but as a practical program it is impossible. Changes in the course of history may in time so close the gap between an utopia and social reality that it may become an ideology. Augustine's *City of God,* which was an utopia in 426 A.D., had become an ideology by the time of Gregory the Great.[5] The state church tends to rationalize the ideal in the form of an ideology, the sect in the form of an utopia. The ideal of the former must be organically related to society; the ideal of the latter not only transcends reality but tends to disrupt it.

Ideals are conservative, idealistic, or radical according as they stress the past, the future, or the present. The ideals of early Christianity and of the radical sects that took early Christian teachings literally belong to the explosive or radical type of utopia. The kingdom of heaven, when first proclaimed by Jesus, was radically utopian in character because it was accompanied by chiliastic ideas that conditioned the attainment of the kingdom upon the immediate and supernatural overthrow of the existing social order. The essence of the chiliastic utopia is a breathless waiting for the stroke of doom when the ideal is to be realized. The present absorbs past and future. The goal is achieved by a sudden crowding of the ideal into the little saddle-back of time of which we are immediately aware. The

---

[5] See Mannheim's suggestive discussion in his *Ideologie und Utopie,* pp. 169 ff.

utopian ideal of early Christianity stressed the child-like and receptive attitude of mind facilitating ready entrance into the kingdom, together with a watchful waiting for the coming of the Lord. The chiliastic type of ideal dropped into the background as the medieval church-state culture took shape, only to emerge in radical and explosive form in the Taborites, an offshoot of the Hussite movement, Thomas Muenzer, a contemporary of Luther, and the Anabaptists of the early sixteenth century.

This explosive sectarian ideal is distinctly an expression of the disinherited. Profound political and economic disturbances, such as the Peasants' War of 1525, stirred the lower classes as never before so that for the first time they manifested something like class consciousness. Some scholars find in the Anabaptist movement the first premonition of the disruptive proletarian movements of modern times.[6] Traces of the explosive type emerged also among the early Quakers. Its fundamental characteristic is an inarticulate up-surge of undisciplined emotions due to profound social unrest. Ideas have little to do with the inception of the explosive type. As these movements progress they sooner or later secure an ideology usually borrowed from the cultural heritage. At first it is outstanding individuals, such as a Melchior Hoffmann, the Anabaptist leader, that give direction to the unreasoned urges involved, later crude symbols taken from the Bible or elsewhere are added and finally, as the need for rationalization becomes strong, thinkers devise an ideology to justify the movement. Modern post-war movements, such as Fascism and the Nazi, show striking similarities with the explosive sectarian movements of the late Middle Ages and the early Reformation. Fascism now boasts a phi-

---

[6] Mannheim, *op. cit.*, p. 193.

losophy,[7] while the Nazis have as yet only a leader, Hitler, and a symbol, the swastika.

In the churchly type the ideal is conceived of not as something to be attained suddenly through the radical disruption of existing society but as already implicit in the institutionalized life of the state-church. Origen as early as the first half of the third century opposed the chiliastic ideal. Augustine in the first quarter of the fifth century definitely suggested in his *City of God* that the ideal is already in process of realization. As the *civitas dei* gradually lost its utopian cast and became the ideology of the Middle Ages, the ideal became more and more a part of concrete reality. A similar concreting of the ideal is found in the theocracies modeled after the pattern of Geneva. Sects such as the Baptists that developed in close contact with Calvinism showed the influence of the Calvinistic ideal. The church of the sect was a select body of saints, separate from the world to be sure, and yet it tended to become an epitome of the Calvinistic holy community embodying in its corporate life a phase of the ideal. Owing to its insistence upon separation of church and state, the corporate life of a sect such as the Baptists was not as rich nor as comprehensive as that of the Calvinistic church-state which included the whole of society. The sect, just because of its limited corporate life, was forced to stress the other-worldly note as necessary for the rounding out of the ideal. In the state-church the this-worldly phase of the ideal tends to outweigh the other-worldly.

The ideal of the sects has been profoundly influenced by modern democratic society with its liberal humanitarian conception of life, which is entirely secular. Life is no longer

[7] See W. K. Stewart, "Mussolini and His Mentors," *American Political Science Review*, Vol. 22, pp. 847 ff.

looked upon as merely providing discipline for the final attainment of the ideal in another world. Social values are stressed
for their own sake and the setting of the ideal is distinctly limited to this world. The modern secularized social order has little
or no place for an ideal which looks upon this world as secondary. "Here if anywhere is your America" is the unwritten
philosophy of present-day culture. The great dissenting-revivalistic churches, therefore, find themselves in a trying position.
They are forced through the pressure of modern culture to
adapt their ideal to a secularized social order dominated by
democracy and science, and yet the historic Christianity from
which they sprang knows nothing of an ideal that is not essentially other-worldly in its attainment. The force of circumstances has made them cultural anachronisms.

V

The sociological significance of the sect is vitally affected by
the fact that its psychology is that of the lower disinherited
classes. The lower classes lack the discipline and power of in-
hibition that come with culture so that their religion is always
highly emotional. If this led to dangerous excesses such as
characterized the Anabaptists, the early Quakers, and Methodists, it was also the source of creative energy that registered
itself in new religious forms and movements. Just as the great
creative periods of art are characterized by a simple, direct, and
non-critical attitude that enables the artist to grasp and portray
the great values of life vividly, so the religious imagination
of the simple but devout souls of the sects is able to feel and
portray religious values with a directness, a beauty, and convincing power impossible in a later sophisticated age. Religious
classics such as John's Gospel or Bunyan's *Pilgrim's Progress*

are illustrations in point. The immediacy and convincing power of the religious experience make it possible to claim the authority of divine revelation with a confidence that is impossible in the case of the critical scholar. The highly emotional and naïvely uncritical mentality of the lower classes is congenial to the flourishing of a *fides implicita*, the correlative of which is a religious absolute. It never once occurred to the early Quaker to question the authority of his absolute, the "Inner Light." The very intensity and immediacy of his religious experience made this impossible. The naïve realism of the typical sect turned the printed Bible into a fetish.

The virtues of the sects are always the virtues most in demand in the life of the lower classes, such as poverty of spirit, simplicity in dress and speech, a direct and categorical attitude towards all moral issues, solidarity, sympathy, and self-sacrifice. Owing to the narrow economic margin of the disinherited, a morally ascetic note is always associated with the attainment of the ideal. To be a Christian is to deny oneself and take up the cross. All idea of wealth as making possible a richer and fuller life is excluded. A camel can get through the eye of a needle easier than the rich man can enter heaven. The vices of the rich and favored class more than often become the classic sins of the sects. This is strikingly illustrated in the case of the poverty-stricken eighteenth-century Baptists of Virginia whose list of orthodox sins, such as dancing, horse-racing, gambling, and card-playing, were the forms of amusement of the Virginia aristocracy who opposed their struggle for religious liberty.

The ascetic note, always associated with the sects and of profound importance for the understanding of the influence of the dissenting-revivalistic churches in American life, was not new. It developed naturally from the ethical rigorism of Jesus' teachings. The singleness of devotion demanded by his radical ethical and spiritual ideals either destroyed the appeal of more material interests or made men indifferent towards them. The inference was soon drawn that anything inherently difficult, involving self-denial and the crucifying of the flesh, was agreeable to the Christian ideal. To this was added the prevalent notion that the body is the seat of sin and evil. Paul said, "I keep my body under [8] and enslave it lest having preached to others I should prove a castaway." [9] Pathological ideas as to sex prevalent in late antiquity also intensified the situation.[10]

The rôle of asceticism in the churchly type was quite different from that in the sectarian type. Asceticism in the Middle Ages was confined to the monastic orders which were really specialized institutional forms for capitalizing the ascetic and dissenting spirit within the church. The monks were the "athletes of God" who through their vows of poverty, chastity, and obedience were able to devote themselves with single-hearted devotion to the attainment of the ideal. But they still retained an organic relation to the church and found the attainment of the ideal only within the church, not outside it. Thus did they enrich the life of the church while dutifully submitting to its authority.[11]

In the state-churches of early Protestantism asceticism was transferred to the inner series of reality. Discipline of the spirit took precedence over that of the body, practiced by the medieval saints with their fastings and flagellations. This was especially true of the Calvinistic churches. The Calvinist despised and rejected the world as the seat of sin and yet needed the world

---

[8] The Greek is ὑπωπιάζω, meaning "I hit under the eye," a pugilistic term.

[9] I Corinthians 9: 27.

[10] Troeltsch, op. cit., Vol. I, p. 106.

[11] The writer has discussed the cultural significance of this in an article, "The Passing of the Saint," American Journal of Sociology, Vol. 24, pp. 353 f.

to make his calling and election sure. The world had value but only as a means to an end that was spiritual and otherworldly. Every man's "calling" was the divinely constituted social agency for spiritual discipline. The essence of the Calvinistic ethic was "a rigorous discipline of the instinctive life, a destruction of all merely instinctive feeling, and the limitation of the sense-life to that which is necessary and useful, the practice of self-discipline and self-control in order to lead a holy life in obedience to the Law of God." [12] This ascetic Calvinistic ethics had implications of the utmost importance for every phase of life and provided something like a religious sanction for the modern capitalistic society.[13]

The asceticism of the sect agreed in part with that of Calvinism and differed from that of the Middle Ages in that it limited the problem to the inner rather than the outer series of reality. It was essentially subjective and spiritual. The sects agreed with Calvinism also in that they made the task of spiritual discipline the same for all men, instead of limiting it to the religious orders as in the Middle Ages. The sects differed from the Calvinistic churches in that they went back directly to the teachings of Jesus and made the Christian life to consist primarily in detachment from the world that they might cultivate the pure ideal. They assumed an indifferent or hostile attitude towards social duties as oaths, war, property, and the exercise .of dominion over others. They interpreted the ethical rigorism of Jesus as requiring rejection of the cares of this world. "For whosoever will save his life shall lose it; but whosoever will lose his life for my sake, the same shall save it." For those sects that accepted Jesus' chiliastic ideas this

[12] Troeltsch, *op. cit.*, Vol. II, p. 607.
[13] Max Weber, *The Protestant Ethics and the Spirit of Capitalism.* Troeltsch, *op. cit.*, Vol. II, pp. 604 ff. R. H. Tawney, *Religion and the Rise of Capitalism,* 1926, pp. 211 ff.

was easy; for those who rejected these ideas or minimized them the problem of the world became a pressing one. Simply to detach oneself from the world in order to live the life of an intensive devotion to an inner attitude of self-denying love is like making bricks without straw. Calvinism sought to attain inner purity by utilizing social institutions. It thus found value in the world, while the sects tended to reject the world.

The influence of the great Calvinistic scheme upon sectarian asceticism was of the utmost importance. The ideals of early Baptists and Quakers were drawn directly from the teachings of Jesus. The Quaker doctrine of the "Inner Light" was peculiar to early Christianity and had little in common with Calvinism. But the necessity of blameless conduct within the corporate life of the champions of the "Inner Light" led directly to rules of conduct that approximated Calvinistic asceticism. The Quaker leaders Fox and especially Barclay, the Scotchman, lived in communities dominated by Calvinism and it was impossible for them to escape its cultural impact. We have, as a result, the rather paradoxical situation that the Quakers adopted externally the asceticism of Calvinism while finding theoretical justification for it in the thoroughly un-Calvinistic doctrine of the "Inner Light." [14] Phases of Quakerism suggested the rational thought-out life of Calvinism. The Quaker habit of waiting quietly upon the movings of the "Inner Light" undoubtedly encouraged the careful weighing of courses of conduct and rational appeals to conscience. The Quaker refusal to take an oath or to fight tended to turn his energies into the world of business where these habits of shrewd and reasoned conduct, combined with scrupulous honesty born of sincerity and integrity of soul, soon registered

[14] Max Weber, *op. cit.*, p. 148.

themselves in pronounced business success. It is no accident that by the end of the eighteenth century some of the most successful business men in England and the American colonies were Quakers. The Quakers thus came to compete with the thrifty Calvinistic-minded tradesman.

The Baptists, who at first had much in common with the Quakers, were in the course of time even more completely dominated by the prevailing Calvinistic or Puritan ethics. This was especially true after the Great Awakening when the Baptist churches in America accepted Calvinistic theology as the basis of the "new birth" and, with their small, covenanted, and autonomous congregations, epitomized in their intensive group life the ascetic ethics of historic Calvinism. After the separation of church and state the ascetic sectarian ethics was carried over into a new order by Baptists, Presbyterians, and even Methodists, and made an integral part of the social ethics of the American people. The records of the frontier Baptist, Methodist, and Presbyterian churches are full of instances of church discipline for "telling lies," "swearing," "shooting for liquor," "intoxication," "tattling," or even slapping another brother's face.[15] Here the center of reference is obviously the spiritual and moral integrity of the group; there is little or no regard for society as a whole. The dignity and sense of comprehensive social values that characterized the ascetic ethics of the Calvinistic state churches even in colonial New England were lacking in the sects, though they did emerge in early Quakerism, thanks to the humanizing effect of the doctrine of the "Inner Light." While the note of intimate sympathetic spiritual helpfulness was encouraged in a little brotherhood of love there was also ample opportunity for tale bearing, idle gossip, and personal

[15] W. W. Sweet, *Religion of the American Frontier: The Baptists,* 1931, pp. 49 ff.

spite. The antisocial outlook of the sectarian ethics explains its lack of balance and insight. This became a serious handicap when later these churches swelled to millions and dominated entire communities, as is true of the Baptist church in large areas of the South. The social ethics of Baptists, Methodists, and Presbyterians is still that of the sect.

VI

Since the sect makes no claim to universality and insists upon freedom to live its own life, it must advocate tolerance, at least so far as that term applies to the autonomy of each sect among rival sects. The sect, furthermore, since it is usually born in opposition to some secularized church, is from its very nature a *dissenting* group. But it must be remembered that dissent and tolerance are terms that do not touch the heart of the life of the sect. The sect seeks primarily to defend and perpetuate a certain type of piety. Christian piety of the traditional Pauline-Augustinian type is a form of organization of the emotional life based upon the great doctrines of evangelical Christianity, sin, grace, and regeneration. Sectarian piety is often at first indifferent and even antagonistic to orthodox theology. It seeks primarily the satisfaction of the emotional life rather than any carefully thought-out system of theology or the development of a philosophical or legal apparatus for the defense of rights of conscience. If we consider the sect from the point of view of its demand for freedom of conscience and its protest against persecution we may call the sectarians dissenters. It is more correct to characterize them from the point of view of the type of piety they represent. The spirit of dissent and the struggle for tolerance are of primary importance in any estimate of the social significance of the sect, although the drive back of this dissent may be zeal for a certain type of piety rather than real interest in freedom.

If there is no inherent connection between sectarian piety and the spirit of dissent with its zeal for tolerance, the question may be asked why dissent and tolerance are always intimately associated with the sects. Their association is to be understood in the light of the rise of the sect. The history of the genesis of every sect reveals the presence, more or less, of the following elements. A situation develops within the church or in society which causes maladjustments between the inner series of emotional needs and the outer series of cultural forms and institutions, as in the twelfth and sixteenth centuries. This gives rise to groups, such as the Albigenses and Anabaptists, who are out of sympathy with the traditional church forms through which religious needs were normally satisfied in the past. This state of emotional strain and dissatisfaction would be characterized by the Freudians as "frustration." Leaders arise and rationalize this feeling of "frustration," characteristic of these maladjusted groups and classes, by means of slogans drawn from the Bible or philosophical formulas that look to the attainment of the freedom necessary to the satisfaction of the defeated urges. These symbols and formulas are usually mere fictions of the religious imagination. They often do violence to logic and factual reality but give point and direction to the group desires. They provide programs of action for achieving necessary freedom and tolerance and an ideology for the cultivation of the desired type of piety.

The real issue between the sect and the persecuting state church, therefore, is not that of tolerance versus intolerance but of sectarian versus churchly piety. The established church insists that the piety gained through the discipline of its forms is indispensable for the development of the best citizenship and the maintenance of public morals and education. The sect seeks only sufficient liberty to enable it to cultivate its peculiar type of piety, which it thinks superior to that of the established church. The sect insists that a highly institutionalized and sacramentarian piety inevitably renders impossible spontaneity and sincerity in the religious life. The charge constantly leveled by dissent against the standing orders both in Massachusetts and Virginia during the colonial days was that they were cursed with an "unconverted clergy." After the sects won toleration they were willing to admit liberty of conscience only *between*, not *within*, the various sects. Individual sects are bitterly intolerant of dissenters within their own group.

An established church, by virtue of its close contacts with the entire cultural pattern, may and usually does inevitably absorb liberal tendencies as the community becomes more enlightened. Arminianism crept into the religious establishments of Holland and England. Unitarianism spread in the bosom of the bitterly intolerant religious establishment founded by Winthrop and John Cotton. The Pietists, Spener and Franke, arose within the Lutheran church and in spite of powerful opposition were never crushed but remained to leaven it with liberalism.

Religious liberty may thus become an intimate and organic part of the life of an established church forced to humanize its forms and minimize its dogmatic requirements in order to accommodate widely varying types of belief. This is the solution of the problem of religious liberty suggested by the Anglican, William Chillingworth (1602-1644), in his great work, *The Religion of Protestants*.[16] A genuine spirit of tolerance may

[16] For an analysis, see M. Freund, *Die Idee der Toleranz im England der Grossen Revolution*, pp. 26 ff.; also A. A. Seaton, *The Theory of Toleration under the Later Stuarts*, pp. 51 ff.

thus be attained *within* the life of an established church. Liberty for the sectarian type, however, always remains something *external to the immediate religious life itself*, a tool used to defend the integrity and autonomy of this life. Typical evangelical piety of the sectarian type rarely succeeded in assimilating the humanistic and rationalistic principles to which it constantly appealed to protect its own integrity and independence.

It is thus part of the irony of history that the intolerant and persecuting established church should in the end become liberal in its theology, while the liberty-loving dissenting sect after the attainment of freedom often becomes the stronghold of obscurantism and intolerance. The great Baptist church in large sections of this country, where it practically dominates the religious life of the masses, is utterly oblivious of its noble traditions of liberty formulated by Baptist heroes of the past, such as Roger Williams, John Clarke, Isaac Backus, and John Leland. These are certainly not today the patron saints of what has been contemptuously called "the Baptist belt."

It would seem, then, that the spirit of liberty is incompatible with the genius of evangelical piety. The Quakers, who of all the sects best succeeded in harmonizing liberty and piety, can hardly be called typical representatives of sectarian Protestantism. They really belong to the radical and spiritual type of dissent which is continental and mystical rather than Anglo-Saxon and Calvinistic. In the typical sect, such as the Baptists, piety and the tolerant spirit are never blended. It is indeed a curious paradox that evangelical piety gives rise to a spiritual dynamic that utilizes a philosophy of dissent incompatible with this piety. The sectarian insists upon tolerance as a means of securing the freedom to cultivate a piety that demands the repudiation of tolerance. To be sure, great dissenting leaders, when faced by intolerant state-churches embodying the dogmas of Augustinian piety and forced to choose between pious intolerance and freedom, have not hesitated but have chosen freedom even at the risk of a loss of theological orthodoxy and a diminution of piety. There has always been a saving remnant who, like Roger Williams, have found the adventurous life of soul liberty more precious than the safe and comfortable existence of a pious orthodoxy. These are the real dissenters.

It is not strange, then, that dissent in the past has found some strange bedfellows. The Quakers and Baptists of seventeenth-century England had more in common with the liberal Shaftesbury than with the pious and orthodox and intolerant Anglicanism and Presbyterianism. Before his reputation as a patriot was shattered by the publication of his *Age of Reason* Thomas Paine was constantly praised by dissenting Baptists and Presbyterians. Reverend John Leland, one of the founders of the Baptist church in Virginia, was a friend and admirer of Jefferson. There are passages in Leland's *Rights of Conscience Inalienable*, 1791, which read as though taken from the pages of Paine or Jefferson.

Where dissenting groups have long been forced to adjust themselves to an intolerant establishment, liberalism tends to soften their piety. The General Baptists, the most numerous group of English Baptists, were largely Arminian in theology and "most of their churches became openly Unitarian." [17] The Particular Baptists, so called because of their doctrine of limited election which would tend to affiliate them with the theology of Calvinistic piety, remained a small group with liberal tendencies during the eighteenth century in England. Down to the Great Awakening the Baptists were an insignificant minority both in New England and in Virginia and were not noted for

[17] A. H. Newman, *History of the Baptist Churches in the United States*, 1894, p. 47.

their orthodoxy or their militant piety. There is every reason to believe that but for the Great Awakening the New England Baptists would have followed the example of the Baptists in England and remained a small group more and more affiliated with liberal movements such as eighteenth-century rationalism and humanism. It was the capture of dissent by the revivalistic piety of the Great Awakening that made religious history in this country.

VII

We conclude, then, that persecution and oppression, rather than mutual inherent attraction for each other, brought dissent and sectarian piety together. Dissent is essentially intellectual and critical; it is interested in the determination of rights and the preservation of freedom. Piety is essentially emotional and bent upon maintenance of the integrity and spontaneity of the religious life. It was the suppression of basic urges that provided the drive and created the problems for the solution of which dissent was born. Among the religious sects the primary interest has always been the satisfaction of the emotions rather than the defense of liberties. The great historic formulators of the principles of religious liberty, such as Voltaire, Locke, Paine, Madison, and Jefferson, were not particularly noted for their piety. They were philosophers rather than religious devotees. It was the pressure of circumstances that brought the leaders of the dissenting sects into sympathetic contacts with Paine and Jefferson at the end of the eighteenth century. When the battle for religious and national liberty was finally won and the great principle of separation of state and church was safely embodied in the Constitution, Paine and Jefferson speedily lost their attraction for the dissenting sects. Today the names of Paine, Voltaire, and even Jefferson, who did so much to make their liberties possible, are anathema among the rank and file of the great churches sprung from dissenting backgrounds.

Whenever the pressure of the struggle for freedom is removed, therefore, the inherent conflict between dissent and piety inevitably emerges. Dissent is forced to be critical, rational, impersonal, and more or less disinterested. Piety is from its very nature warm, intimate, personal, and self-centered. Piety seeks to preserve the peace of mind which has been attained through the acceptance of certain dogmas that have become integral parts of the fabric of the emotional life. Dissent is not interested in championing any particular type of piety with its dogmas but rather in maintaining the right to believe as one chooses. The logic of dissent, then, tends naturally to place all forms of belief on a parity. It is of the very nature of piety, however, that it must cherish its particular type of religious loyalties to the exclusion of all others. Piety is inherently intolerant; dissent is inherently liberal. *The pious man believes in order that he may know; the liberal doubts in order that he may believe intelligently.* Piety is more immediately practical as a means of furthering life because men live by their beliefs, not by their doubts. Dissent is a sort of prolegomenon to life, which may become an intellectual pastime; piety is of the very essence of life itself. A measure of dissent is nevertheless necessary to the health and sanity of the intellectual life.

The great modern churches sprung of dissenting traditions, thanks to the results of cultural evolution, find themselves today, in spite of their numbers and material prosperity, in a curiously paradoxical situation. They are through their past nominally committed to the philosophy of dissent, for it made possible their present liberties. With all the outside pressure forever removed, however, dissent has lost all practical importance. The dissenting churches have surrendered, therefore, to the logic of an evangelical piety which in actual life negates what dissent stood for. To be sure, church historians still glorify the dissenting tradition. Baptists and Presbyterians debate the relative claims of their dissenting forbears to be called the authors of religious liberty in Virginia.[18] It is no exaggeration, however, to say that within these great denominations the spirit of dissent is dead. One seeks in vain in their membership for any real interest in religious liberty, save in the external form of legal tolerance. Dissent today is economic and secular rather than religious.

This perhaps was inevitable. With the goal of dissent attained, namely, legalized tolerance, dissent itself lost its reason for being and disappeared as an active force, leaving the intolerant and self-centered tradition of evangelical piety in complete possession of the field. All the energies of the great dissenting churches have been concentrated for a hundred and fifty years upon the cultivation and militant defense of this evangelical type of piety. It may be important for the integrity of Baptist piety that anti-evolution laws be passed by the states. It may be supremely vital for the piety of Presbyterians that the inerrancy of the Bible and the dogmas of the Westminster Confession should be defended at all hazards. But for the modern man these are hardly matters of transcendent importance for the welfare of society. It is quite possible that the great doctrines of evangelical piety, such as sin, heaven and hell, total depravity, predestination, and irresistible grace, may have a certain survival value as symbols of the religious imagination but as factual realities in the external world of time and sense they have been effectually discredited by natural science and

[18] C. F. James, *Documentary History of the Struggle for Religious Liberty in Virginia*, 1900; T. C. Johnson, *Virginia Presbyterians and Religious Liberty*, 1907.

historical criticism. It may be seriously doubted whether they are any longer a suitable basis for the organization of the type of character demanded by a culture based upon democracy and science.

We may summarize the conclusions of this chapter as follows. The churchly type is institutional, a permanent part of the cultural heritage upon which it depends for its continuity and integrity. The sectarian type is voluntary, based usually upon a covenant and dependent for its effectiveness upon the co-operation of individual wills. The churchly type seeks to attain the ideal Christian order by compromising with existing society; the sects oppose all compromise with the world, insist upon separation from the world, and wait patiently for the coming of the Lord, when the ideal will be attained. The sectarian type minimizes all forms of sacramentarianism, insisting that the use of mechanical agencies is inimical to the integrity of the religious life, following in this connection the example of Jesus. The ethics of the churchly type tends to become secular and relativistic, the highest moral perfection being expected of individuals or groups who specialize in the attainment of sanctity, as in the case of the medieval saints. The sects insist upon one standard of morality for clergy and laity, more or less ascetic and puritanical in character. When the sects were small this democratic standard of ascetic ethics was feasible. With the development of the great modern churches of the dissenting-revivalistic type, such as the Baptists and the Methodists, to where they have become nation-wide in their scope, the attempt to force this sectarian ethics upon a nation through social legislation is politically fatuous and morally confusing, as we have been made painfully aware in the farce of national prohibition. Religion is no longer in the position in this country to serve as the protagonist of mass dissent or effective social reform. Finally, the interest of the sects in religious liberty is secondary, being subordinated to the interests of piety. The tolerance they seek is legal and external, not psychological and spiritual.

Chapter III

Dissent and the American Scene

ANY factors conditioned the problem of the dissenter and religious liberty in the American colonies. Primary among them were race, economic interests, the form of colonial government, political changes in Europe, the impact of a pioneer environment, and the theories of government or ideals of religious liberty championed by such leaders as Roger Williams, William Penn, and Lord Baltimore. Even the geographical features of the new world played their part. It was easy to foresee that the region settled by the Puritan colonies, with its narrow coastal plain, its limited economic resources, and its isolation by mountain and river from the regions to the west and north, might very easily and naturally lend itself to an intensive and self-centered life congenial to an intolerant religious establishment. On the other hand, the colonies south of the Potomac, with their broad and fertile alluvial plains and their mild climate, would favor a spread-out agrarian culture inimical to effective supervision by an intolerant state-church. The middle region, with its great rivers such as the Delaware and the Hudson, facilitating ready access to the interior country, would naturally attract a varied population interested primarily in trade and inclined to insist upon religious tolerance as a practical necessity. Outside of New England the natural environment of the colonies was not adapted to the erection of an effective establishment and the persecution of dissenters.

I

As a rule, homogeneity of race and similarity of religious beliefs were prerequisites to religious establishments and the suppression of dissent, as in the Puritan colonies and Virginia; variety of race and divergence of religious beliefs, as in the New Netherlands, Maryland, Pennsylvania, and the Carolinas, rendered establishments difficult and often impossible since they made a measure of tolerance a practical necessity. It was for this reason that the proprietary colonies, as opposed to those under the crown, were inclined to be tolerant. Founded primarily for the purposes of trade, they welcomed any group of immigrants, irrespective of religious affiliations, who were economic assets. Often the tolerant ways of life built up in proprietary colonies persisted after the colonies were transferred to the crown and offered stubborn and effective resistance to all efforts to enforce a religious establishment. This was especially true of the Carolinas, New Jersey, and New York where the Anglican establishment was never more than a mere shell. The same was also true of Maryland where, however, it was not so much the exigencies of trade as the effect of the liberal ideas early inculcated under Lord Baltimore that later proved a hindrance to the effective functioning of the Anglican establishment.

Typical of the effects of a mixed population upon religion was the Dutch colony of the New Netherlands, which at first included all the territory between the Hudson and Delaware rivers. The interests of trade brought together at the mouth of the Hudson the original Dutch settlers, Englishmen, Walloons, French Huguenots, Scotch peddlers, and Jews. On the shores of the Delaware were settled Dutch, Swedes, and, later, English Quakers. The Jerseys, which became a colony in 1664, had, in addition to Dutch, Swedes, and Quakers in West Jersey, a large infusion of New Englanders in East Jersey along the Hudson, to which were added the Scotch Covenanters and later Germans and Scotch-Irish. In 1662, Stuyvesant made the attempt to suppress the Quakers and introduce something like religious conformity. The attempt failed, largely because the traditionally dissenting group of Quakers was able to capitalize the diversity of religious beliefs among the colonists in the interest of religious tolerance. The prevalence of "polypiety," so thoroughly detested by the New England Puritans, made it impossible to secure anything more than a superficial religious conformity. Even after the colony became the permanent possession of England in 1673 and the nominal Reformed church establishment was superseded by the English church, the laws of the colony assured liberty of conscience to all except papists.[1]

Perhaps the nearest approach to the setting up of a precedent for the persecution of the dissenters was made under the corrupt and incompetent governor Cornbury, who was also a religious bigot and hater of the non-conformists. In 1703 he caused two Presbyterian ministers, passing through New York, to be arrested on the ground that they were preaching without permits. The court decided against Cornbury's right to prohibit and the preachers were set free. It was really a question of wise policy and justice rather than of absolute constitutional rights. "To silence one isolated Presbyterian preacher had not even the merit of being part of a consistent policy of extirpating Dissent. It was an irritating act of capricious tyranny, which

[1] J. A. Doyle, *The English in America: The Puritan Colonies*, 1887, Vol. IV, p. 228.

could do nothing but exasperate." [2] This incident merely brought out more clearly the utter impracticability of trying to enforce a religious establishment in a colony founded primarily for trade and composed of a hodge-podge of religious groups who were under the immediate necessity of living together in peace.

II

On the other hand, where there was homogeneity of race and religious beliefs, as in the Puritan colonies and in Virginia, religious persecution was apt to arise. But even here there were subtle and important differences. The "great migration" that peopled the Bay colony and laid the basis for the dominant group among the Puritan colonies came in the two decades lying between 1620 and 1640.[3] The Bay colonists came from the southeastern counties of England where Congregational non-conformity was strong, and they came during the crucial years of the Laudian persecutions, carrying with them the deeply ingrained religious stereotypes of this more or less abnormal period of English history. The charter of the Bay colony, furthermore, gave to a small group, imbued with the ideals of the Hebraistic theocracy of John Calvin at Geneva, practically a free hand in the disposition of the fate of the colony which was destined to determine the traits of New England culture. The ·result was a biblical theocracy, erected by dissenters from the Anglican establishment, which soon surpassed the Anglican church in its narrow bigotry and bitter persecution of dissent. It remained for two hundred years the stronghold of religious intolerance in America.

The Englishmen who settled the southern colonies, in contra-

[2] Doyle, *op. cit.*, 1887, Vol. IV, p. 268.
[3] James Truslow Adams, *The Founding of New England*, 1921, Chap. 6.

distinction to those of the Puritan colonies, were not dominated by Congregational non-conformity. They were simply normal Englishmen seeking primarily to better their economic condition in a new world. They brought with them the Anglican church as part of their traditional English heritage. It was, to be sure, a "transplanted church" and suffered from all the difficulties incident to setting up in the wilderness a religious establishment that presupposed the old and more or less intensified cultural pattern of English life.[4] But the Anglican establishment was to every citizen of the Old Dominion a concrete institutional embodiment of the cultural continuity that bound him to the mother country. Dissent in Virginia, therefore, was not so different from dissent in England. The laws governing the status of dissent in the mother country were taken over naturally and normally, and were embodied in the laws of the colony. The same political sanity and English sense of justice that marked the acts of toleration in England found their echoes in Virginia. The spirit of tolerance was in fact accentuated by the exigencies of an agrarian plantation society, the loosely organized character of which made strict conformity impossible, especially in remote sections. The Virginian was forced to deal with all matters of dissent from the practical common-sense point of view. There was little either in his cultural heritage or in the structure of his agrarian society to encourage religious fanaticism. The heretic in Virginia was more or less of a nuisance; in the New England theocracies he was a son of Belial.

The New England theocracies, if we judge them from the point of view of traditional English culture, were pseudo-establishments. They did not belong to the great stream of English culture but sprang up within the eddies of that stream. They

[4] T. J. Wertenbaker, *The First Americans, 1607-1690,* 1827, Chap. 5.

were by-products and partook of the idiosyncrasies of their origin. They were thrown off during the tremendous era of the Puritan revolution as a result of the centrifugal forces then in evidence. The group who settled the Bay colony speedily lost intimate contacts with the swiftly changing English culture. In the provincial isolation of New England they took root and developed into a commonwealth that was a curious mélange of the biblical theocracy of Geneva and the Congregationalism of English non-conformity. Neither the Genevan theocracy nor English Congregationalism ever won for itself a place in the great pattern of English culture. They modified that culture somewhat but did not determine its general drift. The New England establishments, therefore, from the very beginning were characterized by a note of provincial unreality. They were not only isolated from the culture that gave them birth; they were likewise isolated, geographically and culturally, from the other colonies. The provincialism incident to this fact was not overcome until the second quarter of the nineteenth century, when Massachusetts finally abolished her establishment.

These cultural facts must be borne in mind if we are to understand why the bloodthirsty piety of John Endicott and the Reverend John Norton found no parallels in Virginia and no witch nor Quaker was hung outside the pale of the New England theocracies. Just because of their provincial and upstart character the New England theocracies lacked the sobering effect of experience and the restraint born of a sense of social responsibility that marked the treatment of dissenters by the English establishment. Furthermore, the New England leaders were constantly tormented by a sense of inconsistency due to the clash between their obstinate and unenlightened intolerance and the earlier dissenting traditions which they had brought over with them from England. They had dared to erect a dissenting group into a state church, thus stultifying the philosophy of the English state, and yet they still claimed all the rights and privileges of members of the British Empire. The mother country of course could never acknowledge the right of Massachusetts to fine, imprison, or banish Englishmen for their religious beliefs without at the same time sanctioning the New England establishments. This England never did and the consequence was that the New England theocracies were to all intents and purposes the religious outlaws of the Empire.

The psychological effect of this situation upon the thought and life of New England was not happy. It rendered the representatives of the establishments painfully self-conscious and pugnaciously self-assertive. They were like the southern slaveholders who had to defend their "peculiar institution" in defiance of the political ideals of the Constitution. The New Englanders were forced to defend their pseudo-establishments against the qualms of an uneasy conscience, the antagonism of the traditional English establishment, the criticism of free colonies, such as Rhode Island and Pennsylvania, as well as the protests of the dissenters. Their leaders became adepts in moral casuistry. By constant and vociferous assertions of the righteousness of their cause they sought to convince themselves, largely by the sound of their own voices and the unremitting drumfire of their tiresome theological tomes, that their cause was just. They hated and despised the dissenters for constantly and inconsiderately putting them on the defensive by appeals to the crown and their rights as British subjects against the tyranny of these petty pseudo-establishments. The establishments became the institutional embodiment of suspicion and hatred of England. The logic of the establishments thus forced New Englanders to deny their great heritage as Englishmen and to stultify the traditions of Milton, Sidney, and Locke. The al-

most pathological cruelty with which the Puritan fathers persecuted the dissenters was possibly a passionate attempt to silence
their own doubts, as has been asserted of the leaders of the
Inquisition.[5]

In early Virginia it is a question whether antipathy to heretics
such as the Quakers was not, as in the case of fear of witches,
more a matter of tradition than of theology.[6] New England
antipathy to the Anabaptists of Münster fame and the popular
fears aroused by the antics of the early Quakers were also in
part matters of folklore. The panic fear of the Bostonians at the
arrival of two Quaker women in the Boston harbor [7] was closely
akin to the popular fear aroused by the witches. Virginia shared
these popular antipathies with New England but with an important difference. In New England the clergy played upon
these popular superstitions with terrific effect, steeling the hearts
of men against the unfortunate victims, whether witch or
Quaker, thereby effectually depriving them of the benefits even
of a just trial by law. This did not happen in Virginia, with the
result that the witch or the Quaker was far more apt to secure
justice in the Virginia courts. No community ruled by an orthodox and powerful clergy, as was New England, is ever famed
for its religious tolerance.

Among the communities of pure English stock Rhode Island,
with its famous traditions of religious liberty, is often mistakenly
considered to lie without the circle of the Puritan colonies. On
the principle that every extreme in social evolution tends to
beget its opposite, Rhode Island is to be understood rather as
the result of a natural and inevitable revolt against the excesses

[5] W. E. H. Lecky, *History of Rationalism*, 1867, Vol. I, pp. 78 f.
[6] Wertenbaker, *op. cit.*, p. 148.
[7] George Bishop, *New England Judged*, edition of 1703, reprinted in Philadelphia, 1885, p. 10.

of the establishments, especially in Massachusetts. In a very real sense it may be said that this liberty-loving colony was the despised and disinherited offspring of the intolerant theocracies. From the days of Roger Williams and Anne Hutchinson it became the asylum of free spirits. By the sheer fact of its existence it constituted an unanswerable argument against the correctness of the Puritan political philosophy.

Rhode Island, however, in spite of her independent corporate existence, was never more than a dissenting minority within a militantly intolerant majority. She was poor in this world's goods. Her population was never more than a fraction of that of the Bay colony. Massachusetts, populous, militant, grasping, and stubbornly intolerant in religious matters, was always inclined to brow-beat the little colony founded by what the historians of the "filial piety" school are wont to call the "social sewage" of Massachusetts.[8] Rhode Island was thus never in the position to take a militant attitude on behalf of the persecuted dissenters. She was forced to seek peace and pursue it. Her rôle among the intolerant Puritan colonies was not unlike that of the dissenting minorities within these colonies. Wisely and tactfully she adopted a policy of passive resistance. She was never in the position to take the leadership in the struggle for those great principles of religious freedom which were finally embodied in the national Constitution.

III

The Dutch, next to the English, were most influential in determining the status of dissent in seventeenth-century America. Holland viewed her colonies primarily as trading stations rather

[8] H. M. Dexter, *As to Roger Williams*, 1876, p. 119. See also J. G. Palfrey, *History of New England*, *1858-1875*, Vol. II, p. 343.

than as permanent settlements. There was no great effort to reproduce the culture of the mother country. The result was that religion was subordinated to the interests of trade. In 1662 Stuyvesant attempted to suppress a Quaker meeting house in Flushing, Long Island. When the directors of the company heard of this they administered to Stuyvesant a sharp reprimand. They did not deny the right to suppress the dissenter but they insisted that in actual practice no man should be molested in his religion so long as he did not cause a civil disturbance. From this policy of tolerance as a practical principle, subordinate to the economic interests of the colony, the directors never departed. They thus sanctioned a policy directly the opposite of that of the Puritan colonies.[9] This liberalism born of the needs of trade always characterized New York as contrasted with the provincial and intolerant conservatism of Puritan Boston. For the Puritan town a non-resident merchant was more or less of a suspicious character. Membership in the established church was almost a basic prerequisite to success in business. *Bene orare est bene laborare* was the unwritten philosophy of the Yankee business man.

Due to the fact that their primary interest was trade rather than permanent settlement the Dutch colonies were more or less ephemeral in character and were unable to compete successfully with the English. Holland, like other colonizing nations such as France and Spain, failed to see that in the long run trade itself required permanence and the transplanting of the stable culture of the old world. For this task, to be sure, Holland lacked the rural communities, such as the English villages with their parish churches transferred bodily to America by the sturdy yeomanry of the Bay colony and Connecticut. Holland

---

[9] Doyle, *op. cit.*, Vol. IV, pp. 46 f.

had accumulated far richer traditions of religious liberty than England, thanks to her victorious struggle against the tyranny of Spain. She lacked the incentive and the means, however, for reproducing in the new world the liberties which she had so dearly bought at home. Her contribution to religious tolerance in the new world was the unintentional by-product of the exigencies of trade.

The eighteenth century witnessed the addition of two other great racial groups to the already variegated ethnic pattern of the colonies, namely, the Germans and the Scotch-Irish. Disturbances in Europe, such as the Thirty Years' War, French invasions, and the devastating dynastic struggles which continued up to the treaty of Utrecht in 1713 had profoundly dislocated the life of the peoples of southwest Germany. About 1710 mass migrations began, thirteen thousand immigrants reaching England, five thousand of whom remained in the British Isles while the rest passed on to America.[10] The stream once started began to flow directly from Germany and continued until after the Revolution. At first the immigrants were sectarian in character and strongly tinged with dissent; later arrivals were of peasant stock and members of Lutheran or Reformed churches. After unsuccessful attempts to settle in New York and New Jersey the Germans finally found in Pennsylvania their Mecca. They settled in the exceedingly fertile region included in the half-circle described from Philadelphia as a center and beginning with Easton at the junction of the Delaware and the Lehigh rivers and passing south and west through Allentown, Reading, and Lancaster to the Maryland border. They formed the intermediary layer of population between the Quakers in and around Philadelphia and the Scotch-Irish of the frontier.

[10] H. L. Osgood, *The American Colonies in the Eighteenth Century*, 1924, Vol. II, Chap. 6.

Many of them overflowed down the Cumberland valley into the valley of Virginia and the Piedmont region of Virginia and the Carolinas.[11]

The Germans, like the contemporary immigrant Scotch-Irish, combined political with religious dissent. They came at the time when discontent and unrest due to political and economic conditions were blended with a profound reaction against the dogmatic formalism of the Lutheran church. This reaction, characterized by the vague but comprehensive term Pietism, was the typical form of dissent against the Lutheran establishment. Looked at from one point of view, it was an attempt to return to the intimate, personal, and mystical religious enthusiasm of the early Luther. Under the leadership of such men as Spener, Francke, and Zinzendorf, the founder of the Moravian communion, it approached the proportions of a national movement. Viewed from another angle, Pietism was a return to the earlier sectarian tradition of the Middle Ages that can be traced back to the primitive Christian teachings. The movement as a whole was distinctly popular and democratic; it preferred small and intimate and voluntary groups to establishments; it stressed a return to the reading of the Bible and the guidance of inner spiritual illumination for its understanding; it emphasized the radical religious experience known as conversion; it insisted upon a purer ethics. As opposed to forms of dissent among Anglo-Saxon peoples it was mystical, meditative, and passive rather than militant.[12]

The Germans with their mystical pietistic background encouraged the utmost variety of tenets, and their undisciplined emotional life flowered out in a welter of sects, such as Mora-

---

[11] Fisher, *The Quaker Colonies*, pp. 41 f.

[12] Osgood, *op. cit.*, Vol. II, pp. 500 f. See also E. Troeltsch, *The Social Teachings of the Christian Churches*, Vol. II, pp. 686 f.

vians, Dunkers, Schwenkfelders, Labadists, Mennonites, New Mooners, New Born, Mountain Men, River Men, Women of the Wilderness, and many others.[13] Some of these sects came over as early as 1682, being strongly attracted by Penn and his Quakerism which had intimate affiliations wtih Pietism. The colony founded by Penn thus became an asylum for the persecuted sects all over Christendom. It was no accident, therefore, that the great militant dissenting churches, such as the Baptists and the Presbyterians, selected as their headquarters Philadelphia, the largest, freest, and most cultured city of the colonies. Reverend Makemie, the founder of American Presbyterianism, recognized at once the strategic position of the Quaker city in the colonies and in 1706 founded the Presbytery of Philadelphia. This has been called "a master stroke of wise policy" [14] for, with the coming of the Scotch-Irish in the third decade of the century and the clash with the Virginia establishment caused by the large influx of Scotch-Irish Presbyterians into the valley of Virginia, it was from Philadelphia that the fight for religious tolerance in the Old Dominion was directed. Similarly the Baptists of various stripes early began to foregather in the tolerant Quaker colony and in 1707 the Philadelphia Baptist Association was formed.[15] From this historic body came such revolutionary patriots as John Gano, Hezekiah Smith, and James Manning, the first president of Brown University. From Philadelphia, likewise, was directed the great campaign for religious liberty which the Baptists, in coöperation with the Presbyterians, waged so successfully in Virginia the last half of the eighteenth century.

[13] Fisher, *op. cit.*, p. 42.
[14] H. J. Ford, *The Scotch-Irish in America*, 1915, p. 334.
[15] A. H. Newman, *History of the Baptist Churches in the United States*, 1894, Chap. VII.

IV

The causes of the great Scotch-Irish migration to America were more economic than religious, due to trade restrictions imposed by England. First the cattle of Ireland were excluded from the English markets. Later, when a flourishing wool industry had been built up to where it competed with the English wool manufacturers, it was destroyed by hostile legislation. "It was computed by a contemporary writer that the woolen manufacture, which was ruined in 1699, afforded employment to twelve thousand Protestant families." [16] The linen industry was subjected to similar restrictions which brought about its decline. The admirable harbors looking to America offered possibilities in the shipping industry. These were discouraged by navigation acts which also created havoc in the economic life of Virginia. England, with a strange blindness to the real interests of the Empire, broke the power of the Protestants of Ireland, upon whom she relied for her hold on the island, discouraged further Protestant migrations from England and "inspired the Presbyterians of the north with a bitter hatred of her rule." [17] To this were added the terrible famines of 1740 and 1741, so that migrations to America from Ulster amounted for a time to twelve thousand annually. This continued intermittently up to the American Revolution. In 1773, four thousand sailed from Belfast alone. Of these Scotch-Irish Lecky says, "They went with their hearts burning with indignation and in the War of Independence they were almost to a man on the side of the insurgents. They supplied some of the best soldiers of Washington." [18]

[16] W. E. H. Lecky, *History of England in the Eighteenth Century*, 1878, Vol. II, p. 233.

[17] *Ibid.*, pp. 243 ff.   [18] *Ibid.*, p. 285.

The coming of the Scotch-Irish during the critical period from the fourth decade of the eighteenth century to the outbreak of the Revolution was of far-reaching importance. The great migration of 1620 to 1640, which laid the basis for New England culture, numbered only twenty thousand, while the Scotch-Irish migration amounted to many times that number.[19] They were scattered along the frontier from New England to the Carolinas and with their stubbornly marked traits and pronounced loyalties provided a sort of social cement uniting the diverse colonial groups. It has been contended that they were "the underlying cause of the American Revolution" and that through their stubborn hostility to England they "supplied to colonial resistance a lining without which it would have collapsed." John Hughes, distributor of stamps for Pennsylvania, observed, October 12, 1765, "Common justice calls upon me to say, the body of people called Quakers, seemed to pay obedience to the Stamp Act, and so do that part of the Church of England and Baptists, that are not some way under Proprietary influence. But Presbyterians and Proprietary minions spare no pains to engage the Dutch and lower classes of people, and render the royal government odious." [20]

The traditional dissenting groups, such as the Baptists and Quakers, were often but slightly tinged with political dissent, while the Presbyterians, who clung to a faith diametrically opposed to the spirit of religious dissent, were among the most pronounced of political dissenters. The problem of liberty in the colonies was complicated in that it always presented a twofold aspect. There was the problem of freedom from the mother country which was essentially political and there was the prob-

[19] See Hanna, *The Scotch-Irish in America*, Vol. I, p. 83, for an estimate of their numbers.
[20] Ford, *op. cit.*, p. 466.

lem of freedom from the intolerance and injustice of the colonial governments in their treatment of the persecuted and disinherited groups which was primarily domestic and religious. The motives that prompted these two movements for freedom were not always identical and the solutions of these problems did not always go hand in hand. In Massachusetts and Connecticut, for example, the external problem of political freedom was solved long before the domestic problem. Connecticut did not abolish her establishment until 1818 and Massachusetts not before 1833. They thus presented the curious anomaly of colonies stultifying in their internal domestic policies the ideal of liberty for which they had fought so successfully in the external and political sphere. Of this fact the dissenting Baptists and Quakers constantly and vainly reminded them. In Virginia, on the other hand, the problem of religious liberty was practically solved before the onset of the Revolution.

The dissenting groups were often torn between the political and religious phases of liberty. The Baptists and Quakers in New England might well fear that complete separation from England would place them more at the mercy of the intolerant colonial establishments. The Presbyterians, on the other hand, who had come to America in a spirit of revolt against the mother country, were also members of a church which in its great historic form in Scotland was a powerful and intolerant state church. The intolerance born of this ingrained tradition of state churchism thus made the Presbyterians opposed to all sectarians. Their traditional hatred of political tyranny, however, inclined them to make common cause with dissenting sects oppressed by state establishments in New England or Virginia. Dissenting groups such as the Quakers and Baptists could very easily find religious sanctions for revolt from England and all forms of established religion. The Presbyterian church, on the other hand, was forced to play a dissenting rôle in spite of the inherent incompatibility of historic Presbyterianism with all forms of religious dissent. The Presbyterian church is still the most illiberal of all the great dissenting-revivalistic denominations.

This throws light for us upon the halting attitude which, we shall see, was taken by the Presbyterians in Virginia in the fight for religious liberty. They were not prepared by tradition and experience to sympathize with complete disestablishment. An entire parity of all sects before the law and the complete separation of church and state were not contemplated in historic Presbyterianism. At first, in Virginia the Presbyterians seemed to be content with the measure of freedom assured them by the Act of Toleration. Prior to the Revolution they were willing to leave the established Anglican church to its own devices so long as Presbyterians were assured freedom to preach, organize churches, and worship according to their peculiar faith. This was of course the status of dissent in contemporary England.

In spite of the stern Calvinistic theology of the Ulster Scots, or perhaps because of it, they fitted into the American scene admirably. Back of them lay an early pioneer training acquired when they laid the basis of a flourishing civilization in the wilds of Ulster. The struggle with nature was later supplemented by the struggle against political oppression and combined with a rigid Calvinism to create a people who were pugnacious, resourceful, venturesome, and stubbornly loyal to conviction. No less a lover of liberty than Milton called them "the blockish Presbyterians" from a "barbarous nook of Ireland." Today their descendants in North Carolina are sometimes alluded to by unfriendly critics as "the pig-headed Presbyterians." Governor Knott once said, "The Scotch-Irishman is one who keeps the commandments of the Lord and every other good thing he can get his hands on." [21] This is not the stock from which spring poets, artists, philosophical idealists, or religious mystics. But it was precisely the stock most in demand in the backwoods of America where the Scotch-Irish were forced to settle. There they fought the Indians with one hand and tamed nature with the other. From them in time sprang great captains of industry, lawyers, soldiers, politicians, and pugnaciously orthodox theologians.

The genius of the Scotch-Irish Presbyterians found admirable interpretation in the realistic Scotch philosophy of "common sense" which they taught in the schools and colleges they founded. This more or less half-baked metaphysics offered a safe middle ground between the lofty but logically intransigent theology of John Calvin and the spotted actuality of business and politics.[22] Their common-sense philosophy saved them from the hopeless impasse of Yankee realism versus religious and moral intransigence which gave to New England culture a note of ghostly unreality. It fitted the view of life of the much touted "self-made man," the characteristic product of the American frontier society, with his adaptability, his fund of practical good sense, his facile and shallow idealism, his individualistic ethics, his pathetic lack of social imagination, and his naïve egotism. The conservative Presbyterians have served as makeweights and mediators rather than as innovators and radicals in the melting-pot of American culture. Their philosophy of common sense, their strategic position, their stern Puritan ethics, and insistence upon an educated clergy, when combined with the moral and spiritual dynamic inspired by the Great Awakening, enabled the Scotch-Irish Presbyterians to play a rôle in

[21] Dinsmore, *The Scotch-Irish in America*, p. 29.
[22] McCosh, *Scotch Philosophy*, p. 299. See also Woodbridge Riley, *American Philosophy*, 1907, p. 562.

molding a pioneer society out of all proportion to their numbers. Scotch-Irish cultural traits passed over into other communions and today shape the pattern of the religious life and social ethics of Baptists and Methodists in wide areas of the South and West.

V

The events in colonial history of primary importance for the fate of the dissenters were the Act of Toleration in 1689, the Great Awakening which began with the Edwardean revivals of 1734, continuing intermittently until the end of the century, and finally the American and French Revolutions. The Act of Toleration soon became part of the law of Virginia and the handful of Quakers and other dissenters then enjoyed in Virginia the same liberties as their brethren in England. The Puritan colonies stubbornly ignored the growing spirit of tolerance in the Empire. Massachusetts was deprived of her charter in 1684, thanks to her flouting of the royal mandates requiring her to return dissenting British subjects to England for trial. In the new charter of 1691, abolishing the theocracy, England sought to assure to all forms of dissent in Massachusetts the privileges enjoyed in England. The situation was complicated of course by the fact that the establishment of the Bay colony, unlike that of Virginia, was not recognized in English law. The result was that the clergy, aided by the magistrates, tried to reintroduce the regulations of the old seventeenth-century theocratic establishment. The laws of the Bay colony looking to this end were nullified by the Crown in 1725, and for the next few decades legislation was grudgingly passed looking to the extension to the dissenters of the privileges granted them under the Act of Toleration. Similar privileges were likewise unwillingly granted to dissenters in Connecticut, only to be taken away after the Great Awakening.

The Great Awakening was an event of profound importance for the dissenters both in New England and in Virginia. It originated under the preaching of Edwards, a loyal minister of the establishment, but his emphasis upon the intimate individual religious experience known as the "new birth" contained a deadly menace to the integrity of the establishment. It created a spirit of schism which registered itself within the Puritan establishments in the form of the Separatist movement, which threatened their complete destruction. More important still was the fact that this revivalistic type of Protestantism, though originating within the state church, in time reached the groups of struggling dissenters, especially the Baptists. Baptist evangelists of the Separatist, or radical-revivalistic type went from New England to Virginia where, in conjunction with the New Light or revivalistic wing of the Presbyterians, they were instrumental in initiating a social and political revolution that wiped out the Anglican establishment and made it possible for Jefferson to write his famous Bill of Religious Rights into the constitution of Virginia, the first complete separation of church and state in history.

The Revolution and the subsequent adoption of the first amendment to the Constitution made complete separation of church and state part of the organic law of the land. It did not affect, however, the rights of the states to solve the problem of religious liberty in their own way. Religious establishments still lingered like vestigial remains, especially in the intransigent Puritan colonies. Connecticut did not abolish her establishment until 1818. Only after the slow working of powerful economic forces had effactually broken down the deeply ingrained habits of the Bay state and convinced her that the establishment was a genuine hindrance to the prosperity of the commonwealth did she grant to her citizens complete religious liberty with the abolition of her religious establishment in 1833.

During the entire colonial period a powerful and yet ill-defined set of forces peculiar to a pioneer culture were subtly and silently at work in New England as well as in Virginia, undermining the establishments and breaking their stranglehold upon the masses of the people. This pioneer culture first found an ideology in Jeffersonianism, which worked hand in hand with dissent in the overthrow of the Anglican establishment and offered vigorous opposition to the entrenched Federalism of Massachusetts and Connecticut. It is one of the happy accidents of American history that the highly abstract old-world fictions of natural rights which Jefferson seems to have derived ·from Locke and Sidney and which were clothed with the rich emotional life centering around the struggle for independence, should have so admirably fitted the loosely organized life of the frontier. For the frontiersman there was no break between the lofty phrases of Paine and the Declaration of Independence and the agrarian philosophy of Jefferson. New England, on the other hand, was never sympathetic to Jeffersonianism, in spite of the fact that Jeffersonianism was really the first crude attempt to give expression to an inchoate nationalism slowly taking shape around the pioneer. Where the frontiersman prevailed Jeffersonianism flourished and where Jefferson's ideas were accepted the establishments were doomed. The religious struggle in Massachusetts and Connecticut after the adoption of the Constitution was merely a phase of a conflict between two types of culture, the old outworn town culture of the theocracies and the culture of a rising frontier democracy. The latter finally prevailed and with its victory went the downfall of Federalism and the elimination of the establishments of New England.

Chapter IV: Dissent and "The Unspotted Lambs of the Lord"

COTTON MATHER calls the Pilgrim Fathers "a little flock of kids," reserving the term "lambs" for the founders of the Bay colony.[1] Just why the frolicsomeness of the kid was thought to suit the Pilgrims and the amiable sincerity of the lamb the founders of the Bay colony we are not informed by the garrulous Mather. Possibly he meant that the Pilgrims were immature or adolescent dissenters in contrast with the Bay lambs who were destined to develop into conforming sheep. What impresses us is the grotesque absurdity of such figures of speech. In a very real sense Cotton Mather was a symbol of his community and age. The intellectual and spiritual unreality, so characteristic of the man and of that monumental synthesis of Brahminical lore, his *Magnalia*, long remained a trait of New England culture, although this note of unreality was accompanied by a vigorous and hard-bitten realism at the level of business and politics.

Paradox lies at the heart of New England culture, for it has produced the thrifty, calculating, and shrewdly realistic Yankee as well as the impossible medieval theologian and the heaven-storming reformer with his spiritual abandon and his moral ruthlessness. The Yankee shot or enslaved the Indians while Mather enthused over God's wisdom in founding the theocracy

[1] Cotton Mather, *Magnalia Christi Americana*, 1702, Vol. I, pp. 54, 65.

in the wilderness to rescue the savages from the devil; the Yankee, pursuing a charmingly realistic policy that would have aroused the admiration of Machiavelli, banished or beat or hanged Baptists and Quakers while election sermons thundered of the liberties of the colonists endangered by England; the Yankee insisted that dissenters pay the taxes to support the establishment or go to jail, while an armed mob threw the tea overboard in the Boston harbor in protest against English taxation; Baptists were imprisoned for conscience's sake by indefatigable Yankee tax-collectors while the Massachusetts leaders, John and Sam Adams, joined in the famous declaration of the inalienable rights of the Americans to be free; the Yankee quietly built up a fortune in the slave trade while Sumner, in turgid philippics in the Senate, pilloried the iniquities of the slavocracy; the Yankee shrewdly steered New England, and finally the nation, into a career of studied economic selfishness through the tariff while Emerson and the Concord school engaged in heavenly discourse on the brotherhood of man. The gap between precept and practice is of course always present in individuals as well as in communities. In the New England theocracies, it is merely accentuated by the contrast between the loftiness of the pretensions and the cool and calculating realism at the level of conduct.

I

Many elements entered into the paradox of New England culture but of primary importance for our purpose is the paradoxical fact that "the unspotted lambs of the Lord," who made it such hard sledding for the dissenters in their Bible commonwealth, were themselves originally of dissenting stock. Of the twenty-five thousand English settled in New England by 1640, genealogists and statisticians have estimated that fifty per cent came from Suffolk, Essex, and Herts and twenty per cent from Norfolk, Lincoln, Nottingham, Middlesex, Kent, Surrey, and Sussex. The counties on the Welsh border and next to Scotland supplied very few.[2] We must recall also in this connection that the district from which the population of New England came corresponds very closely to the districts in which Lollardry spread from the days of Wyclif down to the Reformation. Before the death of Richard II, Lollardry was strong in Sussex, Gloucester, Leicester, Northampton, Worcester, and London. It afterwards spread into Middlesex, Essex, Suffolk, Norfolk, and Lincoln.[3]

To what extent this ancient Lollard dissenting tradition permeated the masses of the population of New England we do not know. That it determined the texture of New England culture so far as religion is concerned, we have seen, is claiming too much.[4] The type of dissent embraced by the oligarchy was that which originated among the exiled English of the Continent under Henry Jacob and other leaders of nonseparatist Congregationalism.[5] This dominated the more radical dissent of the Plymouth colony.

This immigration was still further marked by the fact that the bulk of it came between the years 1620 and 1642. The pressure which, during the régime of Charles I and Archbishop Laud, drove men from England to settle upon the inhospitable shores of New England, ceased with the opening of the Long Parliament. That is to say, the stock that came to New England was drawn from a certain locality of England with strong dis-

---

[2] G. M. Trevelyan, *History of England*, p. 437.
[3] See map in G. M. Trevelyan, *England in the Age of Wycliffe*, 1899, p. 352.
[4] See T. C. Hall, *The Religious Backgrounds of American Culture*, pp. 96 ff.
[5] Champlin Burrage, *The Early English Dissenters*, 1912, Vol. I, pp. 281 f.

senting traditions and from a certain segment of the population
of this region, namely, town tradesmen and country yeomanry
with a sprinkling of lesser nobility. This migration was still
further limited by the fact that it took place in the two decades
from 1620 to 1640, when certain nonconforming attitudes had
been impressed upon the immigrants by the conditions prevailing in England at this time.

These are facts of the utmost importance for the understanding of the culture of New England which was not typical of
England as a whole. The name "New England" is really a
misnomer, for there were groups and cultural traditions in
England not represented in the New England stock. The
humanistic Elizabethan tradition, for example, was not in evidence; the great legal traditions of Magna Charta and the
common law were submerged beneath the medieval trappings
of a theocracy; the larger national outlook represented by the
nobility, the crown, and the great princes of the church was
missing. It was, at least so far as its leadership was concerned,
a dissenting group. But the nonseparatist Congregational group
of dissenters to which the leaders of Massachusetts Bay belonged were never more than a small minority even among the
dissenting population, being far outnumbered at the Puritan
Revolution by the Quakers.[6]

Many factors combined to foster in the Roundhead colony
dissent from England. At first the founders of the colony emphatically denied, in answer to the criticism of their enemies,
that they had separated from the Church of England. No sooner
were they settled in New England, however, than they applied
separatism as a *practical principle* to the Brown brothers, who
were among the "first patentees, men of estates and men of

[6] C. E. Whiting, *Studies in English Puritanism, 1660-1688*, 1931, p. 472.

parts," because they had set up the Episcopal worship at Salem. The Governor and council judged this tended "to mutiny and faction" and the Brown brothers in 1629 were forcibly separated from the Bible commonwealth and shipped back to England. This called forth the following shrewd remark from Isaac Backus, the protagonist of the Baptists in New England: "By this and many other instances we may see, that the men who drew off from the national [English] establishment, as soon as they were convinced that truth called them to it [the reference is to John Robinson and the Pilgrims], were not so severe against dissenters from themselves, as were those who stayed until interest and civil power would favor the cause before they separated." [7] Roger Williams asserted bitterly, "The New England churches secretly call their Mother whore, not daring in America to join with their own Mother's children, though excommunicate." This refusal to tolerate the dissenter is not a matter of conscience, says Williams, but is prompted by a selfish fear that if Episcopalians and others "should set up churches after their own consciences, the greatness and multitude of their own assemblies would decay, and with all the contributions and maintenance of their own ministers, unto which all or most have been forced." [8] This selfish opportunistic separatism gradually grew into a fixed attitude towards England on almost every issue. The culmination of dissent in this larger political sense was absolute separation from the mother country in the Revolution. In this Massachusetts was the leader.

The separation which Massachusetts demanded for herself as a colony in order to preserve her liberties against alleged encroachments of England she never extended to her dissenting

[7] Isaac Backus, *History of New England, 1777-1796*, Vol. I, p. 32.
[8] *The Bloody Tenent: Publications of the Narragansett Club*, Vol. III, p. 283.

groups who sought a like liberty by separation from the establishment. The theocracy fell in 1684 but the establishment persisted as part of the social and economic life of the colony. The great struggle for independence was fought and won, and Massachusetts, after much debate, revised her constitution in 1780 but still remained deaf to the importunities of the persecuted dissenters and retained the establishment. Again in 1820 an effort was made to revise the constitution and abolish the establishment. Daniel Webster and other conservative Federalist leaders threw the weight of their influence into the scales in favor of the establishment, and again the dissenters failed to attain their goal. When complete separation of church and state did come in 1833, it came not as a result of the impact of the liberalizing forces of democracy and dissent but through a curious and undreamed-of combination of factors, partly political, partly churchly, but mostly economic. It was a question of taxes that finally set the dissenters free in Massachusetts.

II

Fate transformed the dissenting Congregationalists of the Bay colony into a militant and intolerant Bible commonwealth. The theocracy was not even faintly suggested in the charter, which contemplated merely a trading corporation. At first particularism reigned, due to the dispersed and loosely organized settlements. The General Court merely authorized such matters as providing for a minister or erecting a school, leaving it to the people to devise ways and means. The charter, however, made a dozen men autocrats, to all practical purposes. Determined to maintain unity, they dealt with a high hand from the very start with differences of opinion as to law enforcement, religious beliefs, or public morals.[9] The gay worldling, Thomas Morton of Merrymount, was banished, together with a certain Philip Ratcliffe who for "scandalous speeches" had his ears cut off and was fined forty pounds. The Brown brothers were sent out of the colony for supporting Anglicanism; Roger Williams was banished for being a separatist, as were the Baptists Clarke and Holmes; Ann Hutchinson was exiled because of Antinomianism and the Quakers were whipped at the cart's tail from town to town, banished, or hanged.

After every spasm of repression the social ideal of the oligarchy took on more definite shape. It envisaged a Bible commonwealth, modeled after the Old Testament theocracy, with Reverend John Cotton as its high priest. In 1631 the franchise was limited to the church members; in doing this the oligarchy exercised a right, according to a "filial piety" historian, "of which nobody but a fool would complain." [10] Does this vigorous language conceal a sneaking feeling that this "right" was debatable? After the flurry aroused by Roger Williams it was voted in 1636 that no church should be approved without the sanction of the magistrates and established churches. As a result of the Antinomian controversy associated with the name of Ann Hutchinson, a law was passed that no town could harbor a person for longer than three weeks without the permission of two of the magistrates or one of the council. "In other words, no Englishman could settle in Massachusetts without personal permission from Winthrop, Dudley or Endicott, or two of their eight associates." [11] A law of 1635 made church attendance compulsory, another in 1638 taxed

[9] S. E. Morison, *Builders of the Bay Colony*, 1930, p. 44.
[10] Henry M. Dexter, *The Congregationalism of the Last Three Hundred Years*, 1880, p. 420.
[11] J. T. Adams, *The Founding of New England*, p. 169.

church members and non-church members for the support of the minister.

The culmination was reached in the famous Cambridge Platform of 1648, which placed the power of the state at the disposal of the priesthood so that they were enabled to use the arm of the law for the enforcement of the requirements of their Biblical theocracy. The fundamental thesis of this famous document is that the principles of government both in church and state are given in the Word of God. It was the culmination of half a generation of practical experience in the development of a theocracy. In it we find a curious blend of the churchly and the sectarian elements. The church-state of Calvin was adapted to the peculiar conditions of Massachusetts Bay. The pressure of contemporary events in England is seen in the adoption of the Westminster Catechism as the confession of faith and the closer approximation to the Presbyterian polity.[12] This served all the more to accentuate the churchly type.

III

Buried beneath this hard and fast churchly form were dissenting elements, such as the acceptance of the Bible as final authority in matters of polity and doctrine, the covenant as the basis of local church organization, the autonomy of the individual congregation, and the limitation of control of other churches to fellowship and advice.[13] The original dissenting elements in the New England theocracy were never destined to play any great rôle in the life of the colony. For the best part of two hundred years the genius of the Bay colony was well

[12] Dexter, *op. cit.*, p. 438.
[13] Williston Walker, *History of Congregational Churches in the United States*, 1900, p. 162.

expressed in the sinister motto of the law book of Massachusetts, "Whoso resisteth the power resisteth the ordinances of God and they that resist receive to themselves damnation." [14]

In "the New England way" a church is formed, after the permission of the magistrates is secured, "by public covenanting together . . . of such persons in any town desiring membership as satisfied each other of their mutual fitness; other churches coöperating by their delegated presence, with some formal expression of fellowship." [15] Such a church elects a pastor, a teacher, and two or more ruling elders, and these constitute the presbytery. People and presbytery constitute the church and both accept the will of God as revealed in the Bible as their supreme rule of faith and practice. "The New England way," therefore, looked at from one point of view is a theocracy or a bibliocracy; in a sense it "resembles a democracy"; and if we stress the power of the presbytery it is an aristocracy.[16] The democratic note of a group freely covenanting together is essentially dissenting; the rôle of the presbytery smacks of the church state ideal of Geneva and Scotland.[17]

Cotton sought bravely to preserve a proper balance between the dissenting trait of Congregationalism and the churchly trait of presbytery. "The gospel alloweth no church authority (or rule properly so called) to the Brethren, but reserveth that wholly to the elders; and yet preventeth the tyranny and oligarchy, and exorbitancy of the Elders, by the large and firm establishment of the liberties of the Brethren, which ariseth to a *power* in them." [18] These "liberties" consist of the power of

[14] Backus, *op. cit.*, Vol. I, p. 323.
[15] Dexter, *op. cit.*, p. 448.
[16] *Ibid.*, p. 441.
[17] For the distinction between Presbyterianism and Independency, see T. C. Pease, *The Leveller Movement*, 1916, Chap. 2.
[18] John Cotton, *The Keys of the Kingdom of Heaven*, p. 36; the citations are from the edition of 1843.

covenanting to form the church, of choice of officers, of raising
exceptions to proposed members, of expostulating with members "in case of private scandals," of speaking in meeting or
asking questions with the consent and under the direction of
the elders. Each local church consisting of presbytery and congregation was a complete autonomous group. Other churches
might advise but could not control the individual church.

The real test of power as between congregation and presbytery emerged in the matter of discipline. "The presbytery cannot excommunicate the whole church (though apostate) for
they must tell the church and join with the church in that censure: so neither can the church excommunicate the whole presbytery, because they have not received from Christ an office of
rule, without their officers." [19] Here then is an impasse. The
church cannot express its will except through the presbytery;
any censure expressed by the rulers or the presbytery is not valid
unless it has the sanction of the congregation. The free spontaneity of the Congregational dissenting tradition is "cribbed,
cabined, and confined" by the authoritarianism of the presbytery; the aristocratic presbytery is held in check by the democratic congregation. On the face of things it would seem that
"the New England way" was neither purely dissenting nor
purely churchly in character but, like New England culture, an
artificial synthesis. In its practical working, however, it was
Presbyterian and Calvinistic, not Congregationalist and dissenting.[20]

Dissent characterized by the general term Congregationalism
based its idea of the church upon Matthew 18: 15-17: "Moreover, if thy brother shall trespass against thee, go and tell him
his fault between thee and him alone; if he shall hear thee
thou hast gained thy brother. But if he will not hear thee, then

[19] *Ibid.*, p. 42.   [20] Pease, *op. cit.*, pp. 53 f.

take with thee one or two more that in the mouth of two or three witnesses every word shall be established. And if he shall neglect to hear them, tell it unto the church; but if he neglect to hear the church, let him be unto thee as a heathen man and a publican." These words were interpreted to mean that the individual church is autonomous and a law unto itself. Since the individual church disciplines and controls its members, admission to membership must be carefully guarded. State churches, such as the Presbyterian, admitted to membership those familiar with essential dogmas and free from scandal in private life. The dissenting Congregationalists demanded that the church member have a saving knowledge of the means of grace, for otherwise the intolerable situation would arise where the saints or real Christians would have their lives regulated by unregenerated church members.

This was the Independent ground for opposition to the theocracy of Geneva and the Erastian state of Elizabeth. For the church, in the thought of the dissenting Independent, was not a matter of cultural inheritance but a voluntary creation of regenerated persons who *covenant together* for the attainment of spiritual ends. The fundamental law of Congregationalism was the covenant. The sanctions for the rights and privileges of the church embodied in this covenant flow not from the state but from the perfect law of Christ, the author of the church. The magistrate, therefore, could never settle matters of conscience or punish religious offenses. On the great question of the relation of church and state Congregational dissent was faced with these alternatives. If the magistrate may not be trusted with the decision of matters of conscience, either the church must assert its supremacy over the state to safeguard religious values or the church must maintain its spiritual autonomy and integrity through complete separation of church and state. John Cotton and the Massachusetts leaders chose the first of these alternatives, thus following out the inherent logic of their Calvinistic theology, and sacrificing their heritage of dissent.

The clergy, not church organization, was the real bond of the theocracy. "The New England way" meant in actual practice *"a speaking aristocracy in the face of a silent democracy."* [21] When we recall that the New England town meeting was really the politically active church organization in which the presbytery was paramount, we are inclined to be somewhat skeptical of its much vaunted rôle as a trainer in freedom and democracy. This suspicion is strengthened by the historical facts in regard to the treatment of the dissenters. One seeks in vain for any indication that the dissenting Baptists and Quakers were ever able to tap this original democratic dissenting tradition in the interest of greater freedom and tolerance for themselves. Congregationalism remained a shadowy tradition with little or no cultural significance. The original self-sufficient cultural units of churches composed of presbytery and congregation were completely dominated by the standing order of the church state in which the unifying bond was the clergy. Whenever Winthrop, Endicott, and Dudley wanted to put through some scheme of the oligarchy they invariably called on Cotton and the ministers to find some text in the Scriptures that lent itself to their program, with which to convince the people that what the oligarchy wanted was merely part of the divine will and designed for their good.

IV

The doublings and twistings and questionable casuistical distinctions necessary to maintain the artificial relationship be-

---

[21] This remark is attributed to Samuel Stone of Hartford by Mather, *op. cit.*, Vol. I, p. 437.

tween the dissenting and churchly phases in the thought pattern of the theocracy are nowhere better illustrated than in the utterances of the ablest man of the group, John Cotton. Typical of his thought is the following passage. "In a free state no magistrate hath power of the bodies, goods, lands, liberties of a free people, but by their free consents. And because free men are not free lords of their own estates, but are only stewards unto God, therefore they may not give their free consents to any magistrate to dispose of their bodies, goods, lands, liberties, at large as themselves please, but as God, the sovereign Lord of all, alone. And because the Word is a perfect rule, as well of righteousness as of holiness, it will be therefore necessary that neither the people give consent, nor that the magistrate take power to dispose of the bodies, goods, lands, liberties of the people, but according to the laws and rules of the Word of God." [22]

In this passage Cotton does his best to clothe his essentially illiberal ideas in the bright garments of seventeenth-century liberalism. In a free state the magistrates hold their powers by the consent of the governed. But the people are only free when they act as the stewards of God and dispose of their liberties in accord with God's will. The Bible as the word of God is the "perfect rule," in terms of which they are to determine these rights which they as a free people delegate to their rulers. But the question will inevitably arise as to how a people can be free when they take the will of another, even though that other be God, as final in determining what are the rights they delegate to their rulers. Cotton seeks to avoid the difficulty by a familiar theological subterfuge, namely, the will of God in the Bible (interpreted of course by Cotton and his associates) is so "perfect," so compelling, so unequivocally clear to the mind not

[22] *Publications of the Narragansett Club*, Vol. III, p. 254.

perverted by sin that it is obeyed spontaneously and with no sense of coercion. Interpretation of what this will is and enforcement of it by the magistrate thus become unnecessary in the case of the good man. When a man disobeys this will it is not proof of its inadequacy or illiberalism but merely indicates the presence of a bad and sinful will in the recalcitrant. John Cotton used this argument to justify his banishment of Roger Williams. The will of a free or regenerated people is always perfectly in accord with the will of God. Sin, or disobedience to God's will, is the only real enemy to freedom. It was this "bloodless ballet of theological categories" that constituted the thought world of the Puritan casuist.

Within this narrow theological setting of Cotton's thought it is obvious that separatism, liberty of conscience, and tolerance can have at best very restricted meanings. The separation of church and state for Cotton was primarily one of *function* just as it was in the Middle Ages. The church member has no right, as such, to resist state authority because such resistance should be made through political channels. Political activities and duties are not identical with religious because they belong to a different department of life. Conduct at the polls is different from that at the communion table. Phases of life, such as private morals, may belong now to the church, now to the state. The church intervenes when a man refuses to baptize his children; the state, when he murders his wife. But for Cotton this separation was functional, not absolute. There was for him an *organic* relation between church and state as is shown by the fact that he banned the sects. He dared not admit them for they would "dissolve the continuity of the state, especially ours whose walls are made of the stones of the churches." [23] There can be but

[23] *Ibid.*, p. 279.

one authoritative source for the will of God, namely, the establishment and the clergy. To admit the sects would destroy the fundamental architectonic principle of the theocracy.

Liberty of conscience and tolerance, in the thought of John Cotton, were restricted to "indifferent things" and did not apply to fundamentals. These "indifferent things" included variations in forms of worship, such as kneeling to take the sacrament, or in dress, as in the wearing of the surplice. In these matters Cotton insisted that "no man be forced to submit against his *conscience* (Romans 14: 14, 23) nor be judged of contempt of lawful *authority* because he is not suddenly persuaded of the *expediency* of indifferent things." [24] The words Cotton italicizes indicate the pivots of his thought. "Conscience" functions only in the sphere of the "expedient" and the "indifferent"; "authority" should be restricted to the sphere of "fundamentals."

What Cotton and the theocracy deemed "fundamental" may be seen from the following exceedingly illuminating passage from the laws of the Bay colony dating from Cotton's time. "Although no humane power be lord over the faith and consciences of men, and therefore may not constrain them to believe or profess against their consciences: yet because such as bring in damnable heresies, tending to the subversion of the Christian faith, and destruction of the souls of men, ought daily to be restrained from such notorious impiety, it is therefore ordered," etc. "Damnable heresies" are denials of any of the following doctrines, "immortality of the soul," "resurrection of the body," the saving work of Jesus Christ, "the morality of the fourth commandment." Following Leviticus 24: 15, 16, blasphemy is made a capital crime.[25] This passage is a striking illus-

---

[24] *Publications of the Narragansett Club*, Vol. III, p. 256.
[25] Massachusetts laws, quoted by John Clarke, *Ill News from New England*, pp. 69 f.

tration of the constant confusion of dissenting and churchly traditions by the theocracy. A sweeping assertion of the dissenting principle of liberty of conscience that leaves nothing to be desired is immediately nullified by restrictions inspired by the requirements of a Bible commonwealth.

If the Puritan priests had even a fraction of the intelligence ascribed to them by the "filial piety" school of historians, they must have been aware of the fundamental contradiction involved in this statement. To be intelligible at all such language must mean that the "damnable heresies" enumerated lie outside the sphere of liberty of conscience and hence may be made the subject of legislation. That is to say, liberty of conscience is restricted to what the entrenched theocracy deems "indifferent" while what they deem "heretical" is excluded. They lay down liberty of conscience as a universal principle and then proceed to delimit it by excluding from its sphere all their pet theological beliefs. It is difficult to justify such an attitude either by the laws of logic or by the rubrics of moral common sense. The logic of circumstances turned the dissenter John Cotton into a standpatter. Cotton was, primarily, a political and moral casuist and, secondarily, a theologian with little use for the ethics of the Sermon on the Mount. The historical student gets the impression occasionally that the famous "Puritan conscience" was after all something of a moral monstrosity.

A keen critic of American life asserts that due to lack of psychological penetration the Puritan "does not even rise to the level of the hypocrite." This may be due to a short-sighted "astuteness" born of a realistic concentration upon immediate selfish interests or was "simply naïveté." [26] This criticism is lacking in historical perspective. The Puritan priests were not

[26] André Siegfried, *America Comes of Age*, 1927, p. 36.

conscious hypocrites. They were, however, the victims of two traditions so thoroughly incompatible that they were constantly exposed to the charge of lack of moral and spiritual ingenuousness. This inconsistency was undoubtedly felt by the victims of their intolerance and helps us to understand the extreme scorn and bitterness with which the leaders of the New England theocracy were attacked by Roger Williams and Quaker writers, such as George Bishop in his *New England Judged*. It would be difficult for the courageous and forthright Williams not to feel a measure of contempt for the tergiversations of Cotton, the apologist of the theocracy. For the Quaker, with his simple and ingenuous loyalty to the "Inner Light," the intolerant and casuistical Puritan priest could very easily come to be regarded as the very incarnation of the spirit of Antichrist.

On the great issue of religious liberty the New England leaders, apart from Rhode Island, were never clear but moved in a twilight region of compromise and casuistry. They used the language of the liberty-loving dissenting tradition while conducting the affairs of state along the lines of the realistic and intolerant churchly tradition. This illuminates the dualism alluded to earlier in this chapter between the moral and spiritual ideal and the actual facts of the political and economic life. This explains why Massachusetts bred at the higher level the morally irresponsible reformer and the impractical idealist while at the lower level she produced the shrewd politician, the moral casuist, and the thrifty man of affairs whose ethics often soared no higher than the moral bookkeeping of Benjamin Franklin. The Puritan priests were primarily practical politicians, and secondarily theologians and moral idealists. The pragmatic realism of their political and economic philosophy outlived their theology.

V

It should be evident from the foregoing that the fundamental weakness of the colonial society of New England, with the exception of Rhode Island, was the absence of a healthful dissenting tradition. The difficulties of Rhode Island in establishing a commonwealth based on the philosophy of dissent merely convinced the timorous Massachusetts conservatives of the wisdom of their position. Not only was the original dissenting element, which largely induced the colonists to leave the mother country, submerged and lost sight of, but all forms of dissent coming in from the outside were sternly suppressed. Massachusetts never shared the sentiments expressed by Madison when he said in the debates in the Virginia house of burgesses in 1788, "This freedom [religious] arises from that multiplicity of sects, which pervades America, and which is the best and only security for religious liberty in any society. For where there is such a variety of sects, there cannot be a majority of any one sect to oppress and persecute the rest." [27]

We shall see later that it was the presence of the vigorous dissenting groups in Virginia, more than any other one factor, which enabled the Virginia leaders to appreciate and finally to solve the problem of religious liberty and equipped them to play the leading rôle in shaping the organic law of the land as to religious liberty. It was the absence of this practical experience that explains why the Massachusetts leaders made no contribution whatever to the solution of the problem of religious liberty. Colonial Massachusetts did not understand religious liberty because it had no dissent and permitted none.

[27] Jonathan Elliot, *Debates in the Several State Conventions on the Adoption of the Federal Constitution, 1827, 1836*, Vol. III, p. 376, cited by E. F. Humphrey, *Nationalism and Religion in America, 1774-1789*, 1924, pp. 473 f.

The worst spiritual despotism is that rooted in uniformity of religious sentiments, such as Massachusetts cultivated so assiduously. The stains on Massachusetts history connected with the cruel and bloody treatment of the Baptists and Quakers and the fearfully benighted fanaticism that hanged ignorant charwomen as witches was the price her people paid for taking their Puritan god too seriously and too unanimously.

The crushing of dissent and the unchallenged supremacy for generations of the Puritan priest with his sublimated intolerance had subtle and far-reaching implications for New England culture. What those implications are can be surmised by a perusal of the sermons of the seventeenth and eighteenth centuries. On March 20, 1707, after the theocracy had begun to wane and the softening influences of eighteenth-century rationalism were beginning to make themselves felt, a sermon was preached by Reverend Benjamin Coleman "before his excellency and the general court in Boston" and published at their command on "Imprecations Against the Enemies of God Lawful and a Duty." [28] The preacher stressed the duty "to utter aloud the devout motions and resentments of your minds in ways of homage to the great God." "Imprecations of judgment upon the wicked enemies of God" should be made part of our prayers. The souls of many martyrs in heaven are calling upon God to "avenge our blood on them that dwell on the earth." Truly an interesting diversion for the blest! "Now if prayers are uttered on this account in heaven," argues the preacher, "are they not decent and becoming in the church here below?" An irresistible *a fortiori* argument! We must be sure, however, to keep our hates and imprecations sanctified and holy. "We must be sure that we do simply consider them as God's enemies and

[28] In Boston Public Library.

not our own, otherwise we may spoil our prayers by gratifying our private spleens." Only the privileged individual who lived in the rarefied atmosphere of absolute moral infallibility of "the unspotted lambs of the Lord" could of course follow this advice, yet the conduct of the Puritan leaders indicates that they thought that they qualified.

When we reflect that for generations men and women were subjected to this sort of training from their preachers it affords us food for reflection. It illuminates John Wilson's conduct when he pronounced the blood-curdling sentence of banishment against Ann Hutchinson and his act during the trial of the Baptist Obadiah Holmes, when, as Holmes testifies, he "struck me before the judgment seat and cursed me, saying, The curse of God or Jesus go with thee." [29] This same Wilson, pastor of a Boston church, stood at the foot of the gallows on Boston common and railed at the Quakers Robinson and Stevenson who were being hanged.[30] In such an atmosphere are born absolute hates. Moral reform becomes sublimated moral ruthlessness. It is vastly flattering to be able to damn in God's name. There is such an exquisite thrill gained from hating out of "a sense of duty to God." One is under no necessity to be careful about it or to reflect upon the consequences or to ask if it violates the principle of Christian charity. The Puritan was trained to formulate his conceptions of right and wrong in the remote and unreal realm of theology. He was encouraged to sublimate his antipathies, isolate them from reality, and launch them incontinently at the world in terms of absolutes, such as "God's will." His moral and spiritual hates thus became sacrosanct. The Puritan priest is dead but we often feel that his ghost still stalks among us.

[29] Backus, *op. cit.*, Vol. I, p. 189.
[30] George Bishop, *New England Judged*, p. 103.

Chapter V: A Forthright Dissenter

THE FIRST wolf to seek access to the fold of the "unspotted lambs" was not a bona fide wolf but a sort of unintentional wolf in sheep's clothing. The reputation of the brilliant Roger Williams had preceded him and the leaders of the Bay colony were prepared to receive him as a most welcome addition. It was only after a series of disappointments and much unhappy friction and misunderstanding that they were at last forced sorrowfully to brand him as a wolf and banish him to the wilderness and the Indians where he belonged. Williams preferred the society of the Indians and the beasts of the forest to the pathologically religious atmosphere of the sheepcote of the "lambs." The wilderness made Rhode Island and religious liberty possible. Was Williams' banishment a premonition of the rôle forest and frontier were to play in liberating the spirit of man in the New World? Certainly a medieval theocracy in the American wilderness was a glaring cultural anachronism to Williams, as to all other free spirits, though it took the Bay colony the best part of two centuries to realize that fact.

I

Roger Williams, the spiritual knight errant of seventeenth-century New England, was born about 1603 and emerges first as a stenographer in the Star Chamber, where he won the commendations of Sir Edward Coke who sent him to school.[1] He received his degree from Pembroke College, Cambridge, in 1626, became acquainted with Thomas Hooker and John Cotton and at this early stage developed the radical flair evinced in his arguments with them against the use of the Book of Common Prayer as unscriptural. By 1630 his views, thanks to probable contacts with the Anglo-Dutch Anabaptists, had become so pronouncedly separatist that he sought escape from the tyranny of Laud by going to the Massachusetts Bay colony, arriving on the ship *Lyon* in February, 1631. Here the future champion of the principle of toleration based upon separation of church and state was brought into direct contact with the persecuting and intolerant New England theocracy. It was a situation fraught with many possibilities.

Roger Williams was the typical reformer of the heaven-storming idealistic type. He was fearless and open, magnanimous, even tender towards those who had wronged him, sometimes impatient and intolerant towards those who differed from him, and yet utterly uncompromising in his loyalty to his ideals and a past master of the arts of controversy so dear to the hearts of men in his day. Williams faced the militant and uncompromising Massachusetts theocracy, puzzled and incensed. He had not yet become the conscious champion of religious liberty and yet he felt the challenge to all that was dear to him. With the reckless abandon of youth and inexperience he threw down the gauntlet to the theocracy. His arraignment of the sins of the theocracy, it must be confessed, is not quite convincing. He condemned the Massachusetts churches because they had paused at nonconformity and had not completely separated from the Church of England. He claimed the magistrates could not pun-

---

[1] R. A. Guild, *Biographical Introduction: Publications of the Narragansett Club*, Vol. I, pp. 1 ff.

ish sins of the first table of the Decalogue, such as idolatry, Sabbath-breaking, blasphemy, and the like, because they were offenses against God, not man. He took the disconcerting and impractical position that the settlers had no right to the lands of the Indians. He opposed the use of the oath in secular matters on the ground that an oath is valid only where those who swear are regenerate. It can be well understood why the fathers of the Bay colony were scandalized. Reverend John Cotton called him "a haberdasher of small questions."

Roger Williams was undoubtedly factious. In this he reflected the spirit of his age. He was the ardent champion of ideas which, at that stage in its development, it was entirely impossible to put into practice in the Massachusetts Bay colony. Williams was an uncompromising idealist of the sort for which Massachusetts in later years was to become famous. Yet throughout her history the Bay colony has had little use for any idealism that was not of the home-grown variety and especially for an idealism that directly challenged her vested interests. The result was that, after four stormy and unhappy years, Williams was banished from the colony October 9, 1635. His sickness, which Cotton with amiable Christian charity interpreted as a visitation of God's providence upon Williams for his wicked, heretical ideas, prevented the immediate carrying out of the banishment. Williams remained in Salem proclaiming his ideas in his home. In January, 1636, Williams, finding that the authorities had made provision to put him on board ship and send him to England, fled in midwinter to the Indians of Narragansett Bay where he laid the foundation for a commonwealth based upon the principle for which he had suffered exile.

II

Williams' doctrine of church and state was clearly stated in his reply to Cotton's letter of 1643, which was the beginning of a long controversy between them over the issues arising out of Williams' banishment. Williams maintained that none of the offenses charged tended to "the breach of holy or civil peace of which I have ever desired to be unfainedly tender, acknowledging the Ordinance of Magistracie to be properly and adequately fitted by God, to preserve the civil State in civil peace and order." In other words, the state is an entity in and of itself with its laws and ordinances which have nothing to do with religion. Over against the state with its independent and self-sufficient existence, we have, he says, "a spiritual government and Governours in matters pertaining to his worship and the consciences, of men." Williams maintained that these two sets of "Governments, Governours, Laws, Offences, Punishments are essentially distinct, and the confounding of them brings all the world into Combustion." [2]

Separatism from the organic churchly point of view of Cotton was a radical and dangerous procedure. It is similar to the use of the knife in cutting out in radical and destructive fashion every member of the body which is affected by any ailment. This endangers the health of the whole body. Separatism, therefore, is not only radical and brutal; it is dangerous and stupid. Cotton claimed, "It is not surgery but butchery to heal every sore in a member with no other but abscision from the body." [3] From Williams' point of view, on the other hand, no butchery is involved in the matter of separation, simply because the

[2] *Publications of the Narragansett Club*, Vol. I, p. 335.
[3] *Ibid.*, p. 378.

spheres of state and religion are not organically and inherently related as Cotton contends. Separatism, from Williams' point of view, is merely the normal and necessary withdrawal of a group from the sphere of the state in the exercise of their own inherent right of spiritual autonomy. Instead of weakening the social organism and dealing it a deadly wound, separatism enriches the moral and spiritual life of the community. It is the inevitable result of freedom. As between the two men, Cotton belongs to the Middle Ages and champions a philosophy of society which, even in his own day, was outworn and doomed. Williams talks the language of the free, democratic social order he was instrumental in establishing in Rhode Island.

Implicit in the thought of Roger Williams, as of most of the dissenters, is a dualistic, not to say a pluralistic, philosophy. Taking Cotton's pregnant phrase with regard to the theocracy, "whose walls are made of the stones of the churches," [4] Williams distinguishes four sorts of walls, the "wall spiritual" of the true church, the "pretended wall" of the false church, the "civil wall" of the state, and the "natural or artificial wall," such as the stone wall built to protect the city. The false spiritual wall may injure or destroy the true spiritual wall, that is, religious forces function in the sphere of religion, but the spiritual wall of the realm of religion cannot affect the civil wall of society and the state, and neither religious wall nor civil wall can destroy the natural or artificial wall. "Spiritual may destroy spiritual, if stronger and victorious, but spiritual can not reach to artificial or civil." [5] For Williams, therefore, there were at least three levels of reality, the purely spiritual of the church, the social and civil of the state, and the physical. We may call them the psychological, the cultural, and the physical. The

[4] *Publications of the Narragansett Club*, Vol. III, p. 279.
[5] *Ibid.*, p. 286.

imperative practical necessity for the separation of church and state is based upon a metaphysical separation of the spiritual from the social and the physical.

It is important to remember in this connection that Williams' point of view was essentially religious. The religious man places at the heart of the universe certain values, such as belief in a personal God, and then constructs his philosophy of history, of society, and of nature in terms of the exigencies of these central values. The typical illustration of this is Augustine's *City of God*, in which a symbolic time-scheme is superinduced upon the entire drama of the universe in the interest of the Christian scheme of salvation.

Williams lacked a unified world-scheme such as that of Augustine. In fact his sharp distinction between the spiritual, the civil, and the natural prevented any such scheme. But for Williams, as for every religiously minded man, the field of religion tended to assume the central place in his scheme of reality. The outlying spheres of society and nature occupied a marginal position in his thought and took on inevitably aspects of the unreal. The failure to recognize this central fact weakens many books on Williams, as, for example, the recent *Roger Williams: The New England Firebrand*, by James E. Ernst. It is tacitly assumed by most writers that Williams ascribed to the state a reality and independence and an autonomy which, so far as his words are concerned, seem to make him the forerunner of Madison and Jefferson and Paine. But the underlying philosophy of Paine and Jefferson and Madison was fundamentally different from that of Williams. These statesmen were not especially religious. In fact, they were more or less indifferent to religion and Paine's name at least has become anathema to the champions of traditional orthodoxy. Williams was deeply religious. Religious realities took precedence over those of nature and society. Hence, when Williams talked of natural rights or civic liberties or the validity of a social and secular ethics, he always subordinated them to the laws and liberties and the moral code of the life of the regenerated members of the invisible and world-wide church. This fundamental postulate of Williams' thought must be constantly borne in mind in the discussion that follows in this chapter.

III

The stock Biblical passage often cited by Williams and all other champions of radical separatism is the famous utterance of Jesus, "Render unto Caesar the things that are Caesar's; and unto God the things that are God's." [6] Williams makes much of the fact that Jesus never addressed himself directly to the state nor to state officials as such. Not the external or cultural phase of reality, but the subjective and the psychological, interested him primarily. "The kingdom of God is within you." To this extent the psychological climates of Jesus and of Williams are strikingly similar. But the separatism implied in Jesus' famous dictum was motivated by ideas quite different from those of Williams. Religion and the state were not separated by Jesus because they were essentially different as Williams contended. Jesus' separatism was based upon *indifference* towards existing society, for Jesus, influenced by the prevailing ideas of his time, thought that the present order would speedily give place to a "new heaven and a new earth." This tended to invalidate the existing social order religiously and otherwise. The separatism of Jesus was not, therefore, radical, as in the case of Williams, but was rather an immediate and practical inference drawn from

[6] Matthew 22: 21.

the implications of his belief that the end of the world was near.

The sources of the state for Williams are found not in the religious but in the social and secular order. In fact, state and society are organically related. "All lawful magistrates" are socially derived and created, "hence they can have no more power than fundamentally lies in the bodies or fountains themselves which power, might and authority is not religious, Christian, etc., but natural, human, civil." It follows from this that any officer of the state or any member of society as such neither gains nor loses by being a Christian. "A Christian merchant, physician, lawyer, pilot, father, master, magistrate, etc.," are not better equipped for fulfilling their social functions than are members "of any other conscience or religion." [7] Religious affiliations do not necessarily affect civic duties. "I ask whether or no such as may hold forth other worships or religions, Jews, Turks or antichristians, may not be peaceable and quiet subjects, loving and helpful neighbors, fair and just dealers, true and loyal to the civil government?" [8]

It follows from Williams' position that there can be no such thing as a "Christian" business, a "Christian" legal or medical profession, or a "Christian" state. These are all functions of society. Williams took the famous phrase of Jesus, "Render unto Caesar the things that are Caesar's; and unto God the things that are God's" in the most radical sense. By stressing the complete integrity and independence of the state beyond any power of religion to intermeddle, Williams also laid the basis for the democratic claim of every individual, irrespective of creed, to the fullest enjoyment of the rights and privileges of society. "I say in this respect although that a man is not godly, a Chris-

---

[7] *Publications of the Narragansett Club*, Vol. III, p. 398.
[8] *Bloody Tenent: Publications of the Narragansett Club*, Vol. III, p. 142.

tian, sincere, a church member, yet to deprive him of any civil right or privilege, due to him as a man, a subject, a citizen, is to take from Caesar, that which is Caesar's, which God endures not though it be given to himself." [9] This ideal found its way into the Constitution of the United States, due largely to the strength of the dissenting tradition in this country, but it would hardly be correct to say that even today, among the masses of American citizens, we have arrived at the advanced position reached by Roger Williams almost a century and a half before the Constitution was drafted. Religious beliefs still condition the rights of men.

Flowing from his fundamental assumption that the essence of the state is everywhere identical and that the same principles and rights are at stake wherever the state is found, is the inference that the states of the heathen peoples are legitimate and enjoy a sane and healthful existence. The effectiveness of their laws or the sanity of their community life are in no wise damaged, says Williams, by the fact of their non-Christian character. Williams makes the statement, quite remarkable for a man of his time, that the Christian religion does not necessarily further every sort of public weal. Williams, to be sure, explains this on the assumption that religion from its very nature cannot affect the natural processes involved in the life of the state. For this reason, states with corrupt and erroneous religions, from the Christian point of view, have flourished. He challenges his opponent, Cotton, to explain why "so many stately kingdoms and governments in the world have long and long enjoyed civil peace and quiet, notwithstanding their religion is so corrupt, as that there is not the very name of Jesus Christ amongst them." It is a dangerous assumption, "that the civil

[9] *Bloody Tenent Yet More Bloody: Publications of the Narragansett Club,* Vol. IV, p. 414.

state and the spiritual, the church and the commonweal, they are like Hippocrates' twins, they are born together, grow up together, laugh together, weep together, sicken and die together." [10] Williams weakens his argument by assuming with Cotton and the rest of the thinkers of his time that the Christian religion is the only true religion and all others "corrupt." Heathen states did flourish without any knowledge of Christianity but it does not follow that the decay of their own particular type of religion did not affect the life of the state. The validity of any religion depends upon the cultural situation just as a given culture is affected by its religion.

Williams' doctrine of the state has international implications. No nation can claim superiority over others by virtue of being a "Christian" nation. "The partition wall" that existed in the days of ancient Israel has been broken down so that so far as nationality is concerned "what difference between Asia and Africa, between Europe and America, between England and Turkey, London and Constantinople?" [11] Williams opposed the forceful annexation of the lands of pagan peoples by "Christian kings so-called" who assume the "right by virtue of their Christianity." [12] This of course was directed against the policy of the Massachusetts theocracy towards the Indians. Williams also takes occasion to rebuke the presumption of Cotton and the theocracy in assuming that by virtue of its "Christian" character the Massachusetts commonwealth was superior to the mother country. On the contrary, says Williams, "I acknowledge the land of England, the civil laws, government and people of England not to be inferior to any under heaven." [13] It was in-

[10] *Bloody Tenent: Publications of the Narragansett Club*, Vol. III, pp. 251, 333.
[11] *Ibid.*, p. 111.
[12] *Bloody Tenent Yet More Bloody*, loc. cit., p. 461.
[13] *Mr. Cotton's Letter Examined: Publications of the Narragansett Club*, Vol. I, p. 77.

deed no merit of New England but rather "the mercy of old England, the mother of dissenting consciences," that interfered to stop the religious fanatics of Massachusetts in their bloody excesses.[14]

The unity and independence of the state make it possible to justify any peculiarities or characteristic traits which a given state may embody. Here, as in almost every other instance, Williams opposes Cotton, who would force every form of the state into the mold of the New England theocracy derived from the Old Testament. Williams asserts that there is no truth whatsoever in the claim of Winthrop and Cotton that the Mosaic legislation outlined once and for all the ideal social and political order. In the background of Williams' thought seems to have hovered something quite closely akin to the modern historical conception of the state as a free organic growth. Williams says, "The civil alters according to the constitutions of peoples and nations." [15] This is due to the fact that the state is a function of society, a phase of a culture. It is an agency created by the organic life of a nation to serve its ends. Each state, then, will tend to express, so far as its external traits are concerned, the peculiarities of the life of the people from which it springs.

Separation of religion from the state leaves the state free for the expansion and intensification of its legitimate sphere. In the Bible commonwealth of Massachusetts the state was poverty-stricken and devoid of the dignity and power which were legitimately its own. This was due to the confusion of the scales of values brought about through the fusion of church and state. "The magistrate is to avenge or punish evil," argued Cotton

[14] *Bloody Tenent Yet More Bloody: Publications of the Narragansett Club*, Vol. IV, p. 463.
[15] *Ibid.*, p. 80.

and the theocracy; "heresy being evil ought to be punished civilly." [16] Here the scale of values within religion runs over into the sphere of the state to the confusion and injury both of religion and the state. Again the church refused to permit the state "to prosecute complaints of children against their parents, servants against masters, wives against husbands," all of which properly belongs to the state. For in the structure of society families are "the stones which make up the common building and are properly the objects of the magistrates' care, in respect of civil government, civil order and obedience." [17] The New England state was the subservient tool of the clergy with the result that the rights of citizens suffered. Rights are never safe except when they are defined and safeguarded by a free and enlightened state. Religion and the church are from their very nature unfitted to take care of the rights of men.

IV

Religious persecution for Williams is not only unchristian and immoral but it is stupid and contrary to the nature of things. "An enforced uniformity of religion throughout a nation or civil state, confounds the civil and religious, denies the principles of Christianity and civility." [18] Just as the state in a way transcends religion and receives from religion no increment to its essential power, so religion differs essentially from the state, seeks different ends and makes use of different methods of control. The use of force in religion is, therefore, just as stupid as an appeal to reason to induce nature to alter her course. The state has no organ or set of agencies for dealing with the prob-

[16] *Publications of the Narragansett Club*, Vol. II, p. 162.
[17] *Ibid.*, p. 164.
[18] *Bloody Tenent, loc. cit.*, Vol. III, p. 4.

lems of religion. The state is not irreligious but nonreligious. Persecution is, therefore, a grotesque attempt to apply to the sphere of religion a principle not recognized in religion, namely, force, while on the other hand it introduces into the sphere of the state a set of values which the state from its very nature cannot satisfy.

Hence, for Williams, the most utterly inexcusable form of the state, the most monstrous ruler, is one who sanctions "that blood-killing, soul-killing and state-killing doctrine of not permitting but persecuting all other consciences and ways of worship but his own in the civil state, and so consequently in the whole world, if the power or empire thereof were in his hands." [19] Persecution is for Williams most diabolically destructive to the peace and welfare of mankind. We can understand, therefore, why the persecuting theocracy of New England was to Williams not a state but a political monstrosity. Compare them, he says, "with the rest of the peoples and nations of the world, and we shall not find them ordinary and common, but rather as six fingers, wonders and monsters to all other parts of the world, yea, even to the very Popish Protestant parts of the world also." [20]

For a state claiming to be Christian to persecute involves serious consequences, thanks to the uniformity and inherent integrity of the state in all its forms; for, to concede the right to persecute to the so-called Christian state involves inevitably the right of the non-Christian state also to persecute. There are, in the world, many non-Christian states. They outnumber, in fact, the Christian states. "And if it be granted that the magistrates receive their power of governing the church from the

[19] *Mr. Cotton's Letter Examined, loc. cit.,* p. 44.
[20] *Bloody Tenent Yet More Bloody, loc. cit.,* p. 454. See also *Queries: Publications of Narragansett Club,* Vol. I, p. 35; *Bloody Tenent Yet More Bloody, loc. cit.,* pp. 207, 238.

people, undeniably it follows, that a people, as a people, naturally considered, of what nature or nation soever in Europe, Asia, Africa, or America, have fundamentally and originally, as men, a power to govern the church, to see her do her duty, to correct her, to redress, reform, establish, etc. And if this be not to pull God, and Christ, and Spirit out of heaven, and subject them unto natural, sinful, inconstant men, and so consequently to Satan himself, by whom all peoples naturally are guided, let heaven and earth judge." [21]

The persecuting state, however, presented to Williams a practical problem not easy of solution. He claimed that the state is a law unto itself. It has the right, therefore, where purely political and social matters are concerned, to use coercion. The very nature of religion, however, does not permit the use of force. It belongs to another level of reality. The spiritual wall and the civil wall perform different functions, deal with different sets of values. What shall be done in the case of the ruler who ruthlessly and stupidly ignores these differences and persecutes?

The answer which Williams would seem to be forced to give to this question, if he is to follow out his radical separatism, is that when the ruler has stultified himself as a ruler by using force in the realm of religion this does not justify his victim in committing the same folly and opposing force with force. The Quaker by his patient and passive resistance vanquished Norton and Endicott and the theocracy more effectively than an army with banners. The victory was won by moral and spiritual means, the only means effective in the sphere of religion. It should not be forgotten, however, that the Quaker's victory was more or less a Pyrrhic victory until it was sanctioned by the state, safeguarded by law, and backed by force.

[21] *Bloody Tenent, loc. cit.*, p. 250.

Williams was almost entirely lacking in the mysticism which would have enabled him to sympathize with Quaker pacifism. This came out in his unfortunate controversy with George Fox. Williams, furthermore, had enjoyed the benefits of the practical experiences growing out of the attempt to establish a commonwealth based upon the principle of separation of church and state. These factors combined to make him take a position in regard to the persecuting state which in reality contradicted his basic assumption of the radical separation of church and state. He seems to have sanctioned the use of the power of the state to resist the tyrannical use of force in religious matters. He certainly justified the English revolution as a revolt against persecution. "Although the civil magistrate hath not the power of Christ in matters of religion, yet they that slay the Lord's sheep are not exempted from all judgments. For, if the offenders slay them corporally, the Lord hath armed the civil magistrate with the sword of God to take vengeance on them. In which respect God hath crowned the supreme court of parliament with everlasting honor, in breaking the jaws of the oppressing bishops, etc. Oh, that such glorious justice may not be blemished, by erecting in their stead a more refined, but yet as cruel an episcopacy." [22]

The following would seem to be a good statement of Williams' position on this vexed question, "It is (indeed) one thing to prohibit the Pope, the prelates, the Presbyterians, the Independents, or any from forcing any in the matters of their respective consciences, and accordingly to take the sword from such men's hands, or (as their executioners) to refuse to use it for them: It is another thing to leave them freely to their own consciences, to defend themselves as well as they can, by the two-edged sword of the spirit, which is the word of God, which

[22] *Bloody Tenent Yet More Bloody, loc. cit.,* p. 195.

all the several sorts of pretenders say they have received from Jesus Christ." [23] According to Williams there are, therefore, two ways in which religion may be disturbed or destroyed: "First, when the professors or assemblies thereof are persecuted, that is hunted and driven up and down out of the world: Against such destroyers or disturbers (being tyrants and oppressors) the civil sword ought to be drawn"; and secondly, "by false teachers, false prophets, by spiritual rebels and traitors against the worship and kingdom of Christ Jesus." [24] Religion may be restricted negatively through destruction of property or life or the loss of physical freedom through imprisonment. The state must correct all such evils that make it difficult or impossible to cultivate the religious life. The real enemies of religion are those who flourish in the proper realm of religion and make use of the methods of religion, namely, the false teachers and prophets. This realm lies beyond the purview of the state. Heresy as such is not a civil offense.

The pluralistic or dualistic metaphysics underlying Williams' doctrine of the separation of church and state obviously met with a severe strain when he came to discuss such practical matters as the persecuting ruler. For man, whether saint or sinner, Christian or pagan, belongs to all three levels of the "spiritual," the "civil," and the "natural" walls. He is not only a psychophysical organism but, as Aristotle long ago recognized, he is also a political animal. A radical separation of state and religion would lead to a radical division between man the citizen and man the saint. Williams, who differed from the Quakers in many ways and was among their bitterest opponents, agreed with them in the formlessness and subjectivity of his conception of religion. But Williams, unlike the Quaker, was

---

[23] *Ibid.*, p. 204.
[24] *Ibid.*, p. 320.

more or less of a practical statesman and was forced by the pressure of circumstances to take a position in regard to the use of force in resisting the persecuting ruler that did not harmonize with his general philosophy of church and state. Williams and the Quakers did not realize to what extent the vigor and sanity of the inner life of religious emotions depend upon external cultural forms. The study of human culture shows that the religious beliefs of men are in the main merely psychological correlatives of their external ways of life. The gods were largely anthropomorphic mental patterns that symbolized the values of the group-life. Church and state never have been and never will be as completely separated as Williams' philosophy demanded.

Religious wars, as we should expect, aroused Williams' moral indignation to the highest pitch. "What fearful cries within these twenty years of hundred thousands, men, women, children, fathers, mothers, husbands, wives, sisters, old and young, high and low, plundered, ravished, slaughtered, murdered, famished." And solely for this reason, "that men fling away the spiritual sword and spiritual artillery in spiritual and religious causes and rather trust for the suppression of each other's God, conscience and religion, as they suppose, to an arm of flesh and sword of steele." [25] Religious wars, bloody and exterminating, Williams sees as the inevitable result of the "bloody tenent" of persecution of Cotton and the theocracy. "If Mr. Cotton or any of his bloody judgment wore the imperial crown of the world's majesty, what slaughters shall we imagine the world would feel and hear . . . what an earthly dunghill religion and worship should the Most High God be served with." [26]

[25] *Publications of the Narragansett Club*, Vol. III, p. 60.
[26] *Ibid.*, Vol. IV, p. 337.

The solution of the problem of international peace will follow, thinks Williams, from his idea of the state. Once men come to recognize the essential identity in nature and function of all states and a foundation is laid for international sympathy and understanding. For the conception of a democracy of equal and sovereign state makes it possible to eliminate the dangerous inequalities and differences, economic, racial, or religious, that are such fruitful sources of war. The Christian would thereby enjoy free access to the protection and the rights of citizenship in a non-Christian state. The Jew, Turk, or pagan would have free access to the rights and privileges of the so-called Christian state.[27]

There is something fascinating in the scope and sweep of Williams' imagination as he pictures the effect upon the international situation of the carrying out of his ideas. With the zeal of the prophet and the vision of the seer he sees across the years into the distant future, when wars shall cease and peace shall reign. He dreams of a time when "Caesar, as a civil, supreme magistrate, ought to defend Paul from civil violence and slanderous accusations about sedition, mutiny, civil disobedience, etc. And in that sense, who doubts but God's people may appeal to the Roman Caesar, an Egyptian Pharaoh, a Philistian Abimelech, an Assyrian Nebuchadnezzar, the great Mogul, Prester John, the great Turk, or an Indian Sachem." [28] Not the church nor the peace-loving principles of the Christian ethics are for Williams the ultimate guarantee of world peace but a federation of free and equal and sovereign states who strike hands in a solemn compact to maintain the universal rights of man.

[27] *Bloody Tenent, loc. cit.*, Chap. 27.
[28] *Ibid.*, Vol. III, p. 159.

V

The realm of practical morals likewise presented to Williams a serious problem, due to his radical separatism. He taught that the urges that make social relations and duties possible are complete and self-sufficient and are not to be identified with the urges prompted by religion. Morals born of social relations partake of the natural character of these relations, and therefore find in them their sanction. Hence it follows that religion can provide neither the drive nor the ultimate sanctions for social morality. "Yea, and there is a moral virtue, a moral fidelity, ability and honesty, which other men (besides church-members) are, by good nature and education, by good laws and good examples nourished and trained up in, that civil places of trust and credit need not be monopolized into the hands of church members (who sometimes are not fitted for them) and all others deprived and despoiled of their natural and civil rights and liberties." [29] "A subject, a magistrate, may be a good subject or a good magistrate in respect of civil or moral goodness . . . though godliness which is infinitely more beautiful be wanting." [30] If there is any real and profitable relationship between secular and religious morals it is not recognized in Williams' pages. In fact Williams asserts, "Confounding the nature of civil and moral goodness with religious, is as far from goodness as darkness is from light." [31]

Such a radical separation of religion and morals is of course incompatible with the facts of everyday experience. It is not surprising, therefore, to find other passages in Williams' writings which seem to contradict those cited above. "And it is most

[29] *Bloody Tenent Yet More Bloody, loc. cit.,* p. 365.
[30] *Bloody Tenent, loc. cit.,* p. 246.
[31] *Bloody Tenent Yet More Bloody, loc. cit.,* p. 406.

true, as Master Cotton saith, that the judgments of God legally executed, or more terribly poured forth in the vials of sword, plague and famine, they are as heavenly lights shining out from the Father of Lights, teaching the inhabitants of the world righteousness." [32] The inference here certainly is that the realm of secular morals is directly influenced by religious forces or "judgments of God," whether these "judgments" take the form of acts of magistrates or catastrophes in the realms of society or of nature. That there was no real contradiction in the mind of Williams may be inferred from the following. While "creation itself or each creature are as candles and glasses to light and shew us the invisible God and creator . . . these are not the ordinances of Christ Jesus given to his church. These are not the preaching of the word and the opening of the mysteries of salvation." The civic virtues such as "civil faithfulness, obedience, honesty, chastity, etc.," [33] are not identical with religious virtues, religious obedience, religious honesty, and the like because the latter presuppose all the machinery of salvation through Christ and the regenerating power of divine grace in the heart of the man who illustrates these Christian virtues in his life.

The field of ethics was thus dichotomized by Williams into that of a natural, civil, and secular ethics shared by all good men of whatever creed or race and an inner and subjective and highly selected realm of Christian morals. The plan of Divine Providence of course included both the realm of nature, social and physical, and that of grace. In so far as civil acts of the magistrates, wars, famines, earthquakes, and the like, take place according to the divine plan they take on a religious character and are agencies for "righteousness" in the cosmic order. How

[32] *Ibid.*, p. 88.
[33] *Ibid.*, p. 207.

this cosmic righteousness is related to the morality that springs from regenerated human nature Williams does not say. One seeks in vain in the writings of Williams any intelligent coordination of these three levels of moral values, the cosmic, the secular, and the intimate spiritual sphere of Christian character. Such a coördination was made difficult, not to say impossible, by Williams' underlying pluralistic metaphysics. His pragmatic pluralism clashed with his Calvinistic theology.

It would seem that when there is a conflict between this higher Christian ethics and the social and secular ethics the Christian ethics should prevail. But here Williams' radical separatism makes itself felt. "The conscience of the civil magistrate must incite him to civil punishment, as the Lord Mayor of London once answered, that he was born to be a judge, to a thief that pleaded he was born to be a thief. If the conscience of the worshippers of the beast incite them to prejudice prince or state, although these consciences be not as the conscience of the thief, commonly convinced of the evil of his fact, but persuaded of the lawfulness of their actions; yet so far as the civil state is endammaged or endangered, I say the sword of God in the hands of civil authority is strong enough to defend itself, either by imprisoning or disarming, or other wholesome means, etc., while yet their consciences ought to be permitted in what is merely point of worship, as prayer and other services and administrations." [34]

This passage throws an interesting light upon the thought of Williams. The righteous judge in obeying the secular ethics, whether in dealing with the thief or with the religious fanatic, is fulfilling the will of God (in the broad providential sense) so that in the strict sphere of the state he has divine sanction for coercing the misguided conscience of the religious enthusiast.

[34] *Bloody Tenent Yet More Bloody, loc. cit.*, pp. 143 f.

In the sphere of the purely religious, as in "worship," "prayer" and the like, conscience should be respected. It is obvious that Williams' ideas can only be realized in a social order where separatism has been so thoroughgoing that religion has become mainly a matter of worship and prayer and the state has been developed to such a pitch of wise and tolerant insight that it can decide unhesitatingly when a matter of conscience becomes downright antisocial. In Williams' ideal social order religion will have become so refined, so spiritual, so intimately personal and subjective, so transcendental and other-worldly, and the state will have become so wise and humane and just and so completely adapted to the many-sided social needs of mankind that religion will cease to play its traditional rôle in motivating the conduct of men and become a sort of spiritual luxury, a "Never, Never Land" of the heart's desire, in which dwell for the most part only mystics and dreamers. Winthrop was right when he said that Williams in the last stages of his religious development had become a "Seeker." Did Williams thus foreshadow the ultimate rôle of religion?

VI

Williams' idea of the church is as follows: "The church or company of worshippers, whether true or false, is like unto a body or college of physicians in a city; like unto a corporation, society or company of East India or Turkey merchants, or any other society or company in London; which companies may hold their courts, keep their records, hold disputations, and in matters concerning their society may dissent, divide, break into schisms and factions, sue and implead each other at the law, yea, wholly break up and dissolve into pieces and nothing, and yet the peace of the city not be in the least measure impaired or disturbed; because the essence of being of the city, and so the well-being and peace thereof, is essentially distinct from those particular societies; the city courts, city laws, city punishments distinct from theirs. The city was before them, and stands absolute and entire when such a corporation or society is taken down. For instance, further, the city or civil state of Ephesus was essentially distinct from the worship of Diana in the city, or of the whole city. Again the church of Christ in Ephesus . . . was distinct from both." [35]

The following observations are suggested by this interesting passage. In the first place Williams' illustration drawn from the worship of Diana at Ephesus was unfortunate. A more intimate historical knowledge of the Greco-Roman city state would have enabled him to see that the worship of gods such as Athena at Athens, Zeus at Olympia, Diana at Ephesus, or Mars at Rome, was a most important part of the life of the entire city. The worship of Diana was inseparably connected with the business life of the city as is shown in the protest of the silversmiths that the preaching of the new religion of Christ threatened their livelihood gained through the manufacture and sale of the images of the goddess.[36] Williams, the radical separatist, had little or no appreciation of the tremendous rôle the churchly or institutional type has played in history and the relatively insignificant part played by the sects.

Again one gets the distinct impression from this passage that the church as the external form of religion is transitory and unimportant. It belongs quite at the same level with the ephemeral organizations that are constantly springing up in the busy life of a great city. Christianity for Williams had never attained anything like final formulation in the external series

[35] *Publications of the Narragansett Club*, Vol. III, p. 73.
[36] Acts 19:24.

of reality, and from the nature of the case never could. Churches like human organizations come and go at the bidding of mortal men who covenant together to maintain them for a little while, but the churches they thus organize die when the inner spirit that gives them life is gone. Williams had no place for tradition. He could not appreciate the accumulated religious experience nor the artistic beauty embodied in sacraments such as the Mass. We have no evidence that the wondrous beauty of the medieval Gothic cathedral ever stirred his soul.

This is a criticism that applies to all forms of the dissenting tradition. Art is primarily the embodiment in external form of the values of the inner series of reality. Dissent stressed the inner experiences and minimized the external forms in which they are embodied. The characteristics of the inner series of reality are swift and kaleidoscopic changes, warmth and intensity without stability, conviction curiously blended with relativity, an absolute which at best knows only an eternal NOW. We get form, fixity, authority by an appeal to the external series of reality. Dissent by damning the validity of the external cultural reality in the sphere of religion doomed itself to formlessness and relativity. The very spirituality of religion defied all form for Williams.

In Williams, therefore, the logic of dissent reached its most extreme expression in his assumption of the essential formlessness of religion. Subjectivity and spirituality are raised to the nth power. Religion is so intensified and rarefied that it rejects external forms as possible contaminations of its spiritual purity. Williams almost approaches the logical absurdity of Plato and the Neoplatonists who called matter "non-being" or the negation of being. External social forms are the negation of true religion. The kingdom of God is timeless and spaceless and formless because it is spiritual, absolute, and eternal. To create forms for religion and force religion to assume them is almost equivalent to a violation of the command of the Decalogue against making graven images of God. Just as the graven image negates and stultifies the essence of the deity, so the external social form negates and stultifies the essence of religion.

This insistence upon the essential formlessness of religion led to its radical impoverishment as a social force. Spiritual forces only become effective when embodied in cultural forms. Radical separatism denied the validity of a "Christian" state, a "Christian" profession, a "Christian" education, or even a "Christian" civilization. For Williams "the unseen things alone are eternal." The very spirituality and inwardness of religion prevented it from ever molding society. Every step towards secularization, institutionalization, or socialization meant inevitably decay and degeneration for religion. Holiness is not a term which can be applied to the things of society; a saint in the medieval sense was for Williams a psychological and social absurdity. Saintliness is a matter of the soul. It is a quality that applies solely to the inner subjective series of reality. It is a phase of character that belongs to the sublimated and transcendental realm of religious verities. Thus in his zeal to keep religion pure, spontaneous, and free Williams saw himself forced to render it socially and morally impotent. The logic of separatism demands the complete de-socialization of religion. The more spiritualized a faith, the more socially impotent.

The principle of voluntarism that lies at the very core of the dissenting sectarian tradition seemed to have affected Williams' entire conception of society itself. One misses in his pages any feeling of cultural continuity or cultural integrity. In his mind society seems to have presented the dramatic spectacle of the never-ending rise and decay of voluntary organizations among men. Tradition and veneration for the past play little or no part in this drama. Men spontaneously unite to form a given social organization and devote themselves loyally and whole-heartedly to its preservation and extension only to desert it when the enthusiasm ebbs or to split off from it when it ceases to satisfy and some other combination seems more profitable.

To be sure, Williams distinguishes between organizations that "voluntarily combine and voluntarily dissolve," as in the case of religion, and "necessary trades, callings, etc.," whose ruin would disturb the peace and welfare of the city.[37] The forms of "civil and humane society" are not to be confused with the forms of "a spiritual society voluntarily uniting" as in the case of the church. The phases of life that have to do with the external series of reality or the forms of culture are necessarily more permanent than the phases that deal with the inner series of reality, with which religion is primarily concerned. The very freedom and spontaneity of the religious life demand that the form be always secondary and more or less transient. Williams tended to assimilate his philosophy of society as a whole, how-ever, to this voluntarism so dear to the separatist heart. To what extent is the triumph of the dissenting-revivalistic type of Protestantism responsible for the American disregard of tradi-tion and precedent?

VII

Williams' thought culminated in his idea of tolerance, the most famous statement of which perhaps is in his letter to the town of Providence, January, 1654, in reply to a seditious paper circulated among the citizens of Providence in which it was asserted that "it was blood guiltiness and against the rules of the Gospel to execute judgment upon transgressors against the public or private rule."

[37] *Bloody Tenent Yet More Bloody, loc. cit.,* p. 69.

In his letter Williams states frankly that he at no time preached "an infinite liberty of conscience," and then continues: "There goes many a ship to sea with many hundred souls in one ship, whose weal and woe is common, and is a true picture of a commonwealth, or human combination of society. It hath fallen out sometimes that both papists and protestants, Jews and Turks may be embarked in one ship; upon which supposal I affirm, that all the liberty of conscience that ever I pleaded for, turns upon these two hinges—that none of the papists, protestants, Jews or Turks be forced to come to the ship's prayers or worship nor compelled from their own particular prayers or worship, if they practice any. I further add that I never denied, that notwithstanding this liberty, the commander of this ship ought to command the ship's course, yea, and also command that justice, peace and sobriety, be kept and practiced, both among the seamen and all the passengers. If any of the seamen refuse to perform their services, or passengers to pay their freight; if any refuse to help in person or purse towards the common charges or defence; if any refuse to obey the common laws and orders of the ship concerning their common peace or preservation; if any shall mutiny and rise up against their commanders and officers; if any should preach that there ought to be no commander or officers, because all are equal in Christ, therefore no masters nor officers, no laws, nor orders, nor corrections, nor punishments;—I say, I never denied but in such cases, whatever is pretended, the commander or commanders may judge, resist, compel and punish such transgressors, according to their deserts and merits." [38]

In this famous figure of the ship, tolerance may be considered as a principle supplementary to the law. Considering the ship

[38] *Letters of Roger Williams: Publications of the Narragansett Club*, Vol. VI, p. 278.

with its captain, crew, and passengers as a figure of the state, tolerance arises out of the need for safeguarding the various activities of the groups and individuals concerned so that they may all freely coöperate in the interest of the common good. Rights are safeguarded by law in essentials where there is unanimity of opinion. There is, however, an intangible and highly debatable realm to which law cannot be applied and here tolerance is called upon to extend and supplement law. Law assures in part to each group the enjoyment of its privileges and the liberty for the exercise of its functions. Tolerance seeks through sympathetic insight and mutual understanding to carry the principle of freedom and differentiation of activities into the higher and debatable realm where religion is primarily concerned. Just as law observance is the test of a social order at the lower level, so tolerance is the test at the higher level. Tolerance merely supplements law.

The justification for separatism and the tolerance it seeks lies much deeper in the thought of Williams than mere expediency. His figure of the three walls, the spiritual, civil, and physical, indicates that in his thought religion and the state are separate by virtue of their inherent differences. The religious life takes place upon another and higher level of reality than that of the state. For this reason religion has laws and principles and a scale of values peculiarly its own. Separation of religion and state is not, therefore, a matter of expediency but of necessity. Tolerance is merely the recognition of fundamental incompatibilities. Intolerance is but another name for stupidity. Tolerance thus becomes not a human makeshift, a rubric of conduct cultivated by intelligent men in the interest of peace and goodwill, but rather something that is natural and necessary. One tolerates the weather primarily because one is not in the position to do anything about it. Much in the same way religion must tolerate the state and the state must tolerate religion because neither is in the position to do otherwise. The methods and agencies of the state cannot be made to function in religion; the principles and values of religion cannot be made to work successfully in the sphere of the state.

It is the weakness of dissent of the Baptist type, to which Williams belongs, that it sees in separation pure and simple the final solution of the problem of tolerance. This conception of tolerance, which is essentially negative, has become embodied in the Constitution and is admirably illustrated in Williams' figure of the ship at sea. Williams' figure of the ship breaks down, however, when applied to a democracy where public sentiment, not the captain of a ship, is the source of control. Where this public sentiment has become strongly tinged with religious ideas, such as anti-Catholicism or anti-evolutionism, the problem of religious tolerance becomes vastly complicated. It then ceases to be a matter of differentiation of function or of different levels of reality and becomes a very practical psychological problem of getting into the public sentiment patterns of thought, or what Burke called "wise prejudices," that will assure the proper delimitation of the spheres of state and religion. Any justification of tolerance upon the basis of an arbitrary functional or metaphysical separation between state and religion immediately impinges upon the practical difficulty that in a democracy the principle of tolerance depends upon an enlightened public sentiment. To put through legislation, in the interest of a theoretical notion of tolerance that is not sanctioned by public sentiment, stultifies the principles of democratic rule.[39]

Williams pleads for tolerance again because of the limita-

[39] J. M. Mecklin, "Religion and the Social Conscience" in a symposium on *Religion and Conduct*, edited by G. H. Betts, F. C. Eiselin, and G. A. Coe, 1930, p. 132.

tions of human knowledge and the uncertainties of life. In a letter to Endicott in 1651 protesting against the treatment of the Baptists, Holmes, Clarke, and Randall, Williams writes, "Yea, Sir, I beseech you remember that it is a dangerous thing to put this to the may-be, to the venture or hazard, to the possibility. Is it possible, may you well say, that since I hunt I hunt not the life of my Savior, and the blood of the Lamb of God. I have fought against many several sorts of consciences, is it beyond all possibility and hazard, that I may have fought against God, that I have not persecuted Jesus in some of them?" [40] Life is too transitory and uncertain to warrant such colossal assurance as that of Endicott and the theocracy in matters religious. "I humbly desire to remember with you, that every grey hair now on both our heads, is a Boanerges, a son of thunder, and a warning piece to prepare us for the weighing of our last anchors, to be gone from hence, as if we had never been." [41]

As in the case of all great souls who have gained a deep insight into life there is in Williams' writings a note of devout agnosticism, not entirely free from a practical and pragmatic tinge. Disgusted as he was with the grievous wrongs that arise through the union of church and state and wearied with endless theological bickerings, he was inclined to stress the least possible connection between the state and religion as necessary to freedom. As a consequence, Williams' thought naturally drifted towards a minimum of belief as necessary to such a separation. Obviously, where a creed is made comprehensive and where liberty of conscience is demanded in connection with such a creed, the danger of friction with the state is increased. The practical problem of maintaining liberty of conscience through

[40] *Letters of Roger Williams, loc. cit.*, p. 225.
[41] *Ibid.*, p. 227.

separatism thus combined with a vivid awareness of the mysteries and uncertainties of life to encourage in Williams a devoutly skeptical and agnostic note. Tolerance flourishes best in a psychological climate where religious absolutes are lacking. Paradoxical as it may seem, tolerance for Williams holds only for the purely secular sphere and not for the strictly religious. Cotton, with his broader secularized notion of the church, permitted saints and sinners to dwell together until the great day when sheep and goats shall be separated. Williams' idea of the church as an invisible and elect body of the saints did not permit of any such moral and spiritual confusion. Lack of moral and spiritual ingenuousness within the church was as deadly as in the life of the individual. The church was merely the saint writ large, a holy community of the elect. The integrity of the life of the spirit demands that it be at one with itself. Williams insisted that "every bit and parcel of leaven is to be purged out of the house of God." [42] Tolerance within the church would be a confession of difference and the presence of differences would imply the presence of sinners, for the life of the saint is one and the same and universal. Homogeneity is a proof of saintliness, at least in fundamentals. Tolerance, therefore, had as little justification within the church as between church and state. Within the dissenting-revivalistic churches of today there is no place for tolerance.

Thus did Williams again anticipate the final logical form that religion was destined to take in American life, thanks to the triumph of the dissenting-revivalistic type of Protestantism. The right of the group to insist upon unity of belief on the part of all its members and likewise the right of the individual to withdraw when he finds himself no longer in sympathy with the beliefs of the group is a basic principle of the politico-

[42] *Publications of the Narragansett Club*, Vol. IV, p. 101.

religious philosophy of American life. For the dissenter of the Williams type, the individual church is merely the enlargement of the life of the individual and just as the health and sanity of the individual's religious life demand that he should have a strong faith, so also the individual church must have unity of faith. "The church of Christ," says Williams, "is a congregation of saints, a flock of sheep, humble, meek, patient, contented, with whom it is monstrous and impossible to couple cruel and persecuting lions, subtle and hypocritical foxes, contentious biting dogs or greedy and roving swine, so visibly declared and apparent." [43]

VIII

Every great genius is more or less a paradox and Williams is no exception. In the last analysis intolerance is only of relative importance in his thought in spite of all he has to say about it. Intolerance, he says, assumes as a vital principle of conduct the Arminian doctrine of free will, "as if it lay in their own power and ability" for men to believe "upon the magistrate's command." The Papist assumes that he alone has the truth and that men can be made to believe of their own free will, and so uses coercion to make them exercise this power. From the Calvinistic point of view of Williams, however, "Since God only openeth the heart . . . it seems to be high presumption to suppose, that together with a command restraining from or constraining to worship, God is also to be forced or commanded to give faith to open the heart, to incline the will." [44] Viewed from the point of view of Williams' theology, the notion that intolerance is injurious to the life of competing religions in the

[43] *Ibid.*, Vol. VI, p. 143.
[44] *Ibid.*, Vol. III, p. 258.

state is meaningless. Unregenerated men of the world, being in a natural state, are dead in sin. They are incapable of a living faith. Intolerance or any form of spiritual coercion as applied to them is absurd. Tolerance in the negative sense thus becomes the natural thing because intolerance based upon the assumption that men can believe of their own accord is meaningless. At the same time it must be observed that, from this point of view, tolerance ceases to have any moral or spiritual significance.

Thus, after having patiently followed the intricacies of the essentially theological thought of Williams, we get at the end a queer feeling of disillusionment and unreality. The tremendous drama acted out between Cromwell and Charles I in England, the bloody persecutions of Baptists and Quakers by the Puritan priests, the Odyssey of his own soul in its long search for liberty and peace were to Williams "the seeker" but the unsubstantial fabric of a dream. There is no true church. The sons of God are scattered; "they are mingled amongst the Babylonians." Tolerance and intolerance are but empty phrases in a shadow world. Thus does our courageous champion of soul liberty suddenly lose the vigorous and red-blooded character history has always ascribed to him and become strangely like the wandering friar of the Middle Ages who had fled this world and sought, staff in hand, a far country of his heart's desire. Tolerance he deemed in the last analysis a meaningless rule among unregenerate men given over to the flesh and the devil and incapable of intelligent and moral exercise of their reasons. In his deepest soul Williams had little faith in tolerance. Persecution at best was but the seal and sign of the spiritually elect. Men play around with tolerance and intolerance in a fleeting and unreal world while God stands within the shadow, "keeping watch above his own." Leaving it to an infinite God to take revenge in his own wise way and time upon those who spilled the blood of the innocents, Williams, with the characteristic ingrained egoism of the dissenter, is primarily concerned to save his own soul out of "the lamentable shipwreck of mankind." He stood for a type of piety which from his day down to the Reverend Billy Sunday has preached a gospel of "each for himself and God for us all." [45]

It is, however, part of the irony of history that the "bloodless ballet of theological categories" that milled around in the troubled brain of Roger Williams and out of which he sought to fashion a "land of the heart's desire" where his courageous spirit might finally be at peace, has become almost as remote and dead and meaningless to the modern man as the bones of a dinosaur, while the story of his struggle for religious liberty, which he thought so futile, has become part of our most precious spiritual heritage.

[45] M. Freund, *Die Idee der Toleranz*, p. 265.

Chapter VI
Ann Hutchinson and the Baptists

N O SOONER had the Bay colony disposed of Roger
Williams, the wolf in sheep's clothing who sought
entrance into the sheepfold of "the unspotted lambs,"
than a much more serious danger threatened in the person of
a very intelligent and attractive she-wolf, Ann Hutchinson.
"It is the mark of seducers," said Cotton Mather, "that they
lead captive silly women, but what will you say when you hear
of subtil women becoming the most remarkable of the seducers?" The devil from the beginning has always had "designs
upon the weaker sex." "Simon Magus traded with his Helena,
and Montanus with his Maximilla." Arius began his wicked and
blasphemous career "by first proselyting seven hundred vir-
gins." In fact it would seem that "a poison does never insinuate
so quickly, nor operate so strongly, as when *women's milk* is
the *vehicle* wherein 'tis given. . . . Behold, reader, *nulla fere
causa est, in qua non foemina litem moverit* (there are few
controversies where a woman does not start the quarrel)." [1]
Thus does the garrulous Mather somewhat ungallantly introduce his account of the Ann Hutchinson episode.

[1] Cotton Mather, *Magnalia*, Vol. II, p. 516.

I

The frankly radical character of Williams' separatism and the fact that it was patently incompatible with the safety and integrity of the theocracy made it comparatively easy to deal with his case. The Antinomianism of Mistress Hutchinson was a much more subtle and dangerous form of dissent and temporarily captured John Cotton himself. It aroused tremendous excitement among "the unspotted lambs" and came near disrupting the colony.[2]

Mistress Ann Hutchinson, the chief actor in the famous Antinomian drama enacted in Massachusetts Bay in 1636-1638, was a very unusual woman. She was the daughter of a London preacher and passed twenty years of her life as the wife of William Hutchinson at Alford, Lincolnshire, England. There she came to know the Reverend John Cotton, pastor of St. Botolph's church in the English town of Boston. In 1633 she followed him with her husband to Boston. Mrs. Hutchinson was a woman of wit and intelligence, with a very decided flare for religion. She might be called, in fact, the forerunner of that variegated school of thought in New England called Transcendentalism, which found its finest flower in Emerson and the Concord school of philosophy and attained its *fin de siècle* form in Mary Baker Eddy. The Boston to which she came was little more than an overgrown village, numbering not over two thousand souls.[3]

[2] *Antinomianism in the Colony of Massachusetts Bay, 1636-1638,* Prince Society Publications, Vol. XXI, 1894, edited by C. F. Adams, for the sources. C. F. Adams, *Three Episodes of Massachusetts History,* 1892, Vol. I, pp. 363 ff. R. M. Jones, *The Quakers in the American Colonies,* 1911, Chap. I, "The Pre-Quaker Movement." G. E. Ellis, *The Puritan Age Rule in the Colony of Massachusetts Bay, 1629-1685,* 1888, pp. 300 ff., for a discussion of the term "covenant of works" and "covenant of grace." E. H. Foster, *The Genetic History of New England Theology,* 1907, pp. 31 ff., for the idea of the covenant in New England theology.

[3] C. F. Adams, *op. cit.,* Vol. I, pp. 395 f.

In this simple, hard-working, pioneer community, the cultural and intellectual advantages were limited. Libraries, newspapers, theaters, card parties, dances, and a thousand and one social and cultural activities which go to make up the life of a modern woman, were lacking. The only interest that dominated every phase of their lives was religion. This is a fact of prime importance for those who wish to understand the almost morbid curiosity with which people of that day discussed theological issues which, for the modern man, are both unintelligible and tiresome. Mrs. Hutchinson, being a woman of sympathetic nature, skilled as a nurse and of inquiring mind, soon became a social leader. Following a practice already existing, she started weekly meetings, attended by fifty or more women, at which she recapitulated and discussed the sermons. These meetings proved a great success. People flocked to hear her. In a community given over to religious interests her influence spread rapidly. She soon passed from the stage of mere expositor to that of critic and set up as an expounder of the Word, rivaling the regular minister.

Mistress Hutchinson soon discovered two types of religion in the community, namely the one based on the "covenant of works" and the other on the "covenant of grace." She placed herself, her brother-in-law, Reverend John Wheelwright, Sir Harry Vane, the governor of the colony, and Reverend John Cotton, the ablest intellect of the community, in the category of the "covenant of grace." She classed the conservatives of the colony, John Winthrop, her pastor, Reverend John Wilson, Reverend Hugh Peters, Endicott, and Dudley as exponents of the "covenant of works." In a community where religion dominated every issue, it was merely a question of time until the distinction drawn by Mistress Hutchinson between these two types of religion affected, first, the church at Boston and, in time, the entire colony.

The issue reached an unpremeditated climax in a famous, fast-day sermon delivered by Wheelwright in 1636.[4] This resulted, after months of excited debate, in the trial and expulsion of Wheelwright from the colony. Later, Mrs. Hutchinson was also tried and banished from the colony, her pastor, Reverend Mr. Wilson, reading the sentence of ex-communication couched in the following amiable Christian terms: "In the name of the Lord Jesus Christ, and in the name of the Church, I do not only pronounce you worthy to be cast out, but I do cast you out; and in the name of Christ I do deliver you up to Satan. I do account you from this time forth to be a heathen and a publican. I command you in the name of Jesus Christ and of this Church as a leper to withdraw yourself out of this congregation." Mistress Hutchinson and her sympathizers were forced to find a home on the island of Aquidneck, now called Rhode Island, where they formed the real nucleus out of which grew the first colony based upon religious liberty.

II

Many elements were concerned in this famous Antinomian controversy. The jealousy of the haughty clergy towards a brilliant woman who threatened to usurp their functions, the enmity aroused by invidious comparisons between ministers who preached a "covenant of works" and those who preached the "covenant of grace," the fears of the oligarchy led by Winthrop that these discussions would injure the colony, the panic at the mention of Antinomian ideas long associated with the horrors

---

[4] Given in *Proceedings of the Massachusetts Historical Society*, 1867, pp. 256 ff.

of Münster and the Anabaptists—all these factors and more combined to intensify the issue. What influenced the leaders primarily were practical considerations. This appears in the sentence pronounced against Wheelwright: "Mr. John Wheelwright, being formally convicted of contempt and sedition, and now justifying himself and his former practice, being to the disturbance of the civil peace, he is by the court disfranchised and banished, having fourteen days to settle his affairs." It is significant that in this sentence theological ideas are not mentioned. The gravity of the situation is suggested in Winthrop's language: "Every occasion increased the contention, and caused great alienation of minds; and the members of Boston (frequenting the lectures of other ministers) did make much disturbance by public questions and objections to their doctrines; and it began to be as common here to distinguish between men, by being under a covenant of grace or a covenant of works, as in other countries between Protestants and Papists." [5] That is to say, the terms had lost their original meanings and had become slogans of political and social factions. This was dangerous to the integrity of the Puritan theocracy.

It is practically impossible in the perusal of the accounts of the trials and debates to get any clear and connected idea of the theological issue. The chief source, Welde's *Short Story*, is unreliable, being marred by superstition and devoid of even common honesty.[6] It may well be doubted whether the participants themselves understood the meaning of the terms they used. No sooner was an issue raised than the disputants lost themselves in a fog of theological abstractions. Distinctions were drawn which obviously were not clear to those making them, much less to their antagonists. It is impossible to believe that

[5] John Winthrop, *Journal*, 1790, Vol. I, p. 124.
[6] Foster, *op. cit.*, p. 24.

the congregations of those days ever carried away clear and comprehensive ideas from the discourses to which they listened. We are forced to suppose that the atmosphere was surcharged with a sort of pious emotional fervor. The theological clatter of spoken words served merely as so many auditory signs or symbols for arousing the pious emotions of the hearer. They were not schooled to criticize. They easily mistook the earnestness and vividness of their own emotions or of the speaker for effective guarantees of the truth of the theological jargon of the preacher. The scandalous vagueness of their theological terminology finds a tragic parallel in the apparent inability of the leaders to follow the dictates of simple justice. This is strikingly brought out in the conduct of John Cotton.

III

The heart of the issue is evidently to be sought in the sociological implications of the two theological phrases "the covenant of works" and "the covenant of grace." The term covenant, which we have seen play such a large part in the dissenting tradition as well as in Protestant theology, is used in a variety of senses. The idea of the covenant was common in the Old Testament and was a familiar cultural phenomenon of the Semites.[7] It was taken over into the New Testament by Paul and made an integral part of his theology. Thence it passed into the great stream of Christian theology. "The covenant of works" is a term applied to the compact entered into by God and our first parents in the Garden of Eden. Their failure to observe their part of the compact brought them and all their descendants into moral disrepute.

[7] H. C. Trumbull, *The Blood Covenant*, pp. 188 f.

"The covenant of grace" is a compact entered into of God's own free will between Himself and His son, Jesus Christ, by means of which Adam's failure in the Garden of Eden was made good by the sacrifice of Christ on the Cross for the sins of the world. The merit purchased by the sacrifice of Christ is appropriated by faith. The sinner is accepted as righteous in the sight of God because of his faith in this divine sacrifice. The essential difference between the two covenants is that the one is based upon works and the other upon grace or faith that is the gift of divine grace. The test of the "covenant of works" is external, based upon the achievements of the individual. The test of the "covenant of grace" is subjective, based upon inner assurance of salvation and the regenerating work of the Holy Ghost. Here is a theological distinction which suggests the eternal dualism between the outer or cultural and the inner or psychological series of reality. The "covenant of works" is affiliated with the churchly type, the "covenant of grace" with the dissenting type of Christianity.

In view of the fact that the "covenant of works" and the "covenant of grace" were both integral parts of the Calvinistic theology that dominated New England thought, the question naturally arises as to why there should have been an issue raised between Ann Hutchinson and the Antinomian group and Winthrop and the defenders of the theocracy. In the theology of John Calvin the two covenants supplemented each other. The "covenant of grace" made possible the fulfillment of the "covenant of works." But the validity of the "covenant of grace" was made to depend upon an authoritative divine revelation, the ordinances of the church, the ministry, and the accepted form of church government. That is to say, the inner psychological fact of the regenerating work of the Holy Spirit effected by the "covenant of grace" was made to depend upon certain cultural forms, such as dogmas and church ordinances. This is the logic of the institutionalized and churchly type. It is obvious, however, that individuals of strong, mystical inclination, in sympathy with the dissenting tradition, like Ann Hutchinson, might very easily be inclined to stress the inner immediate religious experiences as the primary test of salvation and of religious reality rather than the external forms. In other words, we have here, emerging within the framework of the Massachusetts theocracy, the Antinomianism which has been a characteristic of the dissenting tradition from the beginnings of Christianity. In its most comprehensive sense this term meant opposition to all law as a means of restricting the urges of subjective caprice.

The threat of Antinomianism to the theocracy should be obvious. Antinomianism taught that the inner life of immediate religious experiences is a law unto itself and, consequently, it is necessary that its freedom and integrity be preserved at all costs. In the Bible commonwealth of Massachusetts all issues, whether political, economic, educational, moral, or religious, were approached from the point of view of a church-state, in which religious beliefs and external forms were inextricably interwoven in the agencies of social control. What Antinomianism sought is only possible in a community where social sanctions in law, business, education, and morals are secularized and divorced from religion. Mrs. Hutchinson's emphasis upon the "Inner Light" led inevitably to the discrediting of the established forms of social control because it sought to separate the inner life of freedom and spontaneity from external forms. There was no place for this in the theocracy.

The movement initiated by Mrs. Hutchinson, therefore, while fearfully obscured by the theological jargon used by the various disputants in this memorable controversy, was in reality a most insidiously dangerous attack upon the integrity of the church-state. It presupposed a modern philosophy of society, for the successful carrying out of which the theocracy was utterly inadequate. It was the old, old clash between the demands of the sect-type for inner freedom and spontaneity and the insistence of the medieval churchly type that inner spontaneity and freedom be subordinated to fixed external forms. Wilson, Welde, Winthrop, and the rest belonged to the Middle Ages; Mrs. Hutchinson was modern. She was unfortunate in that the cultural setting for the carrying out of her ideas was lacking.

IV

To understand the treatment of the dissenters by the Puritan priests it is imperative that we know the psychology of the age that made these persecutions possible. The following incredible language as to Mrs. Hutchinson is from Cotton Mather: "The erroneous gentlewoman herself, convicted of holding some *thirty* monstrous opinions, growing big with child, and at length coming to her time of travail, was delivered of some *thirty* monstrous births at once; whereof some were bigger, some were lesser; of several figures; few of any perfect, none of any *humane* shape. This was a thing generally then asserted and believed; whereas, by some that were eye-witnesses, it is affirmed that these were no more *monstrous births* than what is frequent for women, laboring with *false conceptions* to produce." Mather then devotes a page to the solemn account in all its hair-raising details, of another monstrous birth brought forth by "one very nearly related to this gentlewoman and infected with her heresies." [8]

[8] *Op. cit.*, Vol. II, p. 519.

John Winthrop, one of the most humane and enlightened men of the colony, tells how a minister, "by prayer and fasting dispossessed one possessed of a devil. They obtained his recovery while the congregation was assembled." [9] A father (presumably Winthrop himself) dreamed that he saw his wife and three children lying in bed "with most sweet smiling countenances, with crowns upon their heads and blue ribbons." His interpretation of the dream was that "God would take of her children and make them heirs with Christ in his kingdom." [10] He gravely narrates the following as sober fact: "At Watertown there was, in view of divers witnesses, a great combat between a mouse and a snake; and after a long fight the mouse prevailed and killed the snake. The pastor of the Boston church, Mr. Wilson, a very sincere, holy man, hearing of it, gave this interpretation: That the snake was the devil; the mouse was a poor contemptible people which God hath brought hither, which should overcome Satan here, and dispossess him of his kingdom." [11]

In such an atmosphere of naïve, primitive, religious realism heresy was feared much as the modern man fears a hideous contagious disease. Antinomians, Quakers and Baptists were viewed much as we view the carriers of the small-pox or typhoid fever germ. With no knowledge of the laws of nature or the findings of modern science, shut in on all sides by mysterious forces of evil, threatened constantly by devils and witches, placing the emphasis mainly upon the life in another world and accepting implicitly the theological dogma that all values rest ultimately upon religion, it is not surprising that the presence of the heretic caused consternation, persecution was thought neces-

[9] *Journal*, Vol. I, p. 125.
[10] *Ibid.*, p. 121.
[11] *Ibid.*, pp. 83 f.

sary to social health, and toleration meant the spread of deadly poison germs.

Just prior to the coming of the Baptists New England had been flooded with antisectarian literature of highly inflammatory character: such as Featley, *The Dippers Dipt*, 1644; Edwards, *Gangraena*, 1646; Baillie, *A Dissuasive from the Errors of the Time*, 1645; and Paget, *Heresiography*, 1645. These books form a most interesting seventeenth-century parallel to the inflammatory anti-Catholic literature made use of by the Ku Klux Klan in the hectic period that followed the World War.[12]

In 1644 the General Court, fearful of an invasion of the heretical Baptist, passed an ordinance to the effect that "if any person or persons, within this jurisdiction, shall either openly condemn or oppose the baptizing of infants, or go about secretly to seduce others from the approbation or use thereof, or shall purposely depart the congregation at the ministration of the ordinance, or shall deny the ordinance of magistracy, or their lawful right and authority to make war, or to punish the outward breaches of the first table," all aimed at characteristic tenets of the Baptist dissenters, "every such person or persons shall be sentenced to banishment." [13]

V

The first spectacular test of this legislation occurred in 1651 when John Clarke, Obadiah Holmes, and John Crandall, Baptists from Newport, Rhode Island, visited on request a certain William Winter of Lynn, "a brother in the church who by reason of his advanced age, could not undertake so great a

[12] J. M. Mecklin, *The Ku Klux Klan*, 1924, Chap. 5.
[13] Backus, *History of New England*, Vol. I, p. 126.

journey as to visit the church." [14] This seems an adequate explanation of the visit but the "filial piety" historians profess to see in this visit a deep-laid plot of John Clarke to defeat the schemes of William Coddington to induce Rhode Island to join the federation and possibly be annexed to Massachusetts. "He [Clarke] seems to have felt that a little persecution of the Anabaptists—if such a thing could be managed—by Massachusetts, might serve an important purpose in prejudicing the Rhode Island mind against Coddington's schemes. An occasion appears to have been made, accordingly, by which the red flag of the Anabaptistical fanaticism could be flouted full in the face of the Bay bull." [15] There does not seem to be the slightest evidence for this assumption and it is utterly out of keeping with the high character of Clarke who was one of the most influential men of Rhode Island.[16]

While Clarke was preaching in Winter's house, two constables appeared with a warrant and arrested Clarke, Holmes, and Crandall, taking them to the ale-house for safe-keeping. In the afternoon a constable proposed to take them to church. Clarke protested, "If thou forcest us into your assembly, then shall we be constrained to declare ourselves that we cannot hold communion with them." [17] Being forced to attend the meeting, Clarke thus describes his conduct: "At my first stepping over the threshold, I unveiled myself, civilly saluted them, and turned into the seat I was appointed to, put on my hat again, and sat down, opened my book and fell to reading." The constable was ordered to pull off their hats which he did. After

[14] *Ibid.*, p. 178, quoting from Newport Church papers.
[15] Dexter, *As to Roger Williams*, p. 119.
[16] Backus, *op. cit.*, pp. 348 f., for an estimate of his character. For a refutation of Dexter, see H. M. King, *Early Baptists Defended*, 1880.
[17] John Clarke, *Ill News from New England*, Collection of Massachusetts Historical Society, Vol. II, 4th Series, p. 29.

the preaching was over Clarke availed himself of the Congregational custom to explain that his "gesture" in not removing his hat was due to his inability to recognize their worship as "according to the visible order of our Lord," whereupon the officer silenced him.[18]

The three Baptists were taken to jail in Boston. The examination before Governor Endicott was "without producing either accuser, witness, jury, law of God or man."[19] It was more like the trial of heretics by the Spanish Inquisition than that of freeborn Englishmen. "The Governor upbraided us with the name of Anabaptists," and the trial degenerated into a theological squabble. "After much discourse," says Clarke, "we were committed again to prison."[20] Meanwhile, as usual, the high priest of the theocracy, Reverend John Cotton, set forth from the word of God the law in the case. In his sermon immediately before the court gave their sentence against Clarke, Obadiah Holmes, and John Crandall, Cotton "affirmed that denying infant baptism would overthrow all; and this was a capital offence; and therefore they were foul murtherers."[21] Thus fortified by their spiritual adviser and the mouthpiece of God, the prosecutors resumed the trial. The decision of the court was a foregone conclusion. Clarke was fined twenty pounds and Holmes thirty. The Court stipulated in each case, "The said sum shall be paid by the first day of the next Court of Assistants, or else to be well whipped, and that you shall remain in prison till it be paid or security be given for it." Crandall was to pay five pounds or "be well whipped."[22]

Clarke, who was a university graduate and well acquainted

[18] John Clarke, *Ill News from New England*, Collection of Massachusetts Historical Society, Vol. II, 4th Series, p. 30.
[19] *Ibid.*, p. 62.   [21] *Ibid.*, p. 56.
[20] *Ibid.*, p. 31.   [22] *Ibid.*, pp. 32, 42.

with the law, after the pronouncement of the sentence courteously said to Governor Endicott, "We are strangers and strangers to your laws, and may be transgressors of them before we are aware, we would therefore desire this courtesy of you as strangers that you would shew us the law by which we are transgressors." This request had been made by Clarke prior to the trial and the answer was, "When you come to the court you shall know the law." There is a fine irony in Clarke's language, for Endicott as well as Clarke knew that the only punishment sanctioned by the law was banishment and there was always in the background this embarrassing possibility that Massachusetts was denying to citizens of Rhode Island rights to which they were entitled as Englishmen and citizens of the British Empire. Endicott well knew that in delivering this sentence he was truckling to the clergy in violation of his honor as a man and his oath as officer of the law. Under the cool irony of Clarke, who must have enjoyed the situation, the hotheaded Endicott lost his temper "and being somewhat transported broke forth, and told me that I had deserved death, and said he would not have such trash brought into their jurisdiction." [23] The wine of the New England theocracy had transformed this particular "lamb" into a swashbucklering, lawbreaking bigot.

With tactless bluster Endicott told Clarke that he could not maintain his case "before our ministers" and that he was at liberty to try it. Clarke welcomed this challenge to debate and the magistrates seemed to have sanctioned it, but "when their elders were come together there was no small stir (as I heard) about the business." [24] Nothing is so disconcerting to entrenched

[23] *Ibid.*, p. 33.
[24] *Ibid.*, p. 34.

intolerance as an appeal to reason and freedom of speech. The clergy would not consent to a debate without definite restrictions which would have defeated the ends Clarke sought, and the debate fell through.

VI

The conversations between Clarke and the authorities in connection with the proposed debate are most illuminating. The authorities maintained, "The Court sentenced you not for your judgment or conscience, but for matter of fact, and practice." To this Clarke replied, "You say the Court condemned me for matter of fact and practice; be it so, but I say that matter of fact and practice was but the manifestation of my judgment and conscience; and I make account that man is void of judgment and conscience, with respect unto God, that hath not a fact and practice suitable thereunto." The situation was really an impasse; "for in truth if the faith and order which I profess do stand by the word of God, then the faith and order which you profess must needs fall to the ground; and if the way you walk in remain, then the way that I walk in must vanish away, they cannot both stand together; to which they seemed to assent." [25]

With the casuistry that tinged the utterances of the theocracy in all their dealings with the dissenters the authorities ignored the matter of liberty of conscience and stressed "matter of fact and practice," that is, conduct in violation of their laws. The sentence, as we have seen, was not according to law and hence, even on the basis of "fact and practice," was illegal and unjust. Clarke goes further, however, and dispels their casuistical smoke-screen by insisting that "fact and practice was but the

[25] John Clarke, *Ill News from New England*, Collection of Massachusetts Historical Society, Vol. II, 4th Series, pp. 34 f.

manifestation of my judgment and conscience," that is, sincerity in the religious life demands that fact and practice correspond to judgment and conscience. By divorcing liberty of conscience from external acts, they were attempting what is psychologically and ethically impossible. The faith and order one professes and one's way of life are inseparable. If one is false, then the other is false. One cannot be condemned without regard to the other. To claim, as did the authorities, that they could punish Clarke for his external conduct without violating his inner freedom and integrity of conscience, of which this conduct is merely the expression, was therefore absurd.

Clarke thus shows in perfectly clear and coolly logical fashion that the liberty of conscience they championed, as a sort of hangover from earlier dissent, was in reality not true liberty of conscience. It was merely a casuistical subterfuge by which the authorities sought, on the one hand, to cajole themselves into thinking that they were still true to the dissenting tradition while, on the other hand, they strove to bamboozle their dissenting victims with the claim that they were being dealt with according to law and justice. The intellectual and moral indecency of the leaders of the theocracy is not the least unpleasant phase of this whole story.

VII

Nowhere in all the voluminous religious literature of this period is to be found, so far as the writer's knowledge goes, any clearer statement of the eternal problem of the place of religion in a given cultural pattern than in the account of the trial of Clarke, Holmes, and Crandall. Three elements entered into the problem, the word of God accepted by dissent and theocracy alike as final, the faith and order which one professes, and the way in which one walks, that is to say, the Bible and the inner and outer phases of reality. The authorities and Clarke agreed that the facts of the inner series of faith and the facts of the outer series or the way of life must both agree with the Bible. For both there was but one true religious life and that is attained when the whole life both of faith and conduct agrees with the will of God in the Bible. It never occurred to either party that there is no one final and true way outlined in the Bible, but a vast cultural panorama of many ways of life, each more or less final for the group and the age concerned. They were far from surmising that where the symbols of the religious imagination, which any age or group draws from the familiar stories and teachings of the Bible, are faithful and adequate vehicles for the religious needs of the given group or age they are in so far true and final, but only for the age or group.

The limitations of the cultural setting of New England in 1651 prevented even as intelligent and liberal a man as Clarke, a university graduate, from grasping the intricacies of the problem of religion and culture. Clarke and his companions rightly felt that mere faith or inner attitude, apart from conduct corresponding to it, was not enough. They did not see that no valid test of this union of inner and outer was to be found in the Bible. They did not realize, furthermore, that to embody this inner attitude in external acts was not possible without revolutionizing the existing pattern of New England culture. The conduct of Clarke and his companions in refusing to remove their hats in church was, therefore, much more serious than it seems. They could be prosecuted, to be sure, under present-day laws but all such laws presuppose liberty of action in the matter of attending church and also liberty of action in creating forms of worship congenial to one's beliefs. Such freedom did not exist in Massachusetts in 1651. Clarke and his companions could not establish their own worship and were forced to attend church. They could not be silent without stultifying their consciences; the authorities could not permit the dissenters to express their sincere convictions without endangering the entire fabric of existing New England culture.

The founders of the New England theocracy created a social impasse, therefore, when they would not permit a dissenter to absent himself from a worship he did not accept and, after forcing him to attend, would tolerate no conduct which did not imply acceptance of the required worship. The dissenter was thereby shut up to the unpleasant alternatives of keeping quiet and starving and stultifying his own spirit, or of acting according to his conscientious convictions and being banished, beaten, or hanged as a common criminal.

The dissenters, after all, were merely trying to live their own lives with sincere and honest regard for the integrity of personality, which demands that the inner life shall find adequate expression in the outer. The difficulty lay in the fact that the external cultural forms which would have enabled them to do this normally did not exist. They were trying to fly without wings. The complete solution of their problem meant the creation of a new social order, a new cultural pattern, which is no easy task. The very bigotry and cruelty with which this inner urge to be true to themselves was checked by the authorities led them to commit excesses which incline the unsympathetic modern man to brand them as fanatics. The New England theocracy was far more pathological than its victims. The urge which led the Quakers to return repeatedly after each beating or imprisonment or banishment by the Massachusetts authorities was merely the natural manifestation in the sphere of religion of the irrepressible will to live.

VIII

Clarke's fine was paid by friends "without my consent and contrary to my judgment,"[26] so he tells us. Crandall was admitted to bail and Holmes was left to suffer alone. He has given an illuminating account of his whipping.[27] Having refused all aid from his friends he said, after the sentence was pronounced, "I bless God I am counted worthy to suffer for the name of Jesus; whereupon John Wilson (their pastor as they call him) struck me before the judgment seat and cursed me, saying, The curse of God or Jesus go with thee."[28] While in his cell awaiting the whipping he tells us, "Satan let fly at me, saying, Remember thyself, thy birth, breeding and friends, thy wife, children and credit," but the morning found him calm and at peace with the world. Friends brought "refreshment of wine and other comforts," which he refused lest men should say that his courage and strength were due to the fact that he "was drunk with new wine." Permission to address the crowd was refused, the officer in charge saying to the executioner, "Fellow, do thine office for this fellow would make a long speech to delude the people."[29]

Holmes thus describes his experiences during the whipping: "As the strokes fell upon me I had such a spiritual manifestation of God's presence, as the like thereunto I had never had, nor felt, nor can with fleshly tongue express, and the outward pain was so removed from me, that indeed I am able to declare it unto you, it was so easy to me, that I could well bear it, yea, and in a manner felt it not, although it was grievous as the

---

[26] John Clarke, *Ill News from New England*, Collection of Massachusetts Historical Society, Vol. II, 4th Series, p. 38.
[27] *Ibid.*, pp. 45 ff.   [29] *Ibid.*, p. 49.
[28] *Ibid.*, p. 47.

spectators said, the man striking with all his strength (yea, spitting on his hands three times as many affirmed) with a three-corded whip, giving me therewith thirty strokes; when he had loosed me from the post, having joyfulness in my heart, and cheerfulness in my countenance, as the spectators observed, I told the magistrates, you have struck me as with roses; and said moreover, Although the Lord hath made it easy to me, yet I pray God it may not be laid to your charge." [30]

This interesting narrative illustrates the familiar phenomenon, often noted in the stories of the martyrs, that spiritual exaltation induces something akin to anaesthesia or insensibility to physical pain. The "filial piety" school, either through inability to understand the mental state of Holmes or, as is more probable, in their pathetic eagerness to save the reputation of their ancestors, make Holmes' language a basis for asserting that the executioner had been ordered "to vindicate what they thought the majesty of the law at little cost to the delinquent." [31] Governor Joseph Jencks, remarking upon the incident later, said: "Mr. Holmes was whipped thirty stripes, and in such an unmerciful manner, that in many days, if not some weeks, he could take no rest but as he lay upon his knees and elbows, not being able to suffer any part of his body to touch the bed whereon he lay." [32]

IX

The repercussion of this farce of a trial and brutal whipping, both at home and in England, was immediate and significant. The spectators were so moved by the heroism of Holmes that

---

[30] *Ibid.*, pp. 50 f.
[31] Palfrey, *History of New England*, Vol. II, p. 353.
[32] Backus, *op. cit.*, Vol. I, p. 193.

two of them, John Hazel and John Spur, "did shake me by the hand," says Holmes, John Spur ejaculating, "Blessed be the Lord." [33] For thus attempting the rôle of the Good Samaritan they were promptly imprisoned and fined. Public indignation manifested itself in the demand that the surgeon should be sent for to treat his wounds, "but what was done," says Holmes, "I yet know not."

More important was the effect in England when in 1652 John Clarke published there his *Ill News from New England.* Sir Richard Saltonstall, one of the earlier magistrates of Massachusetts then in England, wrote to Cotton, "It doth not a little grieve my spirit to hear what sad news are reported daily of your tyranny and persecutions in New England, as that you fine, whip and imprison men for their consciences. . . . These rigid ways have laid you very low in the hearts of the saints." [34] This is an interesting commentary upon the gap that existed between enlightened religious sentiment in England and in the Bay colony.

John Cotton came to the defense of "the lambs of the Lord" in a letter that does little credit to him and his associates. With the impatience, not to say arrogance, characteristic of the leaders of the Bay colony when under criticism from England, Cotton said, "Be pleased to understand we look at such complaints as altogether injurious in respect of ourselves, who had no hand or tongue at all to promote either the coming of the persons you aimed at into our assemblies, or their punishment for their carriage there." [35] In view of Cotton's sermon prior to the pronouncement of the sentence this language may mean that the actual carrying out of the sentence in the whipping was

[33] Clarke, *op. cit.,* p. 51.   [35] *Ibid.,* p. 199.
[34] Backus, *op. cit.,* Vol. I, p. 199.

done by the officers of the law and not by the clergy, in which case Cotton is merely repeating the subterfuge of the church authorities during the Inquisition who, after condemning the heretics, turned them over to the state for their execution. More probably Cotton meant that the laws of the Bay colony were just and necessary and therefore the Baptists did not "suffer an unjust censure."

The infinite self-sufficiency of the leaders of the Bay colony, even at this early period, was not only arousing the suspicion of the home government and the dismay and disgust of their dissenting friends in England but was also subtly poisoning their own moral life with the virus of hypocrisy. To be sure, Cotton, as usual, plasters the ethics of the situation with a thick layer of theological subterfuges. "We believe," he writes, "there is a vast difference between men's inventions and God's institutions; we fled from men's inventions, to which we else would have been compelled; we compel none to men's inventions." Then with a touch of arrogance Cotton adds, "If our ways (rigid ways as you call them) have laid us low in the hearts of God's people, yea, and of the saints (as you style them) we do not believe it is any part of their saintship." [36] The laws we pass and the church forms we adopt *are* "God's institutions" and whatever differs from them are "man's inventions" and so the issue is made up! Within such a vicious theological circle, strict moral integrity was impossible.

Cotton claimed, further, that to compel men in the matter of worship is not to make them sin, as Saltonstall asserted. "If the worship be lawful in itself, the magistrate compelling him to come to it, compelleth him not to sin, but the sin is in his will that needs to be compelled to a Christian duty. If it do

[36] *Ibid.*, p. 200.

make men hypocrites yet better be hypocrites than profane persons. Hypocrites give God part of his due, the outward man, but the profane person giveth God neither outward nor inward man." [37] The mere mechanical performance of an act through the use of divinely sanctioned external forms, though done under coercion, is morally right and spiritually valuable. A man may thus be rendered half-righteous in the sight of God against his will and in spite of the best intentions to be wicked. A dissenter who refuses to perform an external act from conscientious convictions may be a sinner in spite of his best efforts to be a saint. It is in the moral murkiness of such a mental atmosphere that the real hypocrite is born and thrives.

Cotton, the theologian, arguing the case for the theocracy very easily loses all contact with moral common sense. "As for his whipping," Cotton remarks of Holmes, "it was more voluntarily chosen by him than inflicted on him. His censure by the court was to have paid (as I know) thirty pounds, or else be whipped; his fine was offered to be paid by his friends for him freely, but he chose rather to be whipped; in which case if his suffering of stripes was any worship of God at all, surely it could be accounted no better than will-worship." [38] How far Cotton lagged behind the dictates of the sound moral sense of his time appears in Governor Jencks' remarks in this connection, "Although the paying of a fine seems to be but a small thing in comparison of a man's parting with his religion, yet the paying of a fine is the acknowledgement of a transgression; and for a man to acknowledge that he has transgressed when his conscience tells him he has not, is but little, if anything at all, short of parting with his religion." [39] It seems to have been

[37] Backus, *op. cit.*, Vol. I, p. 200.   [39] *Ibid.*, p. 200.
[38] *Ibid.*, p. 200.

psychologically impossible for Cotton and the leaders of the theocracy to enter sympathetically and intelligently into the mental atmosphere of the dissenters, a fact which is largely responsible for the tragedy of the whole situation, and wholly inexcusable in those who were once dissenters.

Cotton closes his letter to Saltonstall with this statement: "I tell you the truth, we have tolerated in our church some Anabaptists and some Seekers, and do so still at this day. We are far from arrogating infallibility of judgment to ourselves or affecting uniformity; uniformity God never required, infallibility he never granted us." [40] Such fine words should not deceive us. It is Cotton talking the language of dissent merely for effect. In the light of the actual facts in the Bay colony we know that no Anabaptist, Seeker, or Antinomian was tolerated for one moment who dared voice his sentiments in overt word or deed. What Cotton and the theocracy tolerated was *silent dissent.* John Clarke could say of the Bay colony in 1652, "The authority there established can not permit men, though of never so civil, sober and peaceful a spirit and life, freely to enjoy their understandings and consciences, nor yet to live, or come among them, unless they can do as they do, say as they say, *or else say nothing* and so may a man live at Rome also." [41] That is to say, they insisted that dissenters could dwell among them only so long as they suppressed or denied in word and deed their inmost beliefs. Was this anything else than to live the life of a conscious hypocrite?

[40] *Ibid.,* p. 200.
[41] *Ill News from New England,* Collection of Massachusetts Historical Society, Vol. II, p. 65.

X

The story of the Baptists during the latter part of the seventeenth century is the story of an impotent and persecuted minority of simple folk striving patiently to maintain liberty of conscience in the face of an all powerful establishment. In 1655, an earnest and devout man, Thomas Gould, developed scruples as to the baptism of his child, which involved him in difficulties with the authorities. In 1665, after ten years of persecution and annoyance, he, together with eight others, organized the first Baptist church in Boston—a Baptist church had already been organized in 1663 in Swansea just across the line from Rhode Island. This of course caused great scandal being, according to Cotton Mather, "a manifest violation of the laws of the Commonwealth relating to the orderly manner of gathering a church, but also with a manifold provocation unto the rest of our churches, by admitting into their own society such as our churches had excommunicated for moral scandals, yea, and employing such persons to be administrators of the two sacred sacraments among them." [42] By such language Mather condemned every dissenting congregation that assembled in England after the passage of the act of uniformity in 1662. Policies that looked black when practiced by the English establishment were somehow washed white by being transferred across the sea to New England and employed by the theocracy.

The eight Baptists were fined and imprisoned but with little effect, for they seemed to thrive under persecution. Fines and imprisonment having failed, the authorities decided to try public debate. So the order was issued for the Baptists, "Thomas Gould, John Farnum, Thomas Osburne and company," to meet

[42] Mather, *op. cit.*, Vol. II, p. 532.

in public debate "in the meeting house at Boston, at nine in the morning," April 14, 1668, the champions of the theocracy, "Reverend Mr. John Allen, Mr. Thomas Cobbett, Mr. John Higginson, Mr. Samuel Danforth, Mr. Jonathan Mitchell, and Mr. Thomas Shepherd." Thus were the ablest intellects of the theocracy pitted against ignorant plowmen and mechanics to decide "in an orderly debate" this momentous question: "Whether it be justifiable by the word of God, for these persons and their company to depart from the communion of these churches, and set up an assembly here in the way of Anabaptism, and whether such a practice is to be allowed by the government of this jurisdiction." [43] According to Cotton Mather, "It was earnestly and charmingly put to them in a great assembly, whether they did own the churches of New England to be true churches; but they would not own it." [44]

The account of the dissenters is slightly different. "When they were met there was a long speech by one of them (Reverend Jonathan Mitchell), of what vile persons they were, and how they acted against the churches and governments here, and stood condemned by the court. The others desiring liberty to speak, they would not suffer them, but told them they stood there as delinquents, and ought not to have liberty to speak. . . . Two days were spent to no purpose." [45] Mitchell then pronounced the decision in the following amiable terms, taken from Deuteronomy 17: 18, "And the man that will do presumptuously, and will not hearken unto the priest that standeth to minister there before the Lord thy God, or unto the judge, even that man shall die: and thou shalt put away the evil from Israel." Gould, Turner, and Farnum were banished as "ob-

---

[43] From the text of the warrant, cited by Backus, *op. cit.*, Vol. I, pp. 300 f.
[44] *Op. cit.*, Vol. II, p. 533.
[45] Backus, *op. cit.*, Vol. I, p. 305, quoting the account of Gould's wife.

stinate and turbulent Anabaptists" on pain of being imprisoned "without bail or mainprise, until he or they shall give sufficient security to the Governor or any magistrate immediately to depart the jurisdiction and not to return, as above said." [46] The dissenters refused to depart and were clapped in jail.

Some idea of the character of these three men thus rudely taken from their homes and their work and incarcerated as dangerous public enemies may be inferred from the letter which they jointly wrote to the authorities: "We thought it our duty and concernment to present your honors with these few lines to put you in remembrance of our bonds: and this being the twelfth week of our imprisonment we should be glad if it might be thought to stand with the honor and safety of the country, and the present government thereof, to be now set at liberty. For wee doe hereby seriously profess, that so farre as wee are sensible or know anything of our own hearts, wee do prefer their peace and safety above our own, however we have been resented otherwise: and wherein we differ in point of judgment wee humbly beseech you, let there be a bearing with us, till god shal reveale otherwise to us; for there is a spirit in man, and the inspiration of the Almighty giveth them understanding, therefore if wee are in the dark, wee dare not say that wee doe see or understand, till the Lord shall cleare things up to us. And to him we can appeale to cleare up our innocency as touching the government, both in your civil and church aftaires. That it never was in our hearts to thinke of doing the least wrong to either: but have and wee hope, by your assistance, shal alwaies indeavor to keep a good conscience void of offence toward god and men. And if it shal be thought meete to afforde us our liberty, that wee may take that care as becomes us, for our

[46] *Massachusetts Records*, Vol. IV, Part II, pp. 373 f., cited by Backus, *op. cit.*, Vol. I, p. 302.

families, wee shal engage ourselves alwayes to be in a readiness
to resign up our persons to your pleasure. Hoping your honors
will be pleased seriously to consider our condition, we shall
commend both you and it to the wise disposing and blessing of
the Almighty, and remain your honors faithful servants in what
we may." [47]

That such a simple, tolerant, and heroic faith was only possible outside of and in opposition to the establishment throws
an interesting light upon Massachusetts society in 1668. From
Cotton Mather's fulsome glorifications of Massachusetts worthies in his *Magnalia*,[48] down to the latest effusions of the filio-
pietistical school, many fine things have been said about the culture and college training of the leaders of the theocracy. John
Cotton, John Norton, John Wilson, Thomas Hooker, Thomas
Shepherd, Charles Chauncy, Peter Bulkly, together with Henry
Dunster, the President of Harvard and the one Baptist black
sheep among the irreproachable Brahmins, were trained at Cambridge. John Davenport and Richard Mather were educated
at Oxford. When one compares, however, the arid scholastic
effusions and brutal theological billingsgate of these men with
the moving utterances of the lowly dissenters, such as the letter
of the three Baptists cited above, one is inclined to find the root
of the matter, so far as the religion of Jesus Christ is concerned,
among the simple and ignorant dissenters.

Just as in the case of John Clarke and his associates, the
treatment of Thomas Gould and his group aroused vigorous
protest both at home and abroad. The feeling of indignation at
the injustice done was stronger than fear of the magistrates
and some sixty-five citizens, including men of such prominence

---

[47] *Massachusetts Archives*, Vol. X, p. 220, quoted by Brooks Adams, *The
Emancipation of Massachusetts*, 1887, pp. 123 f.
[48] Vol. II, pp. 252 ff.

as Captain Edward Hutchinson and Captain Oliver, petitioned the authorities: "Whereas by the censure of this honorable Court Thomas Gould, William Turner and John Farnum now lie in prison deprived of their liberty, taken off from their callings, separated from their wives and children, disabled to govern or provide for their families, to their great damage and hastening ruin, how innocent soever; beside the hazard of their own lives, being aged and weakly men, and needing that succor a prison can not afford; the sense of this their personal and family most deplorable and afflicted condition, hath sadly affected the hearts of many sober and serious Christians and such as neither approve of their judgment and practice; especially considering that the men are reputed godly and of a blameless conversation; and the things for which they suffer seem not to be moral, unquestioned, scandalous evils, but matters of religion and conscience. . . . We therefore most humbly beseech this honored Court, in their Christian mercy and bowels of compassion to pity and relieve these poor prisoners." [49] For their pains the two chief petitioners were fined and the rest made to acknowledge their error "for giving the court such just grounds of offence." [50]

That this official attitude towards the Baptists persisted down to the beginning of the eighteenth century is indicated by the following from Mather's *Magnalia*, published in 1702, "Infant baptism hath been scrupled by multitudes in our days, who have been in other points most worthy Christians. . . . Some of these people have been among the planters of New England from the beginning, and have been welcome to the communion of our churches, which they have enjoyed, *reserving their par-*

[49] Backus, *op. cit.*, Vol. I, p. 304.
[50] *Massachusetts Records*, Vol. IV, Part II, p. 413, quoted by Brooks Adams, *op. cit.*, p. 125.

ticular opinion unto themselves." That is to say they were tolerated so long as they remained *silent dissenters.* "While some of our churches used, it may be, a little too much *cogency* towards the brethren which would weakly turn their backs when *infants* were brought forth to be baptised in the congregation, there were some of the brethren who in a day of temptation, broke forth into *schismatical practices* that were justly offensive to all the churches in this wilderness." [51] Mather could tolerate "weakly" turning of the back by the Baptist when children were baptized but he could not tolerate the attempt to establish an independent Baptist church by Gould and others in 1665. Mather had not advanced beyond the position taken by John Cotton in reply to Saltonstall's letter in 1652 deploring the whipping of Holmes.

The intolerant theocracy never repented and never capitulated. Even after the handwriting was visible upon the wall and all knew the theocracy was doomed, Increase Mather could write, in 1681, "The Anabaptists in New England have in their narrative lately published endeavored to . . . make themselves the innocent persons and the Lord's servants here no better than persecutors. . . . I have been a poor laborer in the Lord's Vineyard in this place upward of twenty years; and it is more than I know, if in all that time, any of those that scruple infant baptism, have met with molestation from the magistrate merely on account of their opinion." [52]

It has been said, "Milton makes his Satan so thoughtful, so persistent and liberty-loving, so magnanimous, and God so illogical, so heartless and repressive, that many perfectly moral readers fear lest Milton, like the modern novelists, may have

---

[51] Mather, *op. cit.*, Vol. II, p. 532.
[52] Preface to Increase Mather, *Ne Sutor*, cited by Brooks Adams, *op. cit.*, p. 127.

known good and evil, but could not tell them apart." [53] One who reads the smug justification of their treatment of the dissenters by the Puritan priests and then turns to the actual facts is inclined to say that they may have known what tolerance and intolerance meant but they were singularly incapable of distinguishing them. The tragedy of the situation was that the leaders were forced to manufacture reasons in justification of conduct that stultified their professions of religious liberty. The real motive of course was the maintenance of the theocracy and of their positions of privilege and power.

[53] Erskine, "The Moral Obligation to be Intelligent," *Hibbert Journal*, Vol. XII, p. 175.

Chapter VII
The Ravening Wolves of Dissent

THE ATTITUDE of the watchful shepherds of "the unspotted lambs" towards the ravening wolves of dissent,
the Quakers, is admirably reflected by the militant
bigot, who more than any other one man is responsible for the
hanging of the Quakers, namely the Reverend John Norton,
in a treatise written at the request of the Court in 1659 with
special reference to the Quakers. "The wolf which ventures
over the wide sea, out of a ravening desire to prey upon the
sheep; when landed, discovered and taken, hath no cause to
complain, though, for the security of the flock he be penned up
with the door opening upon the fold fast shut but having another door purposely left open whereby he may depart at his
pleasure, either returning from whence he came, or otherwise
quitting the place." [1] The door "open whereby he may depart"
seems to have been, then, as in the case of the Antinomians and
Baptists, Rhode Island. In fact the "filial piety" school of
Massachusetts historians, faithfully reflecting the amiable Christian spirit of their forbears, state that "the Rhode Island colonies then took the social sewerage of their neighbors—to the
benefit of the latter." [2] That the leaders of the theocracy and

[1] John Norton, *Heart of New England Rent*, p. 56, quoted by Dexter, *As
to Roger Williams*, p. 129.
[2] Dexter, *op. cit.*, p. 119. Palfrey, *History of New England*, Vol. II, p. 343.

their pious apologists were able to see in Roger Williams, Ann Hutchinson, John Clarke, Obadiah Holmes, and the simple-minded but heroic Quakers, only "social sewerage" reflects little credit either upon their intelligence or their Christian spirit. The "social sewerage" dumped into Rhode Island by Massachusetts resulted in the founding of the Providence colony by Roger Williams and the colony on the island of Aquidneck, later called the Island of Rhode Island, by Ann Hutchinson and her sympathizers, Coddington, Nicholas Easton, Coggeshall, William Brenton, and others. In 1641 these social outcasts on Aquidneck in public assembly declared, "This body politick is a democracy; that is to say, it is in the power of the body of freemen, orderly assembled or the major part of them, to make just laws by which they will be regulated." [3] They added this further exceedingly significant statement, "It is ordered that none be accounted a delinquent for doctrine," thereby establishing Rhode Island's claim to being the first commonwealth in history embodying the principle of religious liberty in its foundation. Religious liberty is the child of the dissenting tradition. This Newport group rather than the Providence colony formed the nucleus of the colony of Rhode Island, and together with the Barbadoes became later a center of Quakerism in the New World.

Dissent of every stripe drifted into the Rhode Island colonies as the only asylum offered, so that Cotton Mather could assert, "There never was held such a variety of religions together on as small a spot of ground as have been in that colony." No man needed to go begging for a religion and "if by chance a man had lost his religion he might find it at the general muster of

[3] *Rhode Island Colonial Records*, Vol. I, p. 112, quoted by Jones, *The Quakers in the American Colonies*, p. 23.

the opinionists." [4] Religious liberty in 1641 was a prodigious and dangerous experiment and the authorities of the Rhode Island colonies had their difficulties. New heresies were broached every year according to Winthrop but soon two general types or groups emerged, the one centering around Ann Hutchinson and her sympathizers and the other around John Clarke, who founded a Baptist church.

The Antinomian movement led by Ann Hutchinson undoubtedly paved the way for the coming of the Quakers. After much theological floundering and prolonged badgering of Mrs. Hutchinson by the authorities, the crisis was reached in her trial when she was led to confess that she had "immediate revelations" or "openings." [5] The effrontery of a mere woman setting herself up as a source of divine truth and asserting, as Reverend Peters complained, "that our ministry is legal," that is external and devoid of authority, was something that the haughty clergy could not for one moment tolerate. It meant the destruction of their power and the speedy dissolution of the theocracy. But this emphasis upon an authoritative "Inner Light" or revelation was the very essence of the Quaker philosophy of dissent. From the little we know of the early history of Newport, where the Antinomians settled, Mrs. Hutchinson's ideas were widespread. Here, therefore, six years before George Fox began his activities and fifteen years before the arrival of the Quakers in the Bay colony, there was in Rhode Island "a group of persons who were Quakers in everything but name." [6]

[4] *Magnalia*, Vol. II, pp. 520 f.
[5] C. F. Adams, *Three Episodes of Massachusetts History*, Vol. I, p. 502.
[6] Jones, *op. cit.*, p. 25.

II

The coming of the Quakers, therefore, meant the renewal of the attack upon the theocracy unwittingly initiated by Ann Hutchinson. For dissent really threatened the Bible commonwealth of the Bay colony in two ways. In part, its threat was political and social and was directed against the cultural forms and institutions of the theocracy; in part, it was psychological and subjective and was directed against the philosophy of religion implicit in the theocracy. The first phase of the dissenting tradition was represented by Roger Williams and the Baptists; the second by the Antinomians and the Quakers. Roger Williams and the Baptists sought external cultural forms which would make it possible through the separation of church and state for the individual and the group to live their own lives in religious matters. The fundamental theological conceptions of Williams and the Baptists touching the Bible, the ordinances of the church, such as Baptism and the Lord's Supper, sin, salvation, the Trinity, heaven, and hell, and the final judgment, were practically identical with those of theocracy. This explains why Cotton Mather could say that the Baptists "have infinitely more of Christianity among them than the Quakers and have indeed been useful defenders of Christianity against the assaults of the Quakers." [7] Separatism was the basic issue between the Baptists and the theocracy.

In the case of the Antinomians and the Quakers the issues at stake were far more fundamental. We have seen that Ann Hutchinson with her doctrine of the "covenant of grace" and "immediate revelations" presupposed a conception of religion which tended to base it primarily upon the inner or subjective

[7] *Op. cit.*, Vol. II, p. 531.

series of reality to the neglect of external cultural forms and observances. If the central idea of Williams and the Baptists was separatism, that of the Antinomians and the Quakers was the supremacy of the "Inner Light." It is obvious that it was far more difficult to make a place in the Bible commonwealth for the Quakers than for the Baptists. The basic idea of the Quakers not only threatened the politico-religious structure of the church-state but was also incompatible with traditional Puritan theology and even conventional morality. The Quaker, just because he placed the emphasis upon this individual, subjective and more or less vacillating "Inner Light," deprived himself and his group of the conventional means of discipline and was guilty of excesses that sometimes bordered upon fanaticism. The presence of such a group in their midst aroused hatred mingled with fear in the conservative, unimaginative, middle-class Englishmen of the Bay colony, with their ingrained love of order and decency.

If the Baptist was viewed as we should view the man who is a germ-carrier and yet otherwise rational and well-behaved, the Quaker was looked upon not only as the carrier of poisonous theological germs but also as a dangerous and irresponsible fanatic or madman. It will always be a question as to whether the Puritan fathers were not actuated by downright fear and terror quite as much as by the detestable *odium theologicum* in their fearful maltreatment of the poor Quakers. If as intelligent a man as Cotton Mather was so filled with panic fear that he saw the devil incarnated in poor neurotic and half-witted women and with a zeal bordering upon fanaticism urged that they be hanged as witches, we can well imagine that similar feelings of panic fear might have been aroused by the eccentricities of the ignorant Quakers. Cotton Mather did in fact assert that the conduct of the Quakers could only be explained on the assumption that they were possessed of devils.[8]

George Bishop, in his *New England Judged* even insinuates that their panic fears had turned the Bay leaders into moral cowards. The arrival of "two poor women," Ann Austin and Mary Fisher, in Boston harbor, July, 1656, "so shook ye to the everlasting shame of you . . . as if a formidable army had invaded your borders." This betrays small confidence in the stability of the divinely constituted Bible commonwealth. "And what was your peace and order and how established that the shadow of two women or the hearsay of their moving should so shake you?" Conduct inspired by panic fear is always stupid. "If ye meant anything that might satisfy the understanding of men," the way to go about it was not "to go and put men to death and then apologize for what ye have done." Self-respecting courts of justice do not act in this wise. "Justice needeth no apology." Their protests betrayed them. "Had ye been wise men ye would have been silent." As it was, crazed by theological fears and blinded by bigotry, "working backward and forward, up and down, now here and now there," they behaved "as men drunk, indeed, with the blood of the innocent, whom guilt suffers not to be silent; and yet, when ye speak, ye manifest your guilt." [9]

III

The persecution of the Quakers extended over a period of approximately twenty-one years, beginning with the appearance of Ann Austin and Mary Fisher in Boston harbor in 1656 and ending with Margaret Brewster's appearance in 1677 in sackcloth in the meeting house "in sermon time," for which she was

[8] *Op. cit.*, Vol. II, p. 528.
[9] Bishop, *New England Judged*, pp. 12, 30 f.

"stripped and most inhumanly and cruelly whipped." [10] This was the last whipping. The persecution of the Quakers ceased after this to be physical and became economic and political in character. It is possible to divide these twenty-one years into three periods. The first period closed with the mandamus of Charles II in 1661 forbidding the Massachusetts authorities from further punishments of Quakers and requiring that they be sent to England to be tried, a royal command which Massachusetts coolly ignored. This period is marked by constantly increasing severity in the laws, culminating in the hanging of four Quakers during 1659 and 1660. The second period ended with the death of Endicott in 1665 and was marked by the atrocious Cart and Whip Act of 1661, which was an attempt to suppress the Quakers by other means than hanging. This period, dominated by the melancholy John Norton and the truculent Endicott, witnessed some of the most brutal treatments of Quakers, especially women. The last twelve years were marked by a gradual cessation of whippings.

Besse in his Quaker *Sufferings* gives the New England list as follows: "1. Two honest and innocent women stripped stark naked and searched in inhuman manner. 2. Twelve strangers in that country, but freeborn of this nation, received twenty-three whippings, most of them with a whip of three cords with knots at the ends. 3. Eighteen inhabitants of the country, being freeborn English, received twenty-three whippings. 4. Sixty-four imprisonments 'of the Lord's people,' amounting to five hundred and nineteen weeks. 5. Two beaten with pitched ropes, the blows amounting to one hundred and thirty-nine. 6. An innocent old man banished from his wife and children, and for returning put in prison for a year. 7. Twenty-five banished upon

[10] *Ibid.*, p. 473.

penalty of being whipped, or having their ears cut or a hand branded. 8. Fines, amounting to a thousand pounds, laid upon the inhabitants for meeting together. 9. Five kept fifteen days without food. 10. One laid neck and heels in irons for sixteen hours. 11. One very deeply burned in the right hand with an H after he had been beaten with thirty stripes. 12. One chained to a log for the most part of twenty days in the winter time. 13. *Five appeals to England denied.* 14. Three had their right ears cut off. 15. One inhabitant of Salem, since banished on pain of death, had one-half of his house and land seized. 16. Two ordered sold as bond-servants. 17. Eighteen of the people of God banished on pain of death. 18. Three of the servants of God put to death [William Leddra's execution after this was written brings the list of those hanged to four]. 19. Since the executions four more banished on pain of death and twenty-four heavily fined for meeting to worship God." [11]

It is no part of the purpose of this study to enter into all the harrowing details of the persecutions of the Quakers but to stress only those phases that throw light upon the place of the dissenting groups in the culture of colonial New England. One who reads the story of these persecutions is impressed by the inhuman cruelty with which they were perpetrated, a cruelty that cannot be explained solely in terms of the customary barbarous treatment of the victims of the law in that age. One or two examples will suffice to bring out what is meant.

IV

In the famous Quaker ship, the *Woodhouse,* that brought the earliest apostles of Quakerism to New England in 1657

[11] Joseph Besse, *The Sufferings of the Quakers,* 1753, Vol. I, pp. xxx-xxxi.

was William Brend, "an ancient and venerable man" but "of iron constitution and an indomitable spirit," [12] who, after a short sojourn in Newport, Rhode Island, the Quaker headquarters, made his way to Salem and thence to Boston in 1658. There Brend and the other Quakers with him were jailed and told that they could have food only on condition that they worked for it. The Quakers refused to work for food while in prison, as this might seem to sanction the imprisonment. So they were confined for four days without food and on the fourth day the jailer gave them "ten stripes apiece with a knotted threefold corded whip" and locked them up again without food thus thinking to break their spirits. After whipping Brend and the others and keeping them in close confinement for five days, the jailer said, "They were clear on paying their fees, who owed him none, and hiring the marshall to convey them out of the country; which they could not do in obedience to the Lord, who sent them thither, or as Englishmen in their own country." [13]

This stubborn resistance seemed so to exasperate the jailer that "the next morning he put Brend, a man of years, into irons, neck and heels, and locked so close together that there was no more room between each than the horse-lock which fastened them on; and for the space of sixteen hours kept him so in irons, as the jailer himself confessed, for not working; and all this time without meat, whilst his back was torn with the whipping of the day before." This still failed to break the spirit of the brave old Quaker, so the next morning the jailer "laid him on with a pitched rope twenty blows over his back and arms with as much force as he could drive, so that with the fierceness of the blows the rope untwisted." The cruel jailer then provided himself with another rope "and having haled

[12] Jones, *op. cit.*, p. 47.
[13] Bishop, *op. cit.*, p. 56.

him down stairs with greater fury and violence than before, gave his broken, bruised and weak body fourscore and seventeen blows more, foaming at the mouth like a madman and tormented with rage; unto which great number he would have added more blows, had not his strength and rope failed him, for now he cared not what he did." [14]

As a result of this terrific mauling, during which Brend received one hundred and seventeen blows with a pitched rope, his "flesh was beaten black as into a jelly, and under his arms the bruised flesh and blood hung down, clotted as it were into bags; and it was so beaten into one mass, that the sign of one particular blow could not be seen." After this performance the jailer locked the bruised and bleeding Brend "in a close room and then went to his morning sacrifice with his hands thus defiled with blood." The strain was too great for the courageous and aged Brend, who after having been without food for five days and cruelly whipped "being kept in a close room without bed, food, or sustenance, soon fainted away, lying upon the boards." [15]

When the story of this barbarous cruelty was noised abroad there was an uproar, the prison was stormed, and the authorities, now thoroughly frightened, made every effort to save Brend's life, the governor sending his son and surgeon to the rescue. The surgeon's judgment was that Brend could not recover "but that his flesh would rot from off his bones." The people demanded that the jailer be dealt with by the courts. Just at this juncture appeared Reverend John Norton, "unto whom as the fountain or principal, most of the cruelty and bloodshed, herein rehearsed," says Bishop, "is to be imputed." With a haughty and cold-blooded callousness, which to the

---

[14] Bishop, *op. cit.*, pp. 56 f.
[15] *Ibid.*, p. 57.

modern man seems utterly incomprehensible in a clergyman, Norton said, "W. Brend endeavored to beat our gospel ordinances black and blue; and, if he was beaten black and blue, it was just upon him, and said he would appear in the jailer's behalf." [16] It should be remembered that the man who thus placed a damper upon the righteous indignation of the masses of the people at this inhuman treatment of Brend held a degree from Cambridge University and had succeeded to the place of John Cotton as the spiritual leader of the theocracy. Norton later succeeded in getting a law passed sanctioning the death penalty for Quakers who returned after banishment. Under this law William Robinson, Marmaduke Stevenson, Mary Dyer, and William Leddra were hanged on the Boston common. Norton thereby gained for Boston the melancholy distinction of being the only spot on American soil where men were hanged for their religion. Massachusetts had yet to realize the truth of Isaac Backus' words in a letter to President Washington in 1790, "Religious ministers, when supported by force, are the most dangerous men on earth." [17]

V

The outburst of indignation among the people at the treatment of William Brend, the murmurings that followed the hanging of Stevenson, Robinson, and Mary Dyer, together with the royal decree forbidding further persecution of the Quakers, made it necessary for the authorities to devise new laws which would attain the ends sought without offending the crown or the sensibilities of the people. The result was the atrocious Cart and Whip Act of 1661. This law required that confessed

[16] *Ibid.*, p. 57.
[17] Alvah Hovey, *Life and Times of Isaac Backus*, 1859, p. 252.

Quakers "be stripped naked from the middle upwards and tied to a cart's tail and whipped through the town, and from thence immediately conveyed to the constable of the next town, towards the borders of our jurisdiction, and so from constable to constable till they be conveyed through the outwardmost towns of our jurisdiction." [18]

In Dover, then part of the Bay colony, a group of Quakers were hailed before the magistrates by "priest Rayner" and the Cart and Whip Act was applied to them in the following order by the magistrate Richard Walden, "To the constable of Dover, Hampton, Salisbury, Newbury, Rowley, Ipswich, Wenham, Lynn, Boston, Roxbury, Dedham, and until these vagabond Quakers are carried out of this jurisdiction. You and every one of you are required in the king's majesty's name [a curious bit of unconscious irony for by this very act they were violating the mandamus of the king] to take these vagabond Quakers, Ann Coleman, Mary Tomkins, Alice Ambrose, and make them fast to the cart's tail, and driving the cart through your several towns, to whip them upon their backs, not exceeding ten stripes apiece on each of them, in each town, and so to convey them from constable to constable till they are come out of this jurisdiction, as you will answer it at your peril, and this shall be your warrant." [19] This bore the date of December 22, 1662, the beginning of winter.

Being haled before the authorities on this warrant, Alice Ambrose was asked her name. "My name," she said, "is written in the Lamb's book of life," to which Walden replied, "Nobody here knows this book." [20] The women were then stripped to the waist, tied to the cart's tail and whipped, "while the priest stood

[18] *Records of the Massachusetts Collection*, Vol. IV, Part II, p. 2, cited by Jones, *op. cit.*, p. 102.

[19] Bishop, *op. cit.*, p. 230.

[20] *Ibid.*, p. 231.

and looked on and laughed at it." When the authorities sought
to send the women to the next town they refused to go. The
attempt was made to put them on horses "but they slid off."
"Then they endeavored to tie each to a man on horseback" but
this likewise failed. The combination of Quaker and woman
was proving quite a problem "insomuch that the constable professed that he was almost wearied of them." Finally they
reached Hampton where they were whipped and, "through dirt
and snow . . . half-way the leg-deep," they were forced at
the cart's tail to Salisbury. Here the constable Fifield said that
they could not make a fool of him as they had of the constable
in Dover, to which the women replied that they were as "able
to deal with him as the other." He wished to whip them early
the next morning before daylight but they said they were "not
ashamed of their sufferings." The constable then proposed to
whip them with their clothes on but the incorrigible Quakers
said, "Set us free, or do according to thy order," that is, whip
them on their naked backs. The constable then asked one of
the women to take off her clothes. "She said she would not
do it for all the world," the other women agreeing with her
heartily. The embarrassed officer "stripped them and then
stood, with a whip in his hand, trembling as a condemned man,
and did the execution as a man in that condition." [21]

At Salisbury one William Barefoot induced the constable to
make him deputy and set the three women free. The indomitable Quakers at once returned to Dover "to look your cruel
law in the face." The two constables, the Roberts brothers,
whom Bishop calls "Sons of Belial," "put on their old clothes
with their aprons" in preparation for the carrying out of their
brutal designs and "laid hands on Alice Ambrose as she was

21 *Ibid.*, p. 232.

in prayer, and taking the one by the one arm and the other by the other arm, they unmercifully dragged her out of doors, with her face toward the snow, which was knee-deep, over stumps and old trees near a mile, in the way of which, when they had wearied themselves they commanded two others to help them, and so laid her up prisoner in the house of one T. Canny, a very wicked man." Returning they took Mary Tomkins "whom they also dragged with her face toward the snow." The old father of the two constables, T. Roberts, followed them crying, "Wo that ever he was the father to such wicked children." [22]

In the bitter cold of the next morning the constables procured a rude boat "or kind of trough hewn out of the body of a tree which the Indians use on the water" with the intention of taking the women to the mouth of the harbor that they "might be troubled with them no more." When the women refused to go "they forced them down a very steep place through the deep snow and then furiously took Mary Tomkins by the arms and dragged her on the back, over the stumps of trees, down a very steep hill to the water-side, so that she was much bruised and often fainted away, and Alice Ambrose they plucked violently into the water, and kept her swimming by the canoe, being in danger of drowning or of being frozen to death." A storm prevented the carrying out of the plans of the constables so "they had them back to the house again and kept them prisoners there till near midnight, and then they cruelly turned them out of doors in the frost and snow, Alice Ambrose's clothes being before frozen like boards." [23] While this brutal performance was taking place, "Hate-evil Nutter, a ruling elder, was present stirring up the constables to do this thing, for which

22 Bishop, *op. cit.*, pp. 233 f.
23 *Ibid.*, p. 236.

they had no warrant, as ever could be known or did appear." [24]
Instances might be multiplied to illustrate the inhuman, one
might almost say the pathological, cruelty with which the Quakers were treated.

VI

The "filial piety" school and others assert that the cruelty of
the age together with the exasperating conduct of the Quakers
suffice to explain, if not to justify in a measure, the conduct of
the authorities. This, however, ignores the hatred, the utter lack
of sympathy, especially on the part of the authorities, and the
outrageous disregard for law everywhere in evidence where
Quakers were dealt with. The real explanation is to be found
in the fact that the Quakers were an outcast group with a philosophy of life totally antagonistic to that of the theocracy.
Quaker and Puritan priest cherished world-views as far apart
as the poles. They cultivated mental attitudes and moved in
universes of discourse that had practically nothing in common.
This tragic lack of insight into each other's views led to suspicion, fear, and bitter animosity. In the Quaker and the leaders
of the theocracy we see the most striking illustration in the
history of this nation of the opposition of the dissenting to the
churchly tradition.

It is the boast of Massachusetts that her people are law-
abiding and the history of the Bay state in the main bears out
that boast. But in the support of that claim references to the
treatment of the Quakers are conspicuous for their absence. In
five instances the Quakers appealed to their rights as British
subjects only to have these appeals ignored. The mandamus of
Charles II forbidding further persecution of the Quakers and

[24] *Ibid.,* p. 235.

asking that they be sent to England for trial was entirely disregarded. In their "Petition and Address of the General Court," by which the theocracy sought to justify its conduct in the hanging of the Quakers, the great traditions of Magna Charta and the common law are ignored and there is a studied attempt made to blacken the character of the Quakers in terms of the theological jargon of the clergy. They were "open blasphemers," "seducers of the glorious Trinity," "Jesuits." The shuffle made use of by John Norton and Bradstreet, when questioned in London by George Fox and others, that the law against the Quakers in Massachusetts was no worse than the English law against Jesuits, brought this question from Fox, "Whether they had put them (the Quakers) to death as Jesuits?" To this Bradstreet replied, "Nay, he did not believe they were Jesuits." Whereupon Fox said that they had murdered the Quakers since there was no English law by which they could be put to death.[25]

The issue of the legality of the Quaker executions was raised by the courageous Wenlock Christison who, when tried in 1661, demanded, "By what law will ye put me to death?" The reply was, "We have a law and by our law you are to die." "Who empowered you to make that law?" asked Christison. "We have a patent, and are the patentees: judge whether we have not power to make laws." Then came the crucial question, "How? Have you power to make laws repugnant to the laws of England?" "Are you subject to the king? yea or nay?" This brought the evasive reply, "What good will that do you?" The upshot of the whole matter was admirably characterized by Christison, "Your will is your law, and what ye have power to do, that you will do."[26]

Not only were the rights of Quakers as Englishmen ignored

[25] Bishop, *op. cit.*, p. 216.
[26] *Ibid.*, p. 208.

but there was a similar disregard of their rights in domestic matters. The Reverend Seaborn Cotton, son of the famous John Cotton and minister at Dover, "having a mind to a pied heifer [of Eliakim Wardel, a Quaker] as Ahab had to Naboth's vineyard, he sent his servant nigh two miles to fetch her; who having robbed Eliakim of her, brought her to his master, for which his servant not long after was condemned in himself." Subsequently, when Wardel was being publicly whipped while "bound to an oak tree that stood by their meeting house," a crowd gathered, among them the pastor, Reverend Seaborn Cotton. After Wardel had been whipped "with cords nearly as big as a man's little finger" and was released, he chanced to see Seaborn Cotton in the crowd and said, "Seaborn, hath my pied heifer calved yet?" Whereupon this scion of the famous John Cotton "stole away like a thief." [27] Many other instances might be cited of the disregard of property rights both of Quakers and Baptists during this period.

This callous disregard of the rights of the Quakers among a people who were in other matters law-abiding is to be explained by the fact that the Quakers were viewed as outcasts. The radical divergencies between their outlook on life and that of the theocracy made all their conduct essentially antisocial and deprived them of the claims for legal protection normally extended to the ordinary citizen. It is a familiar fact that social sympathy and understanding are the only effective guarantees for the protection of the law to individuals and groups. Given radical distinctions, as in the "color line" of the South, or fundamental divergencies, social and economic, as in the famous Sacco-Vanzetti case, and a strain is immediately placed upon the machinery of justice when the rights of ostracized minorities

[27] *Ibid.*, p. 241.

are concerned. The Quakers were really lynched by the Massachusetts theocracy much as a mob lynches a negro suspect, except that in the case of the theocracy there was a hypocritical veneer of legality.

The barbarous treatment to which the modern mob frequently subjects the bodies of its victims finds a curious and gruesome parallel in the treatment of the bodies of the executed Quakers. When the dead bodies of Stevenson and Robinson "were cut down, they were suffered to fall to the ground, by which the skull of W. Robinson was broken, his body being stiff ere it was cut down." "Their shirts were ripped off with a knife" and their naked bodies were dragged "very barbarously by the legs unto the hole that was digged for them near the gallows" on the Boston common. When the Quakers came and asked to be allowed to put the bodies in coffins and bury them and surround their graves with a fence "because it was an open field where beasts might turn up their bodies and so prey upon them," the permission was refused. So the bodies were left "in a pit in an open field which was soon covered with water." [28] This barbarously unfeeling treatment of the bodies of the despised and outcast Quakers measures the gap, both mental and social, between the Quaker enthusiasts, with their fierce opposition to paid "priests," their mystical "Inner Light," their strange visions and voices, their "openings of the Lord" and the intolerant Puritan church-state championed by the leaders of "the unspotted lambs of the Lord." The fact that the differences were cast in religious form only served to accentuate the callous cruelty and the bitter animosity.

The mental attitude which practically denied to the Quaker all protection by law found its most brutal expression among

[28] Bishop, *op. cit.*, pp. 104, 204.

the college-bred clergy. In a sermon against the Quakers, Reverend Charles Chauncy, the second president of Harvard, himself a graduate of Cambridge, gives us this charming example of Christian charity: "Suppose, said he, ye should catch six wolves in a trap—now those to whom he alluded, were six Friends, all inhabitants of Salem—and ye can not prove that they killed either sheep or lambs, and now ye have them they will neither bark nor bite; yet they have the plain marks of wolves. Now I leave it to your consideration, said he, whether ye will let them go alive, yea or nay?" [29] Such language could only be applied to those who have no status in the community, legal or otherwise. Bishop bitterly objects to the inhumanity of a policy that seeks "to cause a man to suffer not for what he is but for what he may be—to judge a man to death without proof—to kill him lest he may do so and so—to execute law where there is not fact—to deal with a man as with a beast—to put a man who was made after the image of God . . . into the state of a beast which is known by its skin." [30] For the Puritan priest there was no "closed season" on Quakers.

VII

In the face of such fearful cruelty and social ostracism, not the least remarkable fact in the record of the Quakers is their courage. "There is so far as I know," remarks Jones, "no instance in the list of sufferings of any Quaker who 'recanted' or who even gave up his practice of the unimportant Quaker 'testimonies' such as wearing the hat or saying 'thou' in order to win his freedom or to spare himself torture." [31] It cannot be

[29] *Ibid.*, p. 72.   [31] Jones, *op. cit.*, p. 109.
[30] *Ibid.*, p. 72.

said, on the other hand, that the record of the cruel persecutors of the Quakers is conspicuous for courage either moral or physical. Every bully is more or less of a moral coward from the mere fact that through an appeal to force in a stupid effort to solve a problem that can only be solved through sweet reasonableness he stultifies the finer side of his nature. George Bishop, the Quaker historian, early recognized that their theological fears and baseless suspicions had turned the leaders of the theocracy into moral cowards.[32] For moral courage is impossible where reason is fettered by bigotry and superstitious fears. Moral uneasiness is reflected in the impatience and petulance in the face of outside criticism. It appears in their repeated refusals of the Quaker appeal to England. It masquerades beneath a smug self-sufficiency that ill befits one conscious of the moral rectitude of his course. It is seen even in the vindictive cruelty manifested towards helpless and unresisting men and women, for this is merely a confession of the moral weakness of a cause that must depend upon force to carry its end.

The moral unloveliness of the Puritan priest is merely accentuated by the fact that he capitalized his monopoly of the means of access to the divine will to throw the cloak of holy religion over conduct that cannot be defended by the most elementary principles of social justice. It is often said in his defense that like the priests of the Inquisition he was merely the child of his age. The parallel is not convincing. John Cotton and the New England leaders belonged at first to the dissenting tradition. They had a vision of liberty which they lost but it constantly rose like Banquo's ghost to trouble them. No one can read the story of their treatment of Antinomians, Baptists, and Quakers and say of them, as Carlyle said of Socra-

[32] Bishop, *op. cit.*, pp. 12 ff.

tes, that they were "terribly at ease in Zion." The fact that they were not at ease merely proves that they were not quite moral monsters.

How wide the gap that separated Quaker and Puritan priest and how bitter the hatred they cherished for each other may be inferred from the terrific epithets they launched at each other's heads. A Quaker thus expresses his opinion of the famous Oxford divine, John Owen, "Thou fiery fighter and green-headed trumpeter; thou hedge-hog, and grinning dog; thou bastard that tumbled out of the mouth of the Babilonish bawd; thou mole; thou tinker; thou lizzard; thou bell of no metal but the tone of a kettle; thou wheelbarrow; thou whirlpool; thou whirligig. Oh! thou firebrand; thou adder and scorpion; thou louse; thou cowdung; thou mooncalf; thou ragged tatterdemalion; thou Judas; thou livest in philosophy and logick which are of the devil." [33] After this terrific bombardment of epithets, the crime alleged, namely, living in philosophy and logic, is, it must be confessed, something of an anticlimax. In every Quaker there was always something of the child. In his simple and naïve faith and his charming ingenuousness the Quaker was like the child. He resembled a child, also, in that he mistook his inability to follow the processes of the cultured intellect for proof of their futility. The Quaker accepted implicitly the mandate, "Except ye become as little children ye cannot enter into the Kingdom of heaven." He failed to see that the sincerity of the child even when combined with the simple ethics of Jesus could not provide adequate moral, legal, or social technique for the solution of the problems even of seventeenth-century New England. The Quaker like the child had the defects of his qualities.

[33] Cited by Mather, op. cit., Vol. II, p. 531.

The Quaker leaders and writers exhausted their vocabularies in the effort to find epithets adequate to the expression of their detestation of the New England Brahmins. They called them "oppressive priests," "blasphemous priests," "blockish priests," "hireling priests," "bloody priests," "savage brutes," "devilish priests," "notorious thieves and robbers." [34] The philippics of the old Hebrew prophets against the enemies of Jahweh were made use of, such as Isaiah, 59:3 ff.: "Your hands are defiled with blood, your fingers with iniquity; your lips have spoken lies; your tongue hath uttered perverseness. None calleth for justice; nor any pleadeth for truth; you trust in vanity and speak lies; you conceive mischief and bring forth iniquity." The Quaker, in spite of his gentle faith, was human and he found a grim satisfaction in the tortures wreaked upon his persecutors of the Bay colony during King Philip's war when "the unspotted lambs" were dealt with rather harshly, the Indians "hanging up some alive on iron crooks by the under jaw until dead; burning some alive by degrees and skinning others alive." The Indians slightly improved upon the methods of Norton and Endicott in dealing with the Quakers. The pious Quaker saw in this "the fearful day of God's most righteous judgment" visited upon the wicked leaders of the theocracy for their bloody persecutions of "the children of light." [35]

It is impossible to understand the mental attitude that inspired such lurid language without keeping clearly in mind the basic differences between the religion of the dissenting Quaker and the theocracy. The very heart of religion for the Quaker was sincerity, simplicity, absence of restraint, inner integrity of soul, and the freedom necessary for the expression of this perfect ingenuousness in external acts. To the Puritan priest with his exclusive Biblical commonwealth, the Quaker with his "In-

---

[34] See Bishop, *op. cit.*, *passim*.   [35] *Ibid.*, pp. 70 f.

ner Light" was a deadly menace to religion and order. On the other hand, it was likewise true that in the imaginations of the Quakers, distorted and pathologically inflamed as they were through harsh and inhuman treatment, the Puritan priest had become a symbol of the forces of the devil. The essentially individual and subjective nature of the "Inner Light" stressed by the Quaker deprived his emotional nature of the necessary means of discipline and encouraged extravagance in word and act. When we add to this the antagonizing effects of the persistent treatment of the Quakers as social outcasts, their unrestrained and unchristian language is perfectly intelligible. The Puritan fathers set up a social order that was tragically inadequate for the satisfaction of the needs of the free spirit and then beat, banished, or hanged those unfortunates who failed to fit the Procrustean pattern of the Bible commonwealth.

VIII

The Puritan priests, in spite of their university degrees and alleged superior culture, were not one whit behind the Quakers in the vigor of their epithets and the animosity with which they characterized these dangerous dissenters. Reverend John Higginson of Salem, whom Cotton Mather in characteristic fulsome phrase calls "the temple wherein the spirit of God was resident," [36] kindly remarks of the Quaker's most cherished belief that "The Quaker's light was a stinking vapor from hell." [37] Reverend John Wilson, on whose hearse the poet placed this naïve encomium, "John Wilson, Oh! change it not: no sweeter name or thing, throughout the world, within our ears shall ring," [38] said in a sermon, "He would carry fire in

---

[36] *Op. cit.*, Vol. II, p. 365.
[37] Bishop, *op. cit.*, p. 242.

[38] Mather, *op. cit.*, Vol. I, p. 318.

one hand and faggots in the other, to burn all the Quakers in the world." When Quaker books were being burned he cast some into the fire with the remark, "From the devil they came and to the devil let them go." To the jury sitting on the trial of Quakers he said, "Hang them, or else"—and then drew his finger across his throat as a sign of what to do with them if they were not hanged. Wilson stood at the foot of the scaffold upon which Stevenson and Robinson were just about to be hanged and said to the doomed men, "shaking his head in a light scoffing manner, Shall such jacks as you come in before authority with your hats on?" This same Wilson loaned his handkerchief to the hangman to bind the eyes of Mary Dyer on the scaffold.[39] Reference has been made to the brutal remarks of John Norton after the whipping of William Brend and the uproar among the people.[40]

Cotton Mather, who, in spite of his learned ignorance and his childish superstitions, was perhaps the kindest hearted and most tolerant of the early New England Brahmins, could write, "Now I know not whether the sect which hath appeared in our days under the name of Quakers, be not upon many accounts the worst of hereticks; for in Quakerism, which has by some been called the 'sink of all heresies,' we see the *vomit* cast out in by-past ages, by whose *kennels* of seducers, lick'd up again for a *new digestion,* and once more exposed for the *poisoning* of mankind . . . they have been the most venomous of all to the churches of America." [41] One cannot read such language as this without feeling that the culture and education of the Puritan priest, of which so much has been made, was exceedingly crude and limited. Their writings are marked not only by the utter absence of all literary form and good taste but also by a tragic

39 Bishop, *op. cit.,* pp. 102 f., 110.   41 *Op. cit.,* Vol. II, p. 522.
40 *Ibid.,* p. 57.

lack of the profoundly human note found in the great Eliza-
bethans as well as in the Puritans, Cromwell and Milton. In
Roger Williams, "the Seeker," there is a feeling of the mystery
and tragedy of human life which prompted him to plead with
Endicott for tolerance,[42] but no such note anywhere emerges
among the New England Brahmins. Their outlook upon life,
in spite of their university degrees, was not one whit broader,
more humane, or more intelligent than that of the despised
and persecuted Quakers and Baptists. The stunted and acrid
culture of the Bay colony did not encourage magnanimity of
soul, nor profound insight into life.

Why Mather considered Quakerism to be among the heresies
"the most venomous of all to the churches of America" should
now be obvious. Quakerism was a sort of religious leaven. It
was at best a spiritual attitude that did not lend itself to the
formulation of a definite creed. George Fox, its founder, was
not a thinker and lacked both the ability and the inclination to
rationalize his experiences and reduce them to a creed. The
credal and rationalistic point of view, on the other hand, dominated the thought and life of the Puritan priest. The spirit of
George Fox and Quakerism was inimical to all forms of organization. The Quaker saw in a church establishment with its
credal and ritualistic paraphernalia the deadliest enemy to the
freshness and vitality of the inner life. For the Puritan priest
form and organization were not only necessary but came very
near to constituting the .very essence of religion. The beautiful
mysticism of the Quaker with all its humane and liberal implications was utterly lacking in the thought and life of the Puritan
priest. Authority for the Quaker was an ominous word and had
come to be identified in his experience with all the devilish
machinery of priests and rulers for manacling the free spirit of

[42] *Publications of the Narragansett Club,* Vol. VI, p. 225.

man. The religion of Cotton Mather was primarily authoritarian and for the Bible commonwealth the denial of the source of authority in church and state was an unpardonable sin. Quakerism tended to negate everything characteristic of institutionalized Christianity and was doubly sinister where church and state were one. For Cotton Mather, therefore, the "Inner Light" of the Quaker was synonymous with all the forces making for social anarchy. Even to tolerate it was asking the theocracy to take to its bosom a deadly asp whose subtle poison would sooner or later compass its utter destruction.

The Quakers looked upon the "Inner Light" as a source of knowledge and guidance that took precedence over everything else. Objective divine revelations of truth of whatever sort were discounted. Even the Bible became for the Quaker merely a collection of printed symbols instead of the religious fetich the priests made of it. It was dependent for its value to the Quaker upon the illuminating power of the "Inner Light" in the man who read its printed page. This not only contradicted the Puritan doctrine of the Bible as the only source of divine truth, but it very easily encouraged in the Quaker an attitude of spiritual and intellectual arrogance which was especially offensive to the Puritan priest with his claim to a monopoly of the cultural heritage of the community. Quakerism was thus a most dangerous challenge to the position of privilege and power enjoyed by the Puritan priest in the theocracy. The Quaker with his "Inner Light" threatened to do to seventeenth-century New England society what Rousseau did to eighteenth-century French society with his doctrine of the *amour de soi*. For the Quaker doctrine deified ordinary human nature by making God and human nature synonymous. The leveling effects of such a doctrine in religion, and through religion in every phase of the life of the community, were literally unlimited in their scope.

The Puritan priests were dimly aware of this and hence the bitterness with which they sought to destroy the Quaker and all his works.

IX

All are agreed that the darkest blot in the record of the Bay colony is its treatment of the Quakers. Historical estimates of this treatment, however, have been affected by certain anti-Quaker stereotypes dating from the time of their appearance, later perpetuated by Cotton Mather in his *Magnalia* and taken over uncritically and popularized by the "filial piety" school of historians. According to these traditional stereotypes the Quakers are "crazy fanatics." Even Barrett Wendell in his admirable *Cotton Mather, Puritan Priest*,[43] refers to the Quakers as "crazy fanatics." Fanatic is of course a relative term. To many modern men Reverend John Norton, thirsting for the blood of the old Quaker William Brend, or Cotton Mather, raving against witches, would merit the term fanatic. No historian can afford to adopt the point of view of the persecutors of the Quakers and of their apologists without running the risk of a distortion of the facts. It must be remembered that these same "crazy fanatics" were viewed in Rhode Island as peaceable and worthy citizens. The critical student must ask himself the question as to how far the fanaticism of the Quakers was the natural and inevitable psychological reaction against that cultural monstrosity, the Massachusetts theocracy. To assume that Endicott and Norton were sane and their victims "crazy fanatics" is just a little naïve. A generation after the Quaker persecutions, Cotton Mather, the priestly chronicler, dubbed the Quakers "dangerous villains" and called the Quaker leader George Fox "a proud fool who could scarce write his name." His verdict as

[43] P. 7.

to the Quakers is, "That if they had not been *mad* they had been *worthy to die*." [44] Beneath this language lies the smug and complacent assumption which no unprejudiced modern scholar can grant, that the Massachusetts theocracy was a sane and well-balanced social order within whose confines men could live in peace and concord and those who could not were mad.

In most cases those whom we label radicals are merely individuals for the adequate development of whose personalities society has made no provision. The men Massachusetts deemed dangerous radicals became in Rhode Island and Pennsylvania quite harmless and well-behaved citizens. In fact, Rhode Island authorities found them the more harmless just in proportion to the freedom accorded them in religious matters. [45] The Bay colony turned the Quakers into dangerous radicals and rebels against the existing social order by its intolerance, and then blamed the Quakers for its own political and religious stupidities. The founders of the theocracy, after having carefully framed a social order in which only one type of character could thrive, namely, the institutionalized "standpatter," then proceeded to label as dangerous fanatics and radicals all those who demanded for the development of their personalities a larger and freer cultural setting. The very fact that they had labeled their pathological social order a "Bible commonwealth" gave it supernatural sanction that blinded them to its inherent political and social ineptitudes. If supernaturalism is not the original sin of the institution, it is certainly not the least of its besetting sins.

The bias of these anti-Quaker stereotypes has made it exceedingly difficult for "filial piety" historians to sympathize with and properly to evaluate the conduct and character of the Baptists and the Quakers. We are told, "The Baptists of our day

---

[44] *Op. cit.*, Vol. II, pp. 526, 527.
[45] Backus, *History of New England*, Vol. I, p. 250.

are quiet, well-behaved persons, comparing favorably in spiritual attainments and usefulness, in general culture, and in special cases of scholastic eminence, with any other denomination of Christians known to the nineteenth century. While the broad-brimmed and drab-colored Quaker of our time has such marked preëminence in all the peaceful and thrifty virtues, as to make it almost impossible for us to think that any, bearing his distinguished name, could ever have been other than a benediction among his fellows." But the Quaker and often the Baptist of the seventeenth century "was essentially a coarse, blustering, conceited, disagreeable, impudent fanatic; whose religion gained subjective comfort in exact proportion to the objective comfort of which it was able to deprive others."

The Quakers of that day were as "unlike the sleek benignant Friends" of today as "the wild Texas steer, maddened by the fever-torture of thirst and the goading torment of the jolt and clatter of a cattle-train; broken loose and tearing terribly through crowded city streets—tossing children, trampling women, and making dangerous confusion thrice-confounded everywhere, until calmed by some policeman's rifle—is unlike the meek-eyed and patient ox which leans obediently to the yoke, as with steadfast steps he draws the straight dark furrow behind him, along which, by and by, the harvest of autumn is sweetly to smile." [46] To complete this lurid picture John Norton, Endicott, Wilson, and the rest of the leaders of the theocracy should be likened to the Texas cowboys mounted upon fiery bronchos and with shouts and brandished whips rounding the Quaker steers into shape, lassoing them, dragging them in the dust and finally branding them with red-hot irons as social and religious mavericks.

To compare the conduct of the patient old man, William

[46] Dexter, *op. cit.*, pp. 138 f.

Brend, with his flesh hanging in bloody bags from the cruel beatings, lying fainting upon the boards of the Boston prison, or that of the comely Mary Dyer, who when asked upon the gallows if she would not return home, quietly replied, "I came in obedience to the will of God," or that of Obadiah Holmes saying calmly to the executioner after his cruel beating, "I pray God it may not be laid to your charge"—to compare such conduct to that of a "wild Texas steer" is grotesquely ludicrous. This is all the more astonishing since the writer who made this comparison had mastered the historical details of these events as had few before or since. The most insidiously dangerous enemy of historical accuracy is a pious provincialism masquerading under a veneer of scholarship and culture.

The answer to the above characterization of the Quaker of the seventeenth century is, as we have suggested, the records of the Quakers in Rhode Island and Pennsylvania. It has been said, "The difference between New England and Pennsylvania in the seventeenth century is simply the difference between Calvinism and Quakerism applied to government." [47] Pennsylvania, though one of the last of the colonies to secure a charter, grew rapidly under wise and tolerant Quaker leadership. Benjamin Franklin sought refuge from the intolerance and obscurantism of Boston in the Quaker city and together with Priestley, Rush, Rittenhouse, Bartram, Marshall, Audubon, Nuttall, and others, formed a galaxy of scientists and humanitarians who made Philadelphia not only the largest and best-governed city but also the cultural center of the western world.

[47] I. Sharpless, *Quakerism and Politics: Essays,* 1905, p. 107.

Chapter VIII
The Dissenter and the Yankee Tax-Collector

THE CONSTANT flouting of the mandates of the crown in the brutal treatment of dissenting British subjects finally cost the Bay colony its charter. There is a certain irony in the fact that the profligate Charles II took the first move to rescue Quakers and Baptists from the bloodthirsty piety of "the unspotted lambs of the Lord." The charter of 1691, which the Bay province was forced to accept by the crown, apparently abolished the establishment and guaranteed complete liberty of conscience when it stipulated "for the greater ease and encouragement of our loving subjects inhabiting our said province or territory of the Massachusetts Bay and of such as come to inhabit there we do by these presents for our heirs and successors grant and establish and ordaine that *forever hereafter there shall be liberty of conscience allowed in the worship of God* to all Christians (except Papists) inhabiting or which shall inhabit or be resident within our said province or territory." [1] But the liberal Dutch monarch William, who

---

[1] *Acts and Resolves of the Province of Massachusetts Bay*, Vol. I, p. 14. The five volumes of this collection, extending from 1692 to 1780, give the legislative acts that indicate the evolution of the status of the dissenting groups in Massachusetts during the eighteenth century. The most important authorities are P. E. Lauer, *Church and State in New England*, Johns Hopkins Studies in Historical and Political Science, Vol. X, 1892, pp. 93 ff.; S. M. Reed, *Church and State in Massachusetts, 1691-1740*, University of Illinois Studies in the Social Sciences, Vol. III, 1914, pp. 455 ff.; J. C. Meyer, *Church and*

sponsored this declaration, failed signally to take into consideration the mores of the people of Massachusetts, their ingrained
conservatism, and the weakness of the dissenters.

I

No sooner was the new charter promulgated than differences
of opinion arose as to the meaning of the phrases "liberty of
conscience" and "the worship of God." In a sermon of 1693,
Increase Mather, who had much to do with the procuring of
the charter, claimed that according to the charter "you may
worship God in the greatest purity and no one may disturb you"
while, on the other hand, "the General Assembly may by their
acts give distinguishing encouragements unto that religion which
is the general profession of the inhabitants." [2] It is perfectly
obvious that any effective union of these two points of view
into a practical program would prove most difficult in Massachusetts.

Assured of the support of the majority, the friends of the
establishment, led by the Mathers, proceeded to enact laws
that really restored the old establishment and ostensibly in
accordance with the new charter. In November, 1692, a law
was passed placing the responsibility upon the county court of
quarter sessions for providing the towns with "learned orthodox
ministers," "chosen of the major part of the inhabitants at a
town meeting" and supported by the town. [3] It is obvious that
this law reintroduces the regulations of the earlier theocratic
régime. The emphasis now is not on orthodoxy so much as on

State in Massachusetts, 1740-1833, 1930; J. F. Thorning, Religious Liberty
in Transition, 1st Series, New England, 1931; Isaac Backus, History of the
Baptists, Vol. II; Alvah Hovey, The Life and Times of Isaac Backus, 1859.
   [2] Cited by S. M. Reed, op. cit., p. 22.
   [3] Acts, Vol. I, p. 62.

good morals, law and order, and the furthering of vested interests. An act of a few weeks later providing for the collection of ministers' rates contained this sinister provision "and to make distress upon all such (as) shall (neglect or) refuse to make payment. And for want of goods or chattels whereon to make distress, to seize the person and commit him to the common jail of the county, there to remain until he pay the sum upon him assessed as aforesaid, unless the same, or any part thereof, upon application made unto the quarter sessions, shall be abated." [4] This act was destined to deprive unlucky Quakers and Baptists of their sheep and cows and kitchen utensils and cause them to spend weary hours in jail throughout the eighteenth century.

II

Plymouth was absorbed by the Bay colony and the first act in the drama of the struggle for religious liberty in Massachusetts under the new charter took place in the southeastern counties of Plymouth, Barnstable, and Bristol. The actors were primarily the Quakers and a handful of Baptists, the forces of the establishment, and the home government of England. The issue was the attempt of the establishment to maintain a state church in towns such as Dartmouth, which was almost solidly Quaker in its religious affiliations. The struggle was carried on mainly by the Quakers, who numbered about three thousand in the three counties of the old Plymouth colony and were scattered through the towns of eastern Massachusetts. Not until the great accession due to the Great Awakening did the Baptists become numerous enough to make themselves felt. Though few in numbers they made common cause with the Quakers. In this struggle the forces within the colony were not

[4] *Acts*, Vol. I, p. 66.

evenly balanced. The dissenters were hopelessly in the minority. There was lacking the rich diversity, racial, economic, and geographic, that enabled Virginia to solve the problem of religious liberty without outside interference. In Massachusetts it was pressure brought to bear by English Quakers upon the King in council that finally forced the intransigent authorities to relax their grip upon impotent Quakers and Baptists and adopt makeshift legislation in a half-hearted attempt to carry out the spirit and intent of the charter.

Bristol county was the head and front of the opposition to the establishment and in Swansea the county court made its first attempt to enforce the laws of 1692 and 1693. The town already had a Baptist church thirty years old and a pastor. The authorities proposed to force upon the town a Congregational minister according to law. In town-meeting the people approved their Baptist preacher, and matters were at a standstill. In 1798 a grand inquest was made by the county authorities and the towns of Swansea, Dartmouth, Tiverton, Freetown, and Attleboro were reported as violating the law by not providing themselves with a minister of the establishment. This was the beginning of a prolonged struggle that lasted for twenty-six years.[5] When the county authorities failed the General Court was forced to intervene.

The nature of the problem presented to the Court by the dissenting towns of the southeastern counties is clearly seen in the act of 1702 looking to the "more effectual providing for the support of ministers."[6] The preamble of this act also indicates the mental attitude with which the Court approached its task. "Whereas in some few towns and districts within this province divers of the inhabitants are Quakers, and other irreligious persons averse and opposite to the public worship of God and to a

[5] Reed, *op. cit.*, pp. 523 ff.   [6] *Acts*, Vol. I, p. 505.

learned orthodox ministry and find out ways to elude the laws provided for the support of such—to the encouragement of irreligion and profaneness," etc. This intolerant and unchristian note is coupled with a hard businesslike emphasis upon "contract," court "allowance" to the ministers and a shameless appeal to the selfish interests of all involved. Where the assessors failed to collect the taxes for the minister they were to be fined. If this failed "three or more sufficient freeholders" were to assess the town, two justices of the peace were to affix their warrants thereto and direct the constable of each town to collect the taxes "and pay the same unto the minister." One can well imagine the mental attitude of dissenters listening to the spiritual ministrations of a parson whose salary was paid in this fashion! If the constables failed to carry out their instructions they were subject to "pains, penalties and forfeitures." To encourage them to carry out their duties they were to be paid "for their pains and trouble" out of the fines "set upon the delinquent assessors." If any funds were left over from this complicated system of fines they were to go back to the county treasury. The act stipulated that these regulations were to be carried out, "any law, usage or custom to the contrary in any wise notwithstanding," a stern challenge to the traditions and habits of Quakers and Baptists built up under the more liberal policies of the old Plymouth colony. This document with its brutal disregard of all the fundamentals of Christian ethics, its shrewd appeal to selfish pecuniary interests, its clever attempt to pit one group against another in the effort to further the ends of statecraft, strikes the keynote of the policies of the Bay colony in its dealings with the dissenters throughout the eighteenth century.

The high-handed attempt of the Court to coerce the dissenting towns culminated in the law of 1706, authorizing the Court to supply a minister to a town and provide for his salary by an addition to the province tax.[7] By thus surreptitiously adding the salary of the minister to the general tax and ignoring rights of local autonomy, the Court sought to circumvent the recalcitrant towns. The Court, apparently, was ready to stoop to any measures that would enable it to wrest the money from the pockets of the dissenters. Tender consciences were ignored. Taxes, not holy religion, were their goal. It never seems to have dawned upon the benighted Massachusetts authorities that a great principle was at stake. They were apparently utterly devoid of any social vision. The endless squabbles over rates and the constant resort by the authorities to every hook and crook to coerce the stubborn dissenters give us a measure of insight into the sordidness and petty provincialism of a period when "the people of New England touched their lowest point intellectually and spiritually." [8]

Great credit goes to the Quakers for the rôle they played during these days of trial. During the forty years since the Quakers had appeared in Massachusetts popular prejudice against them had not materially changed. They were still considered a godless crew of dangerous radicals. But the intense hatred of the middle of the seventeenth century had abated. "Ranterism" had disappeared among the Quakers. Their thrift and diligence in business had won for them a measure of respect as valuable citizens. In Rhode Island individuals had accumulated large fortunes. The influence of the Quakers in Massachusetts was small but it was immensely fortified by the position of influence occupied by the Quakers in England, not only in business but also in matters of state. The Massachusetts Quakers were not slow in advising their English brethren of

[7] *Acts*, Vol. I, p. 597.
[8] J. T. Adams, *Revolutionary New England, 1691-1776*, 1923, p. 35.

the situation created by the laws of 1692, 1693, and 1706. The English Quakers sought legal advice as to whether these laws were not invalid unless approved by the King in council. They tried in vain to enlist the aid of the English dissenters. Petition after petition was sent to the Massachusetts authorities but fell on deaf ears. The Council was inclined to be conciliatory but the more provincial-minded Assembly was obdurate in its refusal of all leniency to the despised Quakers and Baptists.[9]

III

Failing in all their efforts to get the authorities to modify the obnoxious law of 1706, which had been repeated in 1715 and reënacted in 1722, it was decided to appeal to England. The cause of the dissenters was placed in the hands of the able Quakers, Thomas Richardson of Newport, and Richard Partridge of London. Their object was to secure the invalidation of the tax laws of 1722 and 1723 [10] by the Privy Council. As a result of their efforts the Board of Trade, at the direction of the Privy Council, made the following deliverance: "We think it our duty to represent to your excellencies that by the charter granted to the Massachusetts Bay, the foundation of this colony was laid in an absolute and free liberty of conscience for all Christian inhabitants there, except Papists. But the Presbyterians having absolutely the ascendant in the Assembly of this province have assumed to themselves the authority of an established church, and would compel the Quakers even in the towns of Dartmouth and Tiverton, where they are infinitely the majority, to pay a large maintenance to Presbyterian ministers, whom they call orthodox, for the service of some few Presbyterian

[9] Reed, op. cit., pp. 568 ff.
[10] For details as to these laws see Acts, Vol. II, pp. 271 f.

families there." [11] The Board, therefore, in 1724 disallowed the Acts of 1722 and 1723. Thus did the "Mother of dissenting consciences" come to the rescue.

The dissenting Quakers and Baptists had won, but the showing made by the Massachusetts General Court was exceedingly shabby. Conscious, doubtless, that they had no case and at a loss how to defend their cause, they made no defense but fell back upon the favorite method of Massachusetts when it was a matter of resisting royal interference, namely, delay.

Some light may be thrown upon the mental processes of the stiff-necked provincial-minded leaders of the Bay province by an incident that happened while these negotiations were in progress. In 1722 when Quakers and Baptists were being imprisoned and their goods distrained to support the establishment Massachusetts ministers sent a letter to the authorities of Providence in regard to the Congregationalists in Providence, saying, "We are beholden to the mercy of heaven for the freedom and safety they have enjoyed under the wise and good government of the place" and begging that "if ever it should come to pass that a small meeting-house should be built in your town to entertain such as are willing to hear our ministers we should count it a great favor if you all, gentlemen, or any of yours would please to build pews therein." Governor Jencks interpreted this as a move on the part of Massachusetts "to gain the rule over us" by the missionary activities of Congregational ministers in Rhode Island.[12]

The Providence authorities replied, "We take notice how you praised the love and peace that dissenters of all ranks entertain one another within this government," which peace and love are due to "not allowing societies any superiority over one another." They then added, "Since you wrote this letter the

---

[11] Cited by Reed, *op. cit.*, p. 124.   [12] Backus, *op. cit.*, Vol. II, p. 12.

constable of Attleboro has been taking away the estates of our dear friends and pious dissenters to maintain their minister. . . . Is this the way of peace? Is this the fruit of your love? . . . far be it from us to revenge ourselves or to deal to you as you have dealt to us but rather to say, Father forgive them for they know not what they do." The letter was signed for the town of Providence by one Jonathan Sprague.

The Massachusetts ministers made no attempt to deny the facts as charged in the letter from Providence but spitefully published in a Boston paper a court sentence of 1674, fifty-two years earlier, charging Sprague with "lascivious carriage." Aware, doubtless, of the pathological sensitiveness of the descendants of "the unspotted lambs of the Lord" to all sexual laxities, Sprague replied at length, stating that one of the witnesses in the case alluded to had "asked and received his forgiveness for wronging him in her testimony" and had joined the Baptist church. Then, lapsing into verse, Sprague added:

> My youthful walk I'll not commend,
> Nor go about it to defend;
> But to God's glory do confess,
> I liv'd in sin and wickedness.[13]

This incident raises some interesting questions. Were the Massachusetts ministers conscious of hypocrisy when they wrote their unctuous letter? Why were they not magnanimous enough to acknowledge their inconsistency when it was pointed out to them? Were they aware of the exceeding littleness and spitefulness of trying to discount the truth of the letter by digging up youthful excesses of over a half century ago in the man who happened to sign it? Or was this merely another illustration of the fearful and wonderful workings of a mentality which had

[13] Backus, *op. cit.*, Vol. II, pp. 7 ff.

been rendered impervious to criticism by generations of ingrained moral and spiritual egotism?

IV

The first act in the drama of the struggle for religious liberty
in eighteenth-century Massachusetts closed with the royal mandate of 1724, disallowing the laws of 1722 and 1723. From the
effects of this act of the Privy Council the establishment never
recovered. It fought a stubborn rear-guard battle for over a century. But its history is that of a slow debacle. The victory of
1724, to be sure, was only partial. Delinquent assessors were released from jail and the General Court made no further efforts
to force orthodoxy down the throats of the dissenting citizens of
Dartmouth and Tiverton. Ministers' rates, however, were still
imposed upon dissenters as part of the town tax. Quakers and
Baptists now sought exemption from these. Quakers in England united with Quakers in the province to bring pressure to
bear upon the authorities, resulting finally in the law of 1728.
This law, exempting from ministers' rates, was the first attempt
of Massachusetts to relieve Quakers and Baptists from the
financial oppression of the establishment.

By 1740 Quakers, Baptists, and Episcopalians were enjoying
a measure of toleration doled out to them in a grudging and
half-hearted fashion. No penalties were imposed for failure
of the officials to administer these laws equitably with the result
that when dissenters reminded assessors of any laxity they were
often snubbed or dismissed with a contemptuous answer. It is
not surprising, therefore, that the more unscrupulous assessors,
knowing that they would not be held responsible for unfair-
ness in making out the lists of exemptions, simply neglected
them. The result was that "the lists described in this act (of

1728) were taken in scarcely a single town of the province." [14]
With the renewal of exemption law in 1740, and later in 1747,
these abuses remained and were so exasperating to the dissenters
that they were again on the point of appealing to the crown,
their sole source of relief against the cold-blooded injustice of
the establishment. Whenever the authorities did yield it was
no proof that they had been converted to the great principle of
religious tolerance. They yielded through fear of royal authority, just as John Endicott over half a century earlier had yielded
to the mandate of Charles II staying his hand from being still
further imbued with the blood of the patient Quakers.

The intolerance of Massachusetts was not that of individuals
primarily but was ingrained in her institutions and prevailing
way of life. It is a familiar fact that there is no form of intolerance so truculent and at the same time so insidiously dangerous as that of an institution. The institution must assume its
enduring worth and its authoritative finality. By its very nature
it stands sternly opposed to the fluctuating opinions of minorities. Its motto is *eterna non caduca*. It has been said that "the
supernatural is always a conceit of the institution." [15] One is
tempted to add to this another dictum, intolerance is the besetting sin of the institution. The intolerance of the Bay province
was an integral part of the very spirit and philosophy of its
institutional forms, especially the establishment, resembling in
this respect the intolerance of the Catholic church. There is this
fundamental difference, however, that Catholic scholars concede
the intolerance of their church but offer a respectable philosophy
in its justification. The Bay colony never was equal to this in-

---

[14] Hovey, *op. cit.*, pp. 169, 170.
[15] A. Lloyd, "The Institution and Some of Its Original Sins," *American
Journal of Sociology*, Vol. XIII, pp. 523 f. See also J. M. Mecklin, *An Introduction to Social Ethics*, 1920, pp. 217 ff.

tellectual *tour de force*, primarily because it was always bedeviled by earlier traditions of liberty. The result was that Massachusetts during the seventeenth and eighteenth centuries left an unenviable record of banishments, beatings, and cruel hangings, tiresome theological casuistry, indifference to the warnings of English dissenters, and stubborn resistance to the mandates of the crown, degenerating finally into petty legal quibblings in the sordid effort to wring taxes from a handful of impotent dissenters. No other state can rival this record of consistent pig-headed intolerance. It is not surprising, therefore, to find that among all the political and religious leaders of eighteenth-century Massachusetts it is impossible to point to one who, like Roger Williams, William Penn, or Patrick Henry, had social imagination enough to grasp the tremendous import of the issues raised by the dissenters and the courage and independence to champion their cause. "Do men gather grapes of thorns or figs of thistles?"

V

The fight for religious liberty during the early decades of the eighteenth century was waged primarily in the external series of reality. It was a matter of securing toleration for Quakers and Baptists under an establishment. By the middle of the century the fight had shifted from the external to the inner series of reality. This was due to the New Englander's discovery of the emotional life in the Great Awakening. This movement with its central doctrine of the "new birth" was not concerned directly with the rights of dissenting towns nor did it deal primarily with the question of the status of dissenting groups under an established church. It appealed directly to the individual. It stressed the rights and duties of the individual conscience. It placed feeling above theological dogma or legal status. Whitefield's engaging eloquence and evangelical fervor were suffused with a rank individualism that boded ill for all establishments. He was constantly talking of divine laws that are binding upon the conscience of the individual and take precedence of all man-made ordinances. In a letter to the Bishop of London he said, "Your Lordship knows full well that canons and other church laws are good and obligatory when comformable to the laws of Christ and agreeable to the liberties of a free people; but when invented and compiled by men of little hearts and bigotted principles . . . they may be very legally broken." [16]

Whitefield, together with the other revivalists, preached a radical democracy based upon the "new birth" in which there is "neither Greek nor Jew, circumcision nor uncircumcision, barbarian, Scythian, bond nor free." Such a gospel appealed powerfully to the disinherited for, by implication at least, it placed them on a par with the cultured, the rich, and the powerful. From the balcony of the courthouse of Philadelphia Whitefield proclaimed that in heaven there would be no Episcopalians, Baptists, Quakers, Presbyterians, or Independents, but only Christians.[17] When we recall that men listened to such doctrines, proclaimed with the utmost emotional abandon from one end of the colonies to the other and that even in conservative Boston pious Governor Belcher literally hung upon Whitefield's neck in tearful gratitude for his "message," we can gain some idea of the widespread and insidious menace the Great Awakening carried for the privileged New England establishments.

[16] Whitefield, *Works*, Vol. III, p. 163, cited by A. M. Baldwin, *The New England Clergy and the American Revolution*, 1928, p. 57.
[17] Baldwin, *The New England Clergy and the American Revolution*, p. 58.

The price the New Englander paid for the rediscovery of his emotional life was a corresponding loss of his proverbial poise. It is doubtful whether New England either before or since was ever as thoroughly excited over anything as it was over religion during the New Light and Old Light controversy. Indescribable confusion was introduced into a way of life famous for its emphasis of "law an' order." The most striking illustration of this was the chaos and friction created by the Separatist schism. This was only the largest and most spectacular phase of what was going on in every community. Innumerable splits and petty schisms took place within the old churches of the establishment as a result of this great religious upheaval.

VI

The Great Awakening obviously complicated the whole matter of dissenter and tax-collector. The status acquired by small dissenting groups, such as Quakers and Baptists, who had conscientious scruples against an establishment, was just beginning to find legal sanction when everything was thrown into confusion by a tremendous religious upheaval. The old churches of the establishment were splitting into New Lights and Old Lights. The New Lights were becoming Separatists. The Separatists were taking the form of a dissenting group within the ranks of the Congregationalists who refused to support an establishment because it failed to satisfy intimate personal convictions. The Separatist group did not possess elements of permanence and its members were constantly drifting over into the Baptist fold. Here was confusion worse confounded.

The establishments both in Massachusetts and in Connecticut were keenly aware of the danger threatened. Connecticut had always managed to prevent royal interference in the conduct of its affairs and hence did not have the wholesome fear of England instilled into Massachusetts by the experiences in connection with the new charter of 1691 and the invalidation of province laws by the Crown in 1724. In a series of legislative acts, beginning with the law of 1742, the tolerance that dissent had enjoyed under the Saybrook Platform of 1708 was wiped out and for forty years the Separatists were subjected to bitter persecution by the Connecticut authorities. The act of 1742 has been thus characterized: "The law was an outrage to every principle of justice, and to the most inherent and valuable rights of the subject. It was a palpable contradiction and gross violation of the Connecticut bill of rights. It dishonored the servant of God, stained his good name, and deprived him of all the temporal emoluments of his profession, without judge or jury, without hearing him, or knowing what evil he had done. . . . In other cases, civil and criminal, an appeal is allowed; but here, in a case of great magnitude, in which character, and a man's whole temporal living is at stake, there was no redress." [18] The immediate result of the Great Awakening was thus to threaten the rights the dissenters had won in both establishments during the early decades of the eighteenth century.

There is little doubt that Massachusetts would have followed the example of Connecticut had she dared.[19] But her stubborn provincial pride had been humbled on more than one occasion in her tilts with the mother country over the dissenters and she had become wary. She could not forget that the Privy Council in the deliverance of 1724 had said that in her laws directed against the dissenters she had violated her charter. Furthermore, the relations between Massachusetts and England were growing more and more strained and the province authorities

[18] Trumbull, *A Complete History of Connecticut*, 1818, Vol. II, p. 130.
[19] Backus, *op. cit.*, Vol. II, pp. 42, 53.

were keenly aware that every move against the dissenters might easily make the situation worse. Massachusetts was always inclined to turn a deaf ear to all the pleas of the dissenters until they talked of an appeal to the Crown.[20]

The only Massachusetts law which can be traced directly to the disturbances caused by the Great Awakening is that of 1752.[21] This act stipulated that in making out the lists of exemptions for the assessors the certificates shall be "under the hands of the minister and of two principal members of such church, setting forth that they conscientiously believe that such person or persons be of their persuasion." That is to say, membership rather than mere attendance is made the basis of tax-exemption. Furthermore, the ministers and two other members of a given church who issue these certificates must themselves be certified to by "three other churches commonly called Anabaptists . . . that they esteem such church to be one of their denomination." These certificates had to be renewed every year. The preamble of this act suggests the reasons for it, namely, that "exemption had been extended to many persons to whom the same was never designed to extend" and hence the act sought "to ascertain more effectually what persons shall be esteemed and accounted as Anabaptists." [22] The confusion created by the Great Awakening had given rise to groups of a nondescript character religiously. The act was not concerned primarily with their conscientious scruples but with taxes they were refusing to pay. The Yankee tax-collector had become the keeper of the famous New England conscience in religious matters.

The reasons for this piece of legislation are suggested by the merry squabble introduced by the tax-collector into the lives of

[20] Meyer, *op. cit.*, p. 63.
[21] Lauer, *op. cit.*, pp. 81 ff.
[22] *Acts*, Vol. II, p. 645.

the peaceful inhabitants of the town of Sturbridge in 1750.[23] A Separatist church had gone over bodily to the Baptists. To escape the tax for ministers' rates they must present the assessors with certificates that they were bona fide Baptists. Members of the Second Baptist church of Boston were equal to the emergency and supplied the certificates. The authorities were suspicious that perhaps, to use a phrase often on the lips of the disgruntled champions of the establishment, they had been immersed and joined the Baptists in order to "wash their taxes away." The tight-fisted Yankee publicans "sitting at the receipt of custom" were far more interested in the washing away of taxes than in the washing away of sins, and decided to collect the taxes. The new-born Baptists refused to pay. The tax-collectors adopted the usual sordid method of wringing taxes from the poor but stubborn dissenters.

The minions of the law descended upon the hapless Baptists. "They stripped the shelves of pewter, of such as had it; and others that had not they took away skillets, kettles, pots and warming pans. Others they deprived of the means they got their bread with, viz., workmen's tools and spinning-wheels. They drove away geese and swine from the doors of some others; from some that had cows, from some that had but one they took that away. They took a yoke of oxen from one. Some they thrust into prison, where they had a long and tedious imprisonment. A. A. Bloice had a spinning-wheel taken away in 1750 and was imprisoned in 1751. D. Fisk had five pewter plates taken from him in 1750 and a cow in 1751. John Cory imprisoned in 1750. J. Barstow imprisoned 1750. J. Pike a cow taken in 1750. A cradle in 1750 and a steer in 1751 were taken from J. Berry. Trammel, andirons, shovel and tongs were taken from J. Blunt in 1750 and he was imprisoned the next year. .John

[23] Meyer, *op. cit.*, p. 45. Backus, *op. cit.*, Vol. II, p. 94.

Streeter had goods taken in 1750 and 1751; Benjamin Robbins household goods and carpenter's tools. Household goods and a cow were taken from H. Fisk in 1750 and 1751. Josiah Perry was imprisoned in 1750 and a cow was taken from him in 1751. Nathaniel Smith was imprisoned in 1750. David Morse was imprisoned and a cow taken away in 1750 and a yoke of oxen in 1751. Goods were taken from Phinehas Collier in 1750 and 1751. John Newel, goods taken 1750 and 1751. John Draper imprisoned 1751." [24]

The most unpleasant phase of this and many similar incidents was the callous indifference of the authorities to the rights of the Baptists guaranteed them by law. The Baptists appealed to the law to regain their property. But they were no match for their adversaries with their legal quibbles, and the net result in this case was that "the Baptists were again taxed to pay the expenses of an illegal law-suit against themselves." [25] This spectacle of the representatives of "law an' order" descending to every legal trick to outwit ignorant and poverty-stricken dissenters in the interest of taxes is not one that arouses our admiration. It does not compare very favorably with the treatment accorded dissenters at the same time by representatives of the law in the Old Dominion.[26] The average citizen of Massachusetts was doubtless just as law-abiding as the average Virginian but a narrow provincial attitude had dulled the sense of justice, even of the officers of the law, to the rights of dissenters. Massachusetts never acknowledged the rights of dissenters as British subjects. The Anglican establishment and closer sympathy with English legislation on tolerance assured in Virginia far greater sensitiveness to the rights of dissenters.

[24] Backus, *op. cit.*, Vol. II, p. 94, note.
[25] Backus, *op. cit.*, Vol. II, p. 96.
[26] Jones, *The Quakers in the American Colonies*, pp. 265 ff.

The obnoxious law of 1753, designed to make it more difficult for Separatists and others to "wash their taxes away" by being immersed and joining the Baptist church, failed to accomplish its end. On the contrary, it aroused and unified the Baptists. There was again talk of an appeal to England and the Baptists sent a remonstrance to the General Court so bold that the motion was made to arrest its signers. Governor Shirley, who had returned from England, advised that such a move would be exceedingly unwise. The righteous indignation of the Massachusetts authorities suddenly cooled and "they appointed a committee to confer in friendly way with the Baptists." [27] The law of 1753 was renewed in substantially the same form in 1757 and again in 1761 for ten years.[28] Of this law Backus says, "No tongue nor pen can fully describe all the evils that were practised under it." [29]

The treatment of the Baptist church organized at Montague in 1765 is typical of what Backus had in mind.[30] This church presented certificates according to law but the authorities were in doubt as to "whether these were the Baptists whom the law exempted" and they were assessed with ministers' rates. The money not being forthcoming, the property of the Baptists was seized. Samuel Harvey was deprived of his cow and calf by the inexorable tax-collectors. Brother Harvey sued to get back his cattle. At a parish meeting the assessors were sustained. At the trial it was discovered that Harvey had tried to deceive the authorities. He had committed the enormity of signing a certificate for himself along with two others. Judge Williams with commendable regard for the punctilios of the law sternly refused to accept a certificate signed by two when it should have

[27] Backus, *op. cit.*, Vol. II, p. 140. Meyer, *op. cit.*, p. 49.
[28] *Acts*, Vol. IV, pp. 67, 420.
[29] *Op. cit.*, Vol. II, p. 141.
[30] Backus, *op. cit.*, Vol. II, p. 163.

been signed by three and the plaintiff had to go home without his cow and calf. Harvey appealed to the superior court and appeared supported with witnesses. Again he had blundered. His witnesses were all right in every particular but one—they were Baptists and were not permitted to testify, apparently on the assumption that no Baptist could be trusted to tell the truth about a brother Baptist. The indefatigable Harvey again tried his luck before the superior court, in May, 1771, which re-affirmed the opinion of Judge Williams. "Distress was then fearlessly made by the parish." Brother Harvey lost a yoke of oxen in addition to his cow and calf for his pertinacity.[31] Almost we are tempted to say that Tertullian's famous dictum as to the status of Christians in Rome held for the status of Baptists in Massachusetts, *nomen ipsum crimen.*

VII

The patience of the long-suffering Baptists reached the break-ing point in connection with the treatment of their church or-ganized in the pioneer town of Ashfield in 1761.[32] The pro-longed struggle of the Baptists for their rights in Ashfield, which finally reached the King in council, was complicated by the conditions of a pioneer community, the clash between in-habitants and absent proprietors, and the general strain of the impending storm that finally broke in war and revolution. At the time of the organization of the Baptist church in 1761, four-teen of the nineteen families of the place were Baptists in per-suasion. In 1763 a Congregationalist church was organized and all, including the Baptist preacher, were taxed for its erection.

[31] Hovey, *op. cit.*, p. 182.
[32] *Acts*, Vol. IV, pp. 1017, 1036 ff. for the sources. Also Backus, *op. cit.*, Vol. II, pp. 149 f.; Hovey, *op. cit.*, pp. 178 f.; Meyer, *op. cit.*, pp. 54 ff.

This was in accordance with the act of 1734.[33] When the town was incorporated in 1765, however, it was stipulated "that all taxes already raised for settling a minister, *or that may be raised for his support*, be levied on the inhabitants and proprietors." [34] The Baptists claimed that the word "support" was artfully inserted, and "had no place in their original grant, nor in the incorporating acts of the towns of Charlemont and Lanesborough, passed at the same session." [35] In other words, it was a violation of the province law which exempted the Baptists from ministers' rates after a town had been incorporated and the established minister had been provided for.

This, however, was only a part of the troubles in store for the Baptists in Ashfield. In 1768, in answer to a petition from the proprietors, taxing power was taken out of the hands of the inhabitants, contrary to the principle of town government, and the proprietors were empowered to raise such taxes as they saw fit for the support of the minister and to sell the lands of those who refused to pay the tax.[36] This high-handed law, directed obviously against the Baptists, became the center of a prolonged controversy. The hardy Baptist settlers who had "built a fort and Defended our Selves three years before We had any help by soldger," now saw their lands put up for sale and themselves about to be "turned out from our Houses and Lands." [37] The Baptists protested, "But when we manifest our unesieness to them have been told to this purpose; that it is in vain for us to complain for the authority say they will not favor us Because we are Different Opinuon in Religion from them." Thirteen members of the established church signed a statement protesting against the injustice done their Baptist fellow-townsmen

[33] *Acts*, Vol. II, p. 715.
[34] *Acts*, Vol. IV, p. 815.
[35] Backus, *op. cit.*, Vol. II, p. 151.
[36] *Acts*, Vol. IV, p. 1015.
[37] *Acts*, Vol. IV, p. 1036.

by this law. The simple-hearted Baptists in their petition to the Governor said, "We See nothing but that wee . . . shall be Disinherited for the support of a Society that we Do not belong unto." [38]

In spite of the radical individualism inherent in the Baptist form of dissent, the oppressions to which they were constantly subjected forced them to form some sort of central organization for more concerted action. The result was the historic Warren Baptist Association organized in 1767 under the leadership of James Manning, Pastor of Warren and President of the College of Rhode Island.[39] At first only four Baptist churches were represented, Warren, Bellingham, Haverhill, and Middleborough, "the rest fearing lest the new body would conflict with church independence." [40] In a conference called to consider the problem of the Ashfield church, eleven churches were represented. The committee of grievances of the association in a petition to the General Court recounted the ills of the Ashfield Baptists and with admirable dignity and restraint grounded their appeal for justice upon the "Rights of Mankind" and insisted that taxation be based upon the consent of those taxed, drawing a deadly parallel between England's taxation of the colonies and Massachusetts' taxation of the dissenters.

The attitude of the proprietors in this controversy was not free from the smugness and truculence with which propertied and privileged groups always address the disinherited. They made the usual cheap appeal to popular prejudices against the Baptists. They stressed the contractual obligations which the Baptists were alleged to have assumed when they took up land, and closed with a lame attempt to discount the "plea of conscience." The document is chiefly valuable for the insight it

[38] *Acts*, Vol. IV, p. 1038.   [40] *Ibid.*, p. 154.
[39] Backus, *op. cit.*, Vol. II, p. 154.

gives us into the mental processes of those in control.[41] The proprietors repudiated the doctrine of natural rights as "wholly superseded in this case by civil obligation; and in the matter of taxation individuals can not with the least propriety plead them." To admit such appeals would enable all groups and individuals to refuse payment of public taxes "if they should happen not to be inclined to pay them." This of course was good sound sense but unfortunately it placed statesmen, such as Sam Adams, and ministers of the establishment, such as Mayhew, Chauncy, Gordon, and others, in the same boat with the Baptists, for they appealed to the great fictions of natural rights in justification of Massachusetts' refusal to pay taxes imposed by England.[42] These glittering generalizations, so fascinating to the imaginations of men in the eighteenth century, did not hold for the drab world of the disinherited in which despised Quakers and Baptists lived and moved and had their being. That these fictions did hold for the rights of dissenters in Virginia throws no little light upon the question as to why the problem of religious liberty was solved in the one province and not in the other.

One gets the impression from reading the literature of this transitional period that the issue was not so much a question of principles as the interpretation placed upon principles. The famous fifteenth article in the Virginia Bill of Rights, formulated by Mason and Madison and proclaiming complete religious liberty, was at first largely a glittering abstraction in the minds of men. It took a decade or more of prolonged debate and endless petitioning before this statement was rendered concrete in the complete overthrow of the establishment and the adoption of Jefferson's famous bill in 1785. In the lengthy

---

[41] *Acts*, Vol. IV, p. 141.
[42] J. W. Thornton, *The Pulpit of the American Revolution*, 1860.

statement of the Ashfield proprietors to the House of Representatives we find this language: "The legislature, we humbly conceive, can not with any propriety interpose in matters of religion farther than to secure the good and prevent the ill effects of it to the state. Whenever, then, any religion or profession, wears an ill aspect to the state, it is become a proper object of attention to the legislature." [43] This statement sounds curiously liberal and modern though tucked away in a document replete with bitter class prejudices and provincial intolerance.

This language cannot be taken absolutely but depends entirely for its meaning upon the setting, the mental fringe in the minds of the men who used it. What that mental fringe was must be gained from the context. A group representing the "filth of Christianity," "a high kind of Quakerism," a "poisonous enthusiasm," "which rejects men of learning and ability for teachers," whose minister is not a minister in the legal sense, because he "has not had an education at some university or college," and is not even orthodox unless "orthodoxy and simplicity" are synonymous—such a group was, from the point of view of the Massachusetts authorities of 1767, antisocial and "wears an ill aspect to the state" so that state interference is not only justifiable but necessary in the interests of society. Dissent in Massachusetts lacked the numbers, the political and economic power, and the intelligence and culture to make the community see the far-reaching implications of the sweeping generalization that the state "can not, with any propriety, interpose in matters of religion." Public sentiment in any community can never transcend the persistent and compellingly educative effect of the prevailing ways of life. The cultural context carries the meaning, for the statesman as well as for the average man.

The Council and the House appointed a committee to re-

[43] *Acts*, Vol. IV, p. 141.

port on these petitions. The committee upheld the contentions of the proprietors and the Council voted that the petitions of the Ashfield Baptists and their supporters be dismissed. Matters came to a deadlock when the House refused to concur. It is interesting to note that forty years earlier the House, which reflected the popular mind, was reactionary and the Council inclined to be conciliatory towards the dissenters, while in the Ashfield case the situation was exactly the reverse. Did this indicate that the people were gradually becoming liberalized? The Baptists, meanwhile, wearied by delays and the disregard of their petitions, appealed to the crown. In 1771 the King in council disallowed the obnoxious act of 1767 and directed the Massachusetts authorities "to take notice and govern themselves accordingly."[44] Once again stubborn provincial pride was humbled and the long arm of the mother country was stretched across the sea to relieve the oppressed in "the land of the free."

VIII

Twice within fifty years Massachusetts had been disciplined by the hand of the mother country but she was far from bringing forth "fruits meet for repentance." She was not converted to the principle of religious tolerance. In Montague, in Berwick, in Scarborough, in Warwick, and in Chelmsford men were deprived of their goods or lay in jail for conscience' sake.[45] In Concord, in 1773, hard by "the birth-place of liberty" where soon the shot was to be fired "heard round the world," Baptists lay in jail for conscience' sake.[46] In 1774, the year of the Continental Congress and on the very eve of the great struggle for

[44] *Acts*, Vol. IV, p. 1045.
[45] Backus, *op. cit.*, Vol. II, pp. 163 ff. Hovey, *op. cit.*, pp. 182 ff.
[46] Hovey, *op. cit.*, p. 183.

national liberty, eighteen men were "shut up in the Northampton jail for declining to pay ministerial rates in support of the established worship." [47] The Baptists sought to capitalize the spirit of liberty now in the air in an effort to relieve the Massachusetts dissenters of their ills and decided to send a committee to Philadelphia to present their case to the Continental Congress. Led by the indefatigable Backus and the statesmanlike Manning of Rhode Island, the representatives of the New England Baptists made the fourteen-day journey to the city of brotherly love. There they had the support of the Philadelphia Baptist Association and the influential Quakers.

The Baptists were advised by the Quakers not to press their case before the Congress but to ask for a conference with the Massachusetts representatives and to invite those especially interested in religious liberty. On October 14, 1774, the Massachusetts delegates, Cushing, Sam and John Adams, and Robert Treat Paine, met with Backus, Manning, and others representing the New England Baptists, the Quakers Israel and James Pemberton and John Fox, the Mayor of Philadelphia and certain delegates from New Jersey, Rhode Island, and Pennsylvania.[48] Manning made a short and able presentation of the cause of the Massachusetts dissenters. The Massachusetts delegates found themselves in a most embarrassing situation. They were itching for a break with England and represented the state that precipitated the great struggle, yet they needed the support of the other colonies who stood for religious liberty. Here as always it was outside pressure rather than the inherent rights of the dissenters that influenced Massachusetts.

John Adams sought to show: "There is indeed an ecclesiastical establishment in our province; but a very slender one,

[47] Hovey, *op. cit.*, p. 197.
[48] Hovey, *op. cit.*, Chaps. 15, 16. Backus, *op. cit.*, Vol. II, pp. 200 f.

hardly to be called an establishment." [49] This plea went down before the array of facts presented by Backus and Manning. The Massachusetts delegates then shifted their grounds and contended that the General Court had always patiently heard the complaints of the Baptists and that the supreme authorities of the province must not be held responsible for the injustices that might be done by petty officials. To this, the uncomfortable Backus replied, "I was very sorry to have any accusation to bring against the government which I belonged to, and which I would gladly serve to the utmost of my powers; but I must say the facts prove the contrary of their plea; and gave a short account of our Legislature's treatment of Ashfield," adding not without a touch of humor, "which was very puzzling to them." Sam Adams then sought to draw a distinction between the "regular" Baptists and "enthusiasts who made it a merit to suffer persecution" and insinuated that enemies of the colonies were back of this move. Paine reflected the callous attitude of the propertied and privileged classes when he said, "There was nothing of conscience in the matter; it was only a contending about paying a little money." [50]

On the whole, the representatives of Massachusetts, with the possible exception of Cushing, made a poor appearance during this conference. John Adams, who in his account of this conference confesses that he was "of a temper naturally quick and warm," gives the impression of a pugnacious, choleric, and tactless man who, finding himself in a very delicate and embarrassing position, behaved much like the proverbial bull in the china shop. He found Israel Pemberton, whom he characterized as "a Quaker of large property and more intrigue," especially exasperating and, when the Quaker mildly suggested that at this critical juncture when the colonies were trying to unite

[49] Hovey, *op. cit.*, p. 210.   [50] *Ibid.*, p. 211.

against England it was exceedingly important to remove all "difficulties in the way," among which there were none "of more importance than liberty of conscience," Adams dubbed him an "artful Jesuit" bent upon alienating Pennsylvania from the cause. Adams contended that "the people of Massachusetts were as religious and conscientious as the people of Pennsylvania" and that "the very liberty of conscience which Mr. Pemberton invoked would demand indulgence for the tender conscience of the people of Massachusetts and allow them to preserve their laws." In other words, the tenderness of the consciences of the supporters of the establishment was ample justification for enforcement of laws that ruthlessly disregarded the tender consciences of the Baptists, an argument replete with provincial egotism and as old as John Cotton and Roger Williams. Finally, John Adams, who in the beginning had asserted that the Massachusetts establishment was "the most mild and equitable establishment of religion in the world," lost his temper in the heat of debate and told the conference "they might as well turn the heavenly bodies out of their annual and diurnal courses as the people of Massachusetts at the present day from their meeting-house and Sunday laws." The "slender" and "mild" establishment has now suddenly become as fixed and unalterable as the stars in their courses! This called forth from the patient Backus the following remark, in which we detect a touch of saintly irony, "Such absurdities does religious tyranny produce in great men." [51]

For their pains the Baptists, and especially their chosen agent Isaac Backus, were subjected to bitter criticism. John Adams and Paine asserted that Backus had gone to Philadelphia "to prevent the colonies uniting in defense of their liberties." The Reverend Ezra Stiles, who had sought to foist upon Brown University a

[51] Hovey, *op. cit.*, p. 212

charter placing it under Congregational control, seized upon the occasion to give an exhibition of uncharitable distortion of the facts, which enables us to understand why the Puritan bigot is perhaps the most unlovely figure in American history. Manning quotes Stiles as saying: "That the Baptists had made an application to Congress against the Massachusetts Bay; that the delegates of that province expected only a private interview with some of the Baptists; but instead of that, when they came they found the house full, etc.: that they were attacked and treated in the most rude and abusive manner; that the Baptists pretended they were oppressed, but, after all their endeavors, they could only complain of a poor fourpence; that they were ashamed of their errand, and gave up their point, except one or two impudent fellows, who, with Israel Pemberton, abused them in a most scandalous manner; that all the delegates present were surprised at and ashamed of them, and thought they complained without the least foundation." [52] One is at a loss to know whether the man who said this was actuated by pure spite at the clever move of the Baptists to force Massachusetts authorities to air some of their religious dirty linen before the world or whether it was merely a characteristic fulmination of a purblind bigot. The suggestion that Backus could browbeat John Adams is intriguing.

The Baptists sought to set themselves right with the authorities in a statement by Backus to the provincial congress at Cambridge, November 22, 1774. Hancock, the president of the House, asked "with a smile" whether Backus' petition should be read. The Baptist cause was evidently considered to be something of a joke by the authorities. "One Answered: No, we are no ecclesiastical court and have no business with it. Another, another and another agreed to the same. At last one of the

[52] *Ibid.*, p. 215.

members got up and said: This is very extraordinary, that we should pay no regard to a denomination who in the place where he lived were as good members of society as any, and were equally engaged with others in the defence of their civil liberties and motioned to have it read." The petition was read and after debate it was generally agreed to "throw it out; when Mr. Adams got up and said he was apprehensive, if they threw it out, it might cause a division among the provinces; and it was his advice to do something with it," obviously the move of a political realist indifferent to the real issue. The Baptists were then told to apply to the General Court.[53] And so the eternal argument was continued.

In spite of a successful termination of the great struggle for political liberty in which Massachusetts had played a leading part, in spite of repeated petitions of the dissenters for the alleviation of their ills, and in spite of the final adoption of the new constitution in 1780, after much debate of the articles on religion, the petty persecutions of the Baptists continued down to the end of the eighteenth century. The establishment was still possessed of vitality enough to persist, though in attenuated form, for another generation. The tax-collector was still dogging the heels of the dissenter in a state which had sought to justify in the eyes of the world a war for independence by an appeal to "certain inalienable rights," among which was freedom to worship God according to the dictates of conscience.

[53] Hovey, *op. cit.*, pp. 222 ff.

Chapter IX
Dissent Becomes Revivalistic

I T IS a matter of profound significance for American culture
that the most influential of the dissenting groups were
captured by the revivalistic form of Protestantism. This is
all the more remarkable since revivalism and dissent were opposed in many ways. Revivalism arose within the setting of institutionalized Protestantism. Both Wesley and Whitefield
were members of the Church of England and never broke with
it. Edwards, the real father of the revivalistic type of Protestantism destined to triumph in American life, was born and
reared in the lap of the New England establishment and never
consciously repudiated either its theology or its organization.
The fact that neither Baptists nor Quakers, not to mention
other dissenting groups, had suffered anything but ill at the
hands of the New England standing orders would naturally
make them unsympathetic towards any movement which they
championed.[1] They felt the impact of the Great Awakening
only indirectly and gradually.

Traditional dissent, furthermore, was suspicious of the excesses of the Corybantic piety illustrated by such extremists as
Davenport and defended by the learned Edwards. Almost all
the great dissenting groups, and in particular the Quakers and
Baptists, had learned through sad experience the dangers of

---

[1] Isaac Backus, *History of the Baptists*, Vol. II, p. 41.

unbridled emotions. The Baptists had sought through a sober and restrained way of life to live down the prejudices of a world that could not forget the Anabaptist movement of the days of the Reformation and the tragic outcome of the Münster theocracy. The Quakers under the leadership of George Fox, Robert Barclay, and William Penn had struggled hard to eliminate the radicals in the early stages of the Quaker movement. By the time of the Great Awakening "ranterism" had disappeared and the Quakers had become sober and well-behaved citizens with a more or less recognized status in the community. Long and bitter training in the virtue of self-restraint thus made traditional dissent antagonistic to the extravagances of revivalism.

This inherent antagonism between traditional dissent and the emotionalism of revivalistic piety was illustrated also in the case of the Methodists. Lecky remarks: "Usually the Methodists were denounced as dissenters but their leaders steadily repudiated the designation, and in England at least they met with little sympathy from the real dissenters. The fierce fervor of Methodist devotion was as uncongenial to the spirit then prevailing in dissent as it was to the spirit of the established church; and the dissenters were at this time negotiating with a view to obtain full political privileges, and were therefore peculiarly indisposed to ally themselves with so unpopular a body as the Methodists." [2] In 1776 the Methodists, then numbering approximately three thousand in Virginia, refused to join the Presbyterians and Baptists in the struggle for religious toleration, protesting that although "they may, in the opinion of some, also come under the denomination of dissenters, they beg leave to declare they are a religious society in communion with

[2] W. E. H. Lecky, *History of England in the Eighteenth Century*, Vol. II, p. 580.

the church of England, and do all in their power to strengthen and support the said church." [3] Not until 1784, when they became an independent church, did the Methodists feel free to identify themselves with the dissenters in Virginia and New England in their struggle for religious liberty. Methodism was, however, from its very inception essentially dissenting in spirit.

When the Baptists, under the leadership of revivalistic preachers such as Isaac Backus, Manning, Shubal Stearns, and John Leland, finally became evangelical, they discarded their Arminianism for Calvinism and substituted for the political authoritarianism of the standing orders of Massachusetts and Connecticut, against which they fought so bravely, a much more subtle psychological authoritarianism based upon the immediate uncritical witness of the religious emotions. This form of subtle psychological assurance with its inevitable theological dogmatism we still have with us dominating the life and thought of churches of dissenting antecedents. The New England establishment that gave birth to Edwards and revivalism thus revenged itself upon the dissenting churches, who supported Madison when he wrote separation of church and state into the first amendment of the Constitution, by saddling upon them a much more insidious psychological dogmatism based upon the hectic religious enthusiasms that accompany conversion. As the dissenting churches waxed in numbers and influence through revivalism they paved the way for an uncritical emotional authoritarianism that is an insidious enemy of the intelligent exercise of democratic liberties.

The evangelical fervor which dissenters, such as the Baptists, in time gained from the Great Awakening was not at once exploited in support of a Fundamentalist theology. The times

[3] C. F. James, *Documentary History of the Struggle for Religious Liberty in Virginia*, 1900, p. 75.

were not ripe for this, especially in New England. On the contrary, revivalistic zeal was destined at first to provide the dynamic for effective championship of the rights of conscience and religious liberty. It has been pointed out that in communities with entrenched establishments dissent tended to affiliate itself with liberals in theology and politics and in time became very sedate and well-behaved. On the other hand, in communities where social, political, or economic forces had induced unsettled conditions dissent was able to capitalize unbridled religious enthusiasm in the interest of movements that were often revolutionary. In the England of the time of Wesley and Whitefield dissent, as we have seen, took the former course and tactfully refused to make common cause with the unbridled emotionalism of Methodism. Similarly in New England, even after the Great Awakening, dissenting leaders, such as Isaac Backus, were compelled to pursue a course that was restrained and tactful, avoiding every suggestion of revolution. In Virginia, on the other hand, where conditions were quite different, dissenting revivalism spread rapidly and the Baptists and the Presbyterians were able to capitalize the religious enthusiasm born of the Great Awakening in the interest of a revolution that made complete separation of church and state part of the organic law of the Old Dominion and wrought a transformation in the structure of Virginian society.[4]

II

Of all the forms of historic dissent prevalent in the community at the time of the Great Awakening the Quakers would seem to have had the most in common with the revivalistic type

[4] W. M. Gewehr, *The Great Awakening in Virginia, 1740-1790*, 1930, Chap. 11. H. J. Eckenrode, *The Revolution in Virginia*, 1909.

of piety. Corresponding to the doctrine of the "new birth" with its emphasis upon the inner or psychological series of reality the Quakers stressed the "Inner Light." The Quakers, like the extremists such as Davenport, believed in visions and supernatural revelations. The Quakers also agreed with the revivalists in their depreciation of "book learning" and emphasis on lay religion. It has been said that one of the enduring contributions of the Quakers to the religious life of the nation was a "lay-religion." [5] Just how far the Quakers had succeeded in popularizing a form of religion outside of and independent of the standing orders and had made it a part of the life of the masses prior to the Great Awakening is perhaps impossible to determine. Evidence is not lacking, however, that Quaker ideas were spreading among the people and, in at least one instance, Quakerism influenced the leaders of the Great Awakening.

In 1726 a religious movement sprang up spontaneously in New Milford, Connecticut, inspired primarily by the "dying counsel of a loose young man to his companions." [6] It was a movement among the young and caused a revival of religion in this village of some forty families. The group became exclusive and puritanical and began "to purge their meeting" of those who were "unconverted." They entered into correspondence with the "opinionists," the standing order's term for dissenters such as the Quakers, Baptists, and Rogerenes. "The Anabaptists wrote to them from Rhode Island; and so did the Roger's crew, who afterwards made them a visit and brought them books with which they were very much pleased and captivated." Soon Quaker ideas were in evidence, such as "silent

[5] Jones, *The Quakers in the American Colonies*, p. xxx.
[6] Charles Chauncy, *Seasonable Thoughts on the State of Religion in New England, 1743*, pp. 203 ff.

meetings," the "notion of the Spirit's being in and sensibly and immediately leading them," the complete assurance of salvation, the denial of "the necessity of human learning as a qualification for the Work of the ministry," the despising of the ordinances of baptism and the Lord's Supper, and the minimizing of the authority of the Bible. When the Great Awakening came this group at once expressed their sympathy with it.[7]

From this group came a certain David Ferris who was admitted to Yale college in 1729 after having presumably "forsaken his Quakerish and enthusiastic tenents." But Ferris was no sooner a member of the college than he organized a group for the propagation of his ideas. Their central idea was that the "internal light" was their "sole guide," from which came constant revelations. "Mr. Davenport, Eleazar Wheelock, Pomeroy and others were those who lived with this Ferris most familiarly and have since divulged his errors and filled places where they have preached with the superstitions and groundless opinions they learned from him who was their father and dictator as to their belief."[8] It is a matter of history that the men mentioned above were all representatives of the "New Lights" or radical wing of the Great Awakening. In this instance, at least, there would seem to be some connection between Quakerism and revivalism.

The instance of Ferris and the Yale group was, however, exceptional. On the whole the revivalistic leaders were antagonistic to Quakerism. Wesley alluded to Robert Barclay's *Apology*, the standard work on Quakerism, as "that solemn trifle" and in 1738 wrote a letter in which he asserted that there were some ten points in which Quakerism differed from

[7] Chauncy, *op. cit.*, pp. 20 ff.

[8] These are extracts from letters by men who were in Yale college at the time or had personal knowledge of Ferris. Chauncy, *op. cit.*, p. 212.

true Christianity.[9] Evidence is not lacking, also, that the Quakers themselves were opposed to the revival. At the height of Whitefield's success one Moses Bartlett sent the following challenge to the Quakers of Rhode Island: "There is a wonderful reformation of Connecticut colony among the Presbyterians [the popular name for Connecticut Congregationalists], where the everlasting gospel is preached; but I have heard *some of you blaspheme against it abominably*; but I desire you to dispute me in order to vindicate your orders, which you call Friends' orders, for they are antiscriptural and so consequently of the Devil." [10]

In discussing the great danger of confusing the purely imaginary with the genuinely spiritual, a distinction of which he makes much in his *Narrative of Surprising Conversions*, Edwards remarks, "There has been much talk in many parts of the country, as though the people have *symbolised* with the Quakers, and the Quakers themselves have been moved with such reports, and came here once and again hoping to find good waters to fish in; but without the least success, and seemed to be discouraged and left off coming." [11] This passage is exceedingly illuminating as throwing light upon the fundamental differences between the Quakers and the Edwardean revivalistic type of piety. The Quaker, as we have seen, tended to reduce all external religious forms to the rôle of mere symbols of inner realities in the realm of the "Inner Light." That Edwards with his doctrine of divine immanence and his theory of religious cognition by means of a mystical inner perception of religious realities [12] had very real points of con-

---

[9] R. M. Jones, *The Later Periods of Quakerism*, 1921, Vol. I, p. 269.
[10] S. G. Arnold, *History of Rhode Island, 1859-1860*, Vol. II, p. 138, cited by Jones, *The Quakers in the American Colonies*, p. 128.
[11] Jonathan Edwards, *Works, 1806-1811*, Vol. III, p. 259.
[12] *Ibid.*, p. 71.

tact with Quakerism no one can deny. But Edwards was a loyal son of the church and stressed external church ordinances which the Quaker tended to ignore. Edwards also, like a good Calvinist, stressed the necessity of a supernatural external revelation in the Bible as the necessary prerequisite to grace and salvation and the real indwelling of the spirit of God. The Quaker, on the other hand, made the Bible dependent for its spiritual validity upon the "Inner Light" shared by all men. Edwards' degrading doctrine of human nature and of immoral self-abasement before God for sin hardly fitted into the more spiritual and humanistic Quaker conceptions of God and human nature. The Quaker was far too spiritually sensitive and modern in his outlook ever to fall in with the harsh medieval theology of Edwards and the revivalistic type of piety.

To be sure, even Quakerism was not able in the long run to resist the impact of the revivalistic type of Christianity which had become an integral part of American culture. As their early enthusiasm abated, the orthodox conservative Quaker leaders drew their inspiration more and more from the dominant revivalistic type of piety. In the controversy centering around the person and work of Elias Hicks which resulted in the great schism of 1828, the conservatives in their statement of their position embodied all the great central dogmas of the revivalistic type of piety.[13]

III

While the religious fervor of the Great Awakening did not at first reach the traditional dissenting groups it threatened to

[13] Jones, *The Later Periods of Quakerism*, Vol. I, pp. 482 ff.

add to their number another group of dissenters from within the established churches, namely the Separatists or "New Lights," characterized as "warm-hearted, spiritually minded though ignorant persons, who had been profoundly touched by the revival."[14] The Great Awakening accentuated the antagonism between the institutional and the evangelical types of piety which had been latent in New England from the beginning. Chauncy, the leader of the conservatives or "Old Lights," attacked the excesses of revivalistic piety in a trenchant book, *Seasonable Thoughts on the State of Religion in New England, 1743,* while Edwards provided a scholarly defense. Soon all New England was in the throes of a bitter religious controversy between "Old Lights" and "New Lights." Goaded by harsh repressive legislation, especially in Connecticut, Separatist churches were organized, 1740 to 1750, chiefly in Windham and New London counties adjoining Rhode Island. Similar defections took place in other parts of the colony and in Massachusetts, though not to the same extent. The movement was never extensive, being confined for the most part to some thirty towns of Windham and New London counties. By the end of the century most of these schismatic groups had become Baptists or had returned to the established church.[15] Separatism never attained the dimensions of a dissenting sect with a permanent place in the social order.

The Separatist movement, like all forms of dissent in their earlier stages, was plainly a religion of the disinherited. This

[14] W. Walker, *History of the Congregational Churches in the United States,* p. 262.

[15] Blake, *The Separates or Strict Congregationalists of New England,* 1902. Trumbull, *History of Connecticut,* Vol. I, Chap. 8. J. Tracy, *The Great Awakening, 1842,* Chap. 17. M. L. Greene, *The Development of Religious Liberty in Connecticut,* 1905, Chap. 10. Isaac Backus, *History of New England with particular reference to the denomination called Baptists, 1777-1796,* Vol. II, Chaps. 15, 16, 17.

appears in the pathetic protest which in 1752, after a decade of bitter persecution, the Separatists addressed to the general assembly of Connecticut: "We are of that number who soberly dissent from the church established by Connecticut and though we have no design to act in contempt of any lawful authority, or to disturb any religious society, but only to worship God according to the rules he has given us in his word in that way now called Separation, yet we have suffered the loss of much of our goods, particularly because we could not in conscience pay minister's rates, it appearing to us very contrary to the way that the Lord hath ordained even the present way in which the ministry are maintained—poor men's estates taken away and sold for less than a quarter of their value, and no overplus returned, as hath been the case of your Honor's poor informants; yea, poor men's cows taken away from them when they had but one for the support of their families, and the children crying for milk and could get none, because the collector had taken their cow for minister's rates." [16] It goes without saying that men of influence and social standing in the community would never have been treated in this cruel fashion. Dissent never became respectable in eighteenth-century New England. The dissenters were "despised and rejected of men." The Separatists, like Baptists and Quakers before them, never succeeded in winning champions of their cause among the cultured and propertied classes from which came the real leadership. The Baptists in Massachusetts did not have, as did the Baptists in Virginia, a Patrick Henry, a Jefferson or a Madison to fight their battles. When patient old Isaac Backus appeared before the Continental Congress on the eve of the great struggle for freedom to plead the

[16] Cited by Blake, *op. cit.*, p. 117.

cause of the dissenters in Massachusetts, gruff John Adams could hardly treat him with common courtesy.[17]

The kinship of the Separatists with the great dissenting tradition is unmistakable. They separated from the descendants of men who earlier had separated from the Church of England. The Separatist movement was thus a return to the original separatist or dissenting tradition of the founders of the colonies. The basic incentive of the Separatist movement, as of all dissenting movements before it, was the demand for *spiritual autonomy*. This appears in the statement from Solomon Paine, perhaps the ablest of the Separatist leaders: "The cause of a just separation of the saints from their fellowmen in their worship, is not that there are hypocrits in the visible church of Christ, nor that some fall into scandalous sins in the church, nor because the minister is flat, formal, or even saith he is a minister, and is not, and doth lie; but it is in their being yoked together, or incorporated into a corrupt institution, under the government of another supreme head than Christ, and governed by the precepts of men, put into the hands of unbelievers, which will not purge out any of the corrupt fruit, but naturally bears it and nourishes it, and denies the power of godliness, both in the governing and gracious effects of it." [18]

The issue at stake between the Separatists and the standing orders of New England was thus identical with the old conflict as to the validity of the inner and the outer series of reality in the religious life which emerged in Augustine's controversy with the Donatists. The "new birth," the central doctrine of the Great Awakening,[19] definitely located the seat

[17] Hovey, *The Life and Times of Isaac Backus*, pp. 201 f., 249 f.
[18] Cited by Blake, *op. cit.*, p. 58.
[19] Tracy, *op. cit.*, p. ix.

of religious realities in the inner or psychological series of reality. The implications of this emphasis are clear. The inner life demands freedom from state and standing orders so that it may create for itself congenial religious forms and ordinances. Hence the opposition to a state church always implicit in revivalism. Since conversion, or an inner experience, is the test of membership in the kingdom of God it follows that an "unconverted" ministry is a ghastly incongruity. Hence the bitter tirades of Whitefield, Tennent, Davenport, and the Separatist leaders against the spiritual lukewarmness of the ministry of the standing orders. Since the immediate illuminations of the divine spirit in the "new birth" is the primary source of religious truth it follows that any individual equipped with this experience may preach the gospel. The Separatists, like all forms of traditional dissent, encouraged lay preaching and irresponsible itinerant evangelists. This was perhaps the chief reason for the bitter opposition of the standing orders. The high priest of the "parish despotism," the basic unit of the standing orders of New England, would not tolerate these unwarranted incursions into his domain and invoked the political arm in support of his rights and privileges. Here we find the source of the exceedingly oppressive and unjust legislation between 1740 and 1750 which enabled Connecticut to usurp the leadership in religious intolerance among English-speaking peoples previously enjoyed by Massachusetts.[20]

The insistence upon spiritual autonomy based upon the experience of the "new birth" had many other implications for New England and ultimately for American culture. The Separatists protested against the moral laxity of Stoddardism, or the doctrine preached by the grandfather of Edwards, that so long as a man observed the decencies of polite society and had never

[20] See Blake, *op. cit.*, Chap. 5, and Greene, *op. cit.*, Chap. 10.

been in jail he might join the church and even partake of the Lord's Supper. The good life for the Separatists and all dissenters was not a matter of external decency of conduct but of intent, of purity of soul, of acts inspired by the vivid experiences of a "new birth." Separatism by its emphasis upon the inner spirit tended to quicken the sense of moral responsibility. This quickening of the moral sensibilities, however, when combined with the strict surveillance exercised by the dissenting group over its members, easily became puritanical. It was a puritanism, moreover, that lacked the dignity and sense of civic responsibility always associated with the puritan ethics of early Calvinism. Dissenting ethics has always purchased moral sensitiveness at the price of petty censoriousness and a sad lack of moral common sense. The moral reformer in our modern churches of dissenting-evangelical background is always in danger of becoming the moral fanatic.

The anti-intellectualism which has always been one of the most serious handicaps of dissenting-evangelical Protestantism was distinctly in evidence in the Separatist movement. It sprang logically from their fundamental doctrine of the "new birth." The Separatists held that the revelation of the divine spirit gained through the "new birth" took precedence over all "book learning." Appealing to the logic of their own hectic emotional experiences men judged the preacher according as he furthered or hindered these experiences. Standards of scholarship and even of moral common sense disappeared. "They objected against their pastor using notes and at the same time praying for assistance in preaching." Ministers who studied their sermons were "preaching out of the head" and hence not edifying. "They maintained that there was no need for anything more than common learning to qualify men for the ministry; that if a man had the spirit of God, it was no matter whether he had any learning at all. Indeed the first Separatists at Stonington, Connecticut, held to a special revelation of some facts or future events not revealed in the Scriptures. They elected their first minister by revelation. In less than a year they chose, ordained, silenced, cast him out of the church, and delivered him up to Satan." [21]

This anti-intellectualism springing out of the philosophy of the "new birth" emerged first in the ideas of the Separatists and became an integral part of the revivalistic frontier Protestantism first formulated in the Great Awakening. It proved a deadly handicap to these revivalistic churches in discharging the responsibilities of intellectual and moral leadership which their favored position in American culture imposed upon them. This is illustrated by the rôle of the Baptist preacher in the backwoods of eastern Tennessee during the nineteenth century, described by J. J. Burnett in his *Sketches of Tennessee's Pioneer Baptist Preachers*, 1919. These *Sketches* make it perfectly intelligible why a Scopes trial could take place in Dayton, Tennessee, in the year of our Lord, 1925.

IV

The revivalistic type of piety dating from the Great Awakening found its first logical formulation in Separatism, but neither Separatists nor Quakers were destined to popularize this type of Protestantism. That was to be the work of Baptists, Presbyterians, and Methodists. The New England Baptists, who were later thoroughly identified with this revivalistic type of piety, were at first out of sympathy with the Great Awakening, owing in part to their dislike of its harsh Calvinism and its unrestrained emotionalism. The Baptists, furthermore, had suf-

[21] Trumbull, *op. cit.*, Vol. II, p. 136.

fered too severely at the hands of the established church to feel any great enthusiasm for any movement it initiated. No such prejudices existed among the Baptists of New Jersey and Pennsylvania where the revival spread rapidly.[22] In time these prejudices disappeared in New England and individuals and sometimes entire churches passed from Separatism into the Baptist communion.[23] This transfer was hastened by the fact that the Baptists enjoyed, at least nominally, a measure of tolerance under the establishments which was denied the Separatists.

The story of the gradual infiltration of the Baptists with revivalistic piety by the Separatists is admirably illustrated in the career of Isaac Backus. If the greatness of a man is to be measured not in terms of wealth or learning or power but in terms of the principles that inspired his life, Backus must rank high in the list of Massachusetts worthies. Patient, tolerant, wise, and brave in the face of institutionalized intolerance and petty persecution he illustrated, in simple and unpretentious fashion, principles which were later to become embodied in organic law and made the guarantee of our democratic liberties. John Cotton, Cotton Mather, John Wise, and even Jonathan Edwards belonged to their day and age but Isaac Backus belongs to every age and to all men who love liberty. Out of the long list of Massachusetts leaders, from John Cotton to William E. Channing, Backus alone deserves to be called the worthy successor of Roger Williams and John Clarke in the long, long struggle for religious liberty.[24]

When the Great Awakening reached Norwich, Connecticut, it found there a tradition of "pure Congregationalism" more

[22] Backus, *op. cit.*, Vol. II, p. 41.
[23] Newman, *History of the Baptist Churches in the United States*, pp. 245 f.
[24] Hovey, *op. cit.*

or less antagonistic to the state-churchism of the Half-Way Covenant and the Saybrook Platform of 1708. Among those who opposed the Saybrook Platform and remained loyal to the earlier and purer Congregationalism was the family of Isaac Backus, who was born in Norwich in 1724. Backus was converted in 1741 under the preaching of Eleazar Wheelock, the founder of Dartmouth College, and united with the first Congregational church of Norwich in 1742. It was to be expected that this great religious upheaval would revive the old tradition of "pure Congregationalism" and hence we find the pastor, who stood for the established order, soon at odds with a large group of his parishioners who were opposed to the union of church and state. These withdrew, with young Backus, and formed a Separatist group.

The reasons given by Backus and his associates for withdrawal from the ministry of Reverend Lord were typically dissenting, namely, "that persons were received into the church who gave no satisfactory evidence of conversion; that many were suffered to remain as regular members, without being dealt with, whose walk was evidently contrary to the Gospel; that the pastor declared his strong attachment to the Saybrook Platform, which had been renounced by the church before settling him," and that the nature of true piety and experimental religion "were not clearly set forth" by the pastor.[25] Backus thus found himself identified with a group, more or less transitory in character, who had revived the old dissenting traditions to the extent that they had separated from the established state church. Their dissent, however, as the sequel showed, was not of such a logical and thorough character that it sufficed to assure to them a separate and independent existence as a sect. They preserved along with the elements of dissent other ele-

[25] Hovey, *op. cit.*, p. 43.

ments that indicated they had not completely broken with the standing order. Many still clung to infant baptism and an educated clergy.

Backus, by identifying himself with this more or less nondescript dissenting group of the Separatists, made possible some of the most unhappy and painful experiences of his checkered career. When he began his activities as a Separatist itinerant preacher, his education being "limited to the public schools of his native place," [26] he was exposed to the Connecticut law aimed at the Separatists that only graduates of Harvard, Yale, or some approved foreign Protestant institution could enjoy "the benefit of the laws of this government respecting the settlement and support of ministers." For one not a settled and ordained minister to preach in any parish without the permission of the regular minister was a penal offense.[27] Even as regular pastor of the Separatist group in Titicut parish, Massachusetts, where he was ordained in 1748, Backus was subject to the precinct tax in support of the establishment. Having conscientious scruples against support of religion by the civil authorities, he refused to pay the tax and was seized and threatened with prison. Backus was finding the way of the dissenter hard in New England.

Even more serious were the troubles that arose within the dissenting group with which he had identified himself. Influential Separatists, following out the historic tradition of dissent, accepted Baptist views as to adult baptism and close communion. Backus found it impossible to avoid the issue and after much perplexity decided for the Baptists for the curious reason that "the Baptist principles are certainly right because nature fights so against them." [28] This decision was hasty, for the old churchly

[26] *Ibid.*, p. 31.   [28] *Ibid.*, p. 84.
[27] *Ibid.*, pp. 59, 65.

tradition was still strong within him. In a public confession he retracted his repudiation of infant baptism. This led to infinite confusion in his own church. The Baptist-inclined faction was naturally disgruntled and considered this act a proof of bad faith. After endless bickerings Backus was excluded from the church. Council followed council and conference succeeded conference among the distraught Separatists who were losing members to the Baptist communion. In the hope of uniting his divided flock Backus had a conference called at Exeter, Rhode Island, in 1753. The twenty-five Separatist churches represented reached the following conclusion: "(1) That we do not find it to be a censurable evil for one who had professed and practiced the baptism of minors, to turn from that to baptism of adults by immersion; and (2) That we do not find it to be a censurable evil for one who has professed and practiced rebaptizing by immersion, to turn from it and give up his children or minors in baptism." [29] This was a futile attempt at compromise by accepting both churchly and dissenting traditions as to baptism as valid. It satisfied neither of the factions concerned.

The logic of dissent combined with the logic of events to bring Backus into the Baptist church. The Separatists having arrived at an impasse on the matter of baptism in the Stonington conference of 1754, Backus in 1756 became a Baptist and formally organized a Baptist church at Middleborough, Massachusetts, which he served for fifty years. Backus' motives for making this momentous decision were mixed. Doubtless he realized that his energies were being frittered away by the differences among the Separatists. The dissenting elements, to be sure, far outweighed the churchly among the Separatists, yet the stubbornness of the controversy on baptism prevented the attainment of that peace and harmony necessary to the cultivation

[29] Cited, *ibid.*, p. 108.

of the religious life. These irreconcilable elements had wrought havoc with the religious life of his own church at Titicut. The separatist tradition, ingrained as we have seen in the "pure Congregationalism" of the church of his boyhood in Norwich, was naturally hostile to the idea of a national church suggested by infant baptism.

The logic of the dissenting tradition that insists upon a return to direct teachings of the Bible also played its part in Backus' decision. For the New Testament pictures a voluntary brotherhood with "one Lord, one faith and one baptism." A church, therefore, that tolerated two types of baptism could not possibly be reconciled with the New Testament ideal, so reasoned the unsophisticated dissenter. Thus it was that the dissenting tradition, strong in the Separatist movement from the start and reënforced by his boyhood faith, carried Backus into the Baptist group, the most typical of all the dissenting sects. But in making this momentous decision Backus, together with the host of Separatists who followed him, carried over into the Baptist group the revivalistic type of piety inspired by the Great Awakening. Associated with Backus in his memorable struggle for religious liberty in New England were other leaders such as Manning, the first President of Rhode Island College (later Brown University), Stephen Gano, his nephew, and Hezekiah Smith, who all came from the Philadelphia Baptist group, where they were thoroughly impregnated with revivalistic piety. They had been educated in Princeton, the product of the revivalistic wing of the Presbyterian church. New England Baptists owe a great debt to the New Jersey institution.

The revivalistic piety of the Great Awakening rescued the Baptists of New England from slow and sure decay. In spite of serious handicaps, which were not removed until the abolition of the establishments in the nineteenth century, they began to multiply. When Whitefield began his preaching tour in New England in 1740 the Baptists had but six churches in Massachusetts, eleven in Rhode Island, and four in Connecticut. Fifty years later there were ninety-two churches in Massachusetts and one hundred seventy-four in the rest of the New England colonies. The Baptists were a disinherited group drawn from the lower middle classes and their undisciplined emotional life was powerfully moved by the fear-inspiring theology of Edwards and the revival leaders. From New England Daniel Marshall, Shubal Stearns, John Leland, and others of Baptist persuasion carried the evangelical fervor of the Great Awakening to Virginia, where in the later decades of the eighteenth century they were to provide the submerged and disinherited classes of the Old Dominion with the organization, the leadership, and the liberty-loving zeal for the overthrow of the Anglican establishment and the complete separation of church and state.[30]

V

The controversy between the conservative "Old Side" and the revivalistic "New Side" groups precipitated in the Presbyterian church by the Great Awakening paralleled that between "New Lights" and "Old Lights" in New England with this important difference, that the "New Side" finally gained the upper hand among the Presbyterians. The "Old Side" insisted in 1738 that a man licensed to preach must have a diploma from a European or New England college. The "New Side" insisted that training in the famous "log college" of the Tennents was adequate equipment for the ministry. The "Old Side" stressed learning and character; the "New Side" placed piety

[30] Gewehr, *The Great Awakening in Virginia, 1740-1790*, Chap. 5.

above scholarship.[31] The "Old Side," true to the traditions of the churchly type, insisted that the church courts had the right to enact laws binding upon the conscience and subject to ecclesiastical censure when violated; the "New Side," following the logic of dissent and the spirit of a pioneer democracy, insisted that the church had no power to originate laws binding upon the conscience. It was their duty merely to interpret and administer the laws of Christ. Man-made ordinances were only binding when they met the demands of a good conscience. The revivalistic wing soon lost this free dissenting note and identified orthodox dogmas with the laws of Christ, thus camouflaging their acceptance of the "Old Side" position with pious theological fictions. The Presbyterian church, in spite of or perhaps because of its absorption of the dissenting-evangelical note, has to its credit more spectacularly vindictive heresy trials than any other denomination in America.

The "Old Side," just as the "Old Lights" of New England, charged the "New Side" preachers with making irregular incursions into the pastorates of others without the sanction of the incumbent minister or the authority of the Presbytery to the vast confusion of the church.[32] Matters were brought to a head in 1740 by the famous Nottingham sermon, "The Danger of an Unconverted Ministry," preached by Gilbert Tennent, the leader of the "New Side" party. In scathing language Tennent attacked the "Old Side" leaders as "hirelings," "caterpillars," "letter-learned Pharisees," "men with the craft of foxes and the cruelty of wolves," "plastered hypocrites," "varlets," "dead dogs that can not bark," "daubers with untempered mortar," "moral negroes," "dead drones."[33] The issue here

---

[31] Tracy, op. cit., p. 62.

[32] Ibid., p. 71.

[33] See Chauncy, op. cit., p. 249, for a list of epithets in this remarkable sermon.

raised was of course the central one of the "new birth." The immediate result of this sermon was the schism of 1741. "To no other human agency probably, so much as to this sermon," remarks Tracy, "is it owing that Presbyterian ministers at the present day are generally pious men." [34] This is probably an exaggerated statement. Certainly it must be offset by another fact, namely, that this famous sermon was the forerunner of a literature of revivalistic theological billingsgate to which the Presbyterian church, in spite of its emphasis on a learned ministry, has contributed its share. Compare, for example, the sermons of the Presbyterian revivalist, Reverend "Billy" Sunday.

This hectic emphasis upon the emotional cataclysm known as conversion or the "new birth" as a religious experience essentially individual and hence incommunicable in character, obviously had much in common with the Quaker doctrine of the "Inner Light" with all its insidiously dangerous implications for the ordered life. The "Old Side" were quick to detect this danger and protested against "invisible motions and workings of the Spirit, which none can be conscious or sensible of but the person himself, and with respect to which he is liable to be deceived or play the hypocrit." [35] Here we detect the sober and orderly genius of Calvin who wrote, "It is not the office of the Spirit that is promised to us to make new and before unheard of revelations, or to coin some new kind of doctrine, which tends to draw us away from the received doctrine of the gospel, but to seal and confirm to us that very doctrine which is by the gospel." [36]

The "Old Side," however, had undertaken the impossible task of trying to carry over the ideals of the conservative Ulster

---

[34] Op. cit., p. 70.
[35] Ibid., p. 71.

[36] Institutes, Bk. I, Chap. 9, Sec. I.

Presbyterianism and apply them successfully to a pioneer society. The future was with the "New Side" with their revivalistic emphasis and their missionary zeal. It was the representatives of the "New Side" who penetrated central Virginia and
as itinerant evangelists came into conflict with the colonial
authorities the middle of the eighteenth century and precipitated the struggle for religious liberty which, with the aid of
the Baptists, was to result in disestablishment and revolution.
It was primarily the spiritual dynamic of the "New Side" group
which makes it possible to classify the conservative Presbyterian
church among the dissenting groups who made possible the
triumph of religious liberty in America.

VI

Had the dissenting-revivalistic Protestantism triumphed as
completely in Massachusetts as it did in Virginia the history of
those states and of the nation would have been different. The
unbroken cultural continuity that enabled the Bay state to maintain her traditional intolerance and self-satisfied provincialism
also enabled her to make unique contributions to national culture
in education, literature, and civic life. With her educated, disciplined, and orderly citizenship she provided a necessary prophy-
lactic against the crudities of an inchoate pioneer culture sprawl-
ing enthusiastically over a continent. The revolution in Virginia
destroyed in a measure the continuity of her culture, placed in
power disinherited groups with their dissenting-revivalistic
piety, indifferent if not hostile to the higher values of education, literature, and the sciences. William and Mary declined
with the decline of the Tidewater and the University of Virginia, the creation of the deist Jefferson, was long suspected by
Baptists, Methodists, and Presbyterians as the home of infidelity.

The public school system suffered from the squabbles of the sects for control.[37] The great schools of learning, for which New England is justly famous, sprang from the life of a people whose enthusiasm for the higher values of life had never been shaken by the anti-intellectualism and obscurantism too often closely connected with the dissenting-revivalistic type of piety.

[37] S. Bell, *The Church, the State and Education in Virginia*, pp. 205 ff.

Chapter X: Dissent in Colonial Virginia: Presbyterians and Baptists

ALL AUTHORITIES agree with John Leland that prior to the fourth decade of the eighteenth century members of the dissenting sects in the Old Dominion were "few and peaceable." [1] They consisted primarily of a sprinkling of Quakers in the southeastern counties of Norfolk, York, and Nansemond. The Quakers played no part in the great struggle of the dissenters for religious liberty in the Old Dominion. The fight for complete religious freedom was to be waged by the more militant Presbyterians and Baptists.

I

In 1732 Scotch-Irish Presbyterian families from Pennsylvania and Maryland had begun to settle in the Valley of Virginia and by 1738 their number had increased to the point where it was deemed advisable to secure for them the advantages of the Act of Toleration, now an integral part of the law of Virginia. They, therefore, delegated John Caldwell, the grandfather of John C. Calhoun, to induce the Synod of Philadelphia to intercede in their behalf with Governor Gooch.

Governor Gooch replied that he had always been "inclined to favor the people who have lately removed from other prov-

[1] John Leland, *The Virginia Chronicle*, p. 14.

inces to settle on the westward side of our great mountains, so you may be assured that no interruption will be given to any minister of your profession who shall come among them, so as they conform themselves to the rules prescribed by the Act of Toleration in England, by taking the oaths enjoined thereby, and registering the place of their meeting, and behave themselves peaceably towards the government." [2] This seems to have included pioneer Presbyterians in Campbell and Prince Edward counties east of the mountains. Gooch probably had two motives in writing this letter. He wished for a strong frontier beyond the mountains as a protection against Indians and French. Being of Scotch extraction he knew these people to be hardy and brave. In fact, from New England to the uplands of the Carolinas, the Scotch-Irish were sent to the frontier to level the forests and fight the Indians. He did not consider these dissenters a real menace to the establishment, for many leagues of the still unsettled Piedmont region lay between the Tidewater and the Valley. It cost Gooch nothing, therefore, to extend to these newcomers the benefits of the Act of Toleration.

In the course of time, however, these Presbyterians penetrated the barrier of the Blue Ridge and dribbled into the counties of the southwest and central Piedmont, where they were destined to precipitate the first stage in the struggle for religious liberty in Virginia. Militant dissent, which we have seen was almost entirely lacking in seventeenth-century Virginia, was not possible until the great central area of the Piedmont had been swept by a series of revivals among Presbyterians, Baptists, and Methodists. The submerged and disinherited groups thereby attained the numbers, organization, class-consciousness, and leadership which made dissent formidable. They were particularly fortunate in that their cause was championed by such leaders as Mason, Madison, Jefferson, and Patrick Henry.[3]

The emergence of the revivalistic interest in the Piedmont region seems to have been more or less accidental. In Hanover County, on the border line between the Piedmont and the Tidewater, a group led by Samuel Morris became interested about 1740 in the reading of religious books, such as Luther's *Commentary on Galatians*, Whitefield's *Sermons* and Boston's *Fourfold State*. The reading of this evangelical literature was accompanied by the familiar revivalistic phenomena, such as weeping and crying out. At first they were ridiculed for such extravagances but, as the meetings increased to such an extent that the parish churches fell off in attendance, the authorities became active and arrested some of the group and fined them for non-attendance at church. Hoping to secure relief under the Act of Toleration they claimed to be dissenters but were hard put to it to classify themselves. The only dissenting group they had heard of was the Quakers and apparently they had no knowledge of the Presbyterians. This situation continued for several years until the "New Side" revivalistic wing of the Presbyterians sent Reverend William Robinson south to visit the various Presbyterian groups in Virginia and the Carolinas. While engaged in evangelistic work east of the Blue Ridge Robinson heard of the Hanover group and visited them in

[3] H. R. McIlwaine, *The Struggle of Protestant Dissenters for Religious Toleration in Virginia,* Johns Hopkins Studies in Historical and Political Science, Series IV, April, 1894, Chap. 4. H. J. Eckenrode, *The Separation of Church and State in Virginia,* 1909. W. T. Thom, *The Struggle for Religious Freedom in Virginia,* Johns Hopkins University Studies, Series XVIII, 1900. T. C. Johnson, *Virginia Presbyterianism and Religious Liberty in Colonial and Revolutionary Times,* 1907. C. F. James, *Documentary History of the Struggle for Religious Liberty in Virginia,* 1900. *Source Problems in United States History,* edited by McLaughlin, Dodd, Jernegan, and Scott, 1919, pp. 183 ff. W. M. Gewehr, *The Great Awakening in Virginia, 1740-1790,* 1930.

1743. He was instrumental in capturing this spontaneous revivalistic movement for "New Side" Presbyterianism. The Hanover group was visited later by the "New Side" Presbyterian ministers, John Blair, John Roan, and Samuel Davies, later president of the College of New Jersey. The movement rapidly spread into the adjacent counties of Henrico, Goochland, Caroline, and Louisa, and became at one and the same time the center of Presbyterianism east of the Blue Ridge and the first foothold gained by the Great Awakening in the South.[4]

II

Conservative Presbyterians leagues away in the Valley of Virginia behind the Blue Mountains could be safely tolerated but a militant revivalistic Presbyterianism flourishing in Hanover County in the very heart of the colony and spreading rapidly to adjoining counties presented an entirely different problem. It was characteristic of the essentially English attitude of the Virginia authorities that they ignored this movement and the violation of the law in the matter of securing licensed preaching places until overt acts were committed that threatened public peace and order. These were provided by the tactless abandon of the revivalistic preacher John Roan, who made use of unlicensed preaching places to indulge in the following abusive language against the establishment. "At church you pray to the devil." "Your good works damn you and carry you to hell." "Your ministers preach false doctrine . . . and all who follow them are going to hell." "The Church is the house of the devil." [5] There is no more convincing evidence of the

---

[4] The origins of this Hanover movement are obscure. There are at least three different accounts. See Gewehr, op. cit., p. 45, footnote, for the sources.

[5] W. H. Foote, Sketches of Virginia, 1849-1855, Vol. I, pp. 137 f.

inherent weakness of this frontierized revivalistic Protestantism than that from its very inception it has been characterized by a language and a spirit that stultify the real spirit and purpose of the founder of Christianity. Revivalism did not produce the gentleman.

Governor Gooch viewed this conduct as a menace to public peace and order. In his charge to the grand jury in 1745, Gooch called attention to "certain false teachers that are lately crept into this government, who, without order or license, or producing any testimonial of their education or sect, professing themselves ministers under the pretended influence of new light, extraordinary impulses and such like satirical [fanatical?] and enthusiastic knowledge, lead the ignorant and innocent people into all kinds of delusions." The governor asked that a stop be put to "the devices and intrigues of these associated fanatics." [6]

To the modern American, good-naturedly tolerant towards the methods of the modern revivalist, it is exceedingly difficult to realize the extent to which the excesses of revivalistic piety scandalized the good taste and sense of decency of men and women of gentle breeding in the eighteenth century. The revival today is accepted as part of the familiar pattern of a crude American democracy, a fixed tradition of Protestantism. It was far from being so considered a century ago. When a copy of Gooch's charge to the grand jury reached the conservative "Old Side" Synod of Philadelphia, who in 1738 had secured from Gooch the toleration of the Presbyterians of the Valley, the Synod at once repudiated the conduct of Reverend Roan and the "New Side." Charges were entered against John Roan, William Morris, and others "for reflecting upon and vilifying the established religion" and for unlicensed meetings. Mean-

[6] McIlwaine, *op. cit.*, pp. 46 f.

while Roan returned to Philadelphia. His followers were tried
by the General Court in Williamsburg where the prosecutor
was the district attorney, Sir John Randolph, one of the ablest
lawyers of the colony and no friend of the dissenters. The jury's
verdict was, "We find the people did assemble at the house of
the defendant, but not in a riotous manner, and that John Roan
preached in said house, but not against the canons of the Church
of England as set forth in the information."[7] Small fines were
imposed in two instances for violation of the letter of the law.
This may be interpreted as an evidence of growing sympathy
with the dissenters. More probably it was an indication of religious liberalism born of indifference.

The question of the status of this new group of dissenters
still remained to be settled by the authorities. The issue turned
upon the interpretation of the Act of Toleration made part of
Virginia law in 1699. This act required the taking of the oath
of allegiance, the paying of tithes in support of the established
church, the subscription to articles of religion [certain exceptions being made in favor of Baptists and Quakers], compulsory
attendance upon divine service, licensed ministers and places of
meeting.[8] In the English statute of 1711 a broader interpretation was placed upon the Act of Toleration allowing the dissenting minister "to officiate in any congregation in any county,"
provided he was qualified and the place licensed. This was not
a part of Virginia law.[9]

The number of dissenters at first affected by the Virginia law
of 1699 was not large, being confined mainly to scattered
Quaker groups who under the protection of the Act of Toleration had gained a recognized status as a small and peaceful

[7] McIlwaine, *op. cit.*, p. 49.
[8] *Source Problems*, p. 202, for the sources.
[9] *Ibid.*, p. 204.

minority in the colony. The dissenters showed no appreciable increase in the colony. The Presbyterians in the Valley enjoyed religious freedom, thanks to the letter of Governor Gooch in 1732 assuring them the protection of the Act of Toleration. What was to be the attitude of the authorities as to the status of the growing revivalistic Presbyterians in Hanover and adjacent counties of the Piedmont, who were claiming the same freedom enjoyed by the Quakers, the Presbyterians of the Valley, and the dissenters in England? The Virginia authorities, following a precedent set by Governor Cornbury of New York in 1707, when he arrested and imprisoned the Presbyterian preacher Makemie, were inclined to insist that the Act of Toleration was subject to the interpretation of the colonial authorities. The dissenters stressed the broad interpretation of the act under Queen Anne which granted licenses to dissenting preachers whenever wanted.[10] The governor and his council sought "to differentiate the colonial practice from the English, upholding the power of the general court to decide such cases according to its own interpretation." [11]

III

The Presbyterians were fortunate in having at this critical juncture a man of unusual powers and commanding personality as their leader, the Reverend Samuel Davies, who came to Virginia in 1747. He has been described as "tall, well proportioned, erect and comely; his carriage easy, graceful and dignified, his dress neat and tasteful, and his manners polished." [12] Davies appeared armed with a license from the court to preach

[10] McIlwaine, op. cit., p. 55.
[11] Eckenrode, op. cit., p. 34.
[12] W. W. Henry, Life, Correspondence and Speeches of Patrick Henry, 1890-1891, Vol. I, p. 13.

at four places in Hanover and adjoining counties. Before the end of 1748 he had added three other houses, making a total of seven places. The personality of Davies and his eloquent preaching proved so attractive that members of the establishment came from a distance to hear him and soon began to leave the church and become dissenters. This naturally alarmed the clergy and the authorities. The correspondence that took place between the friends of the establishment and the Bishop of London during 1750 and 1751 clearly indicates the problem that Davies presented. William Dawson, the commissary of Virginia, asked in a letter to the bishop July 27, 1750: "I earnestly request the favor of your lordship's opinion, whether in licensing so many houses for one teacher they have not granted him greater indulgence than either the king's instruction or the Act of Toleration intended? It is not to be dissembled that several of the laity, as well as clergy, are uneasy on account of the countenance and encouragement he has met with, and I can not forbear expressing my own concern to see schism spreading through a colony which has been famous for uniformity of religion." [13]

The attitude of the clergy towards the Hanover movement found expression in a petition to the House of Burgesses in 1751. They asserted that the Hanover Presbyterians were mere irresponsible "lay enthusiasts" or "strolling pretended ministers," who could not legitimately call themselves Presbyterians for they had been excluded from the Synod of Philadelphia for their errors. They were not entitled to be classified as members of the Synod of Philadelphia, "the kirk of Scotland, the Presbyterian dissenters in England, or any other body of Presbyterians whatsoever." They were, in other words, dangerous sectarians, pretending to a greater degree of piety and yet seeking "to inveigle ignorant and unwary people with their sophistry"

[13] *Source Problems*, p. 215.

and "to seduce them from their lawful teachers and the religion hitherto professed in this Dominion." [14] The clergy viewed "New Side" Presbyterianism as a nondescript and upstart phase of dissent not contemplated in the Act of Toleration. The "New Side" dissenting movement in Virginia thus offered an interesting parallel to the Separatist dissenting movement in New England. Both were inspired by the Great Awakening and both were protests against highly institutionalized sacramentarian types of piety. "Old Side" and "New Side" were reunited in 1758.

The authorities were determined to check the spread of dissent by a strict interpretation of the Act of Toleration. Governor Dinwiddie, in a letter to the Bishop of London in 1752, wrote: "I told him (Davies) I thought it impossible for him to discharge the duties of a good pastor to so many different congregations dispersed at so great a distance one from the other . . . and that as he did not discharge these duties, which I conceived he could not do without a close residence with his hearers, I must look on him as an itinerant preacher more out of lucrative view than the salvation of the people." This charge of irresponsible itineracy, destined to be common practice of a revivalistic Protestantism, evidently rankled with Davies. "After a long silence," wrote Dinwiddie, "he desired I would not look on him as an itinerant preacher, which character he abhorred." Dinwiddie thus summed up the position of the authorities: "I told him that the church allowed of no pluralities, and therefore if he would confine himself to one meeting house or to the limits of a county, he should meet with all the protection and indulgence the Act of Toleration allows, while he continued peaceable and quiet." [15] This of course would most effectually

[14] *Ibid.*, pp. 222 f. See also Gewehr, *op. cit.*, pp. 81 f.
[15] *Source Problems*, pp. 220 f.

curtail the evangelizing activity which was the very heart and soul of the "New Side" Presbyterianism.

In a letter to England, 1752, quite characteristic of the tact and courtesy of the man, Davies stated his position: "If it be determined by competent authority that the Act of Toleration does not allow the dissenters to have meeting-houses licensed where they may occasionally meet for public worship, we shall quietly resign our claim 'till some favorable juncture happens when we may petition for our liberty. But if we may legally make this claim, if dissenters enjoy this privilege in England, and if the rulers there judge that the Act of Toleration entitles them to it, then we humbly conceive that pushing the matter to a determination could be attended with no ill consequences; as we only press for an explanation of the Act of Toleration with reference to Virginia according to its true intent and meaning in England." [16]

Thanks to the subsequent triumph of the dissenting-revivalistic type of Protestantism and the separation of church and state, it has been tacitly assumed that in this controversy Davies was entirely right and the authorities entirely wrong. The situation was not so simple as that. Davies claimed as valid for Virginia and the Presbyterians the English law of 1711 which permitted the dissenting minister "to officiate in any congregation and in any county." This phrase he interpreted to mean "to permit the dissenters to worship in their own way," [17] which was equivalent to claiming the right to preach to Presbyterians at any time and anywhere. The practical issue, said Davies in a letter to Benjamin Avery, 1732, was "whether a dissenting congregation, that is very much dispersed, and can not meet in one place, may claim a right by virtue of said act, to have a

[16] Cited by Foote, *op. cit.*, Vol. I, pp. 210 f.
[17] *Source Problems*, p. 218.

plurality of places licensed for the convenience for [of?] the sundry parts of the congregation?" Or, as Davies puts it in a letter to the Bishop of London, "Whether contiguity of residence is necessary to entitle dissenters to the liberties granted by the Act of Toleration?" Davies insisted that the true intent of the act was that dissenters be able to have "as many houses licensed as will render public worship accessible to them all." Where this end is prevented, that is to say, where dissenters are not *"permitted to worship in their own way,"* the principle of religious tolerance sought by the act is defeated and the act rendered null and void.[18]

Obviously Davies was demanding not religious toleration but complete religious liberty, terms by no means identical. The fundamental presupposition of the Act of Toleration, which Davies accepted, was the privileged position of the establishment. The act assumed that in the case of a conflict the needs of the establishment took precedence over those of the dissenters. The dissenters, from the point of view of the Act, were an evil which the law sought to mitigate as far as was possible. The Act did not contemplate the encouragement and possible triumph of dissent. It sought as far as possible to make the lives of dissenters tolerable in a community where church and state were united. To permit the dissenters "to worship in their own way" would be little short of equivalent to placing them on an equality with the establishment and this could only mean the ultimate invalidation of the establishment.

Davies insisted upon an application of the Act of Toleration to Virginia conditions, ignoring the basic assumption of the act both in England and Virginia, namely a fixed relationship between a licensed minister and a licensed place of worship. The dissenters could not claim for themselves a larger liberty than

[18] *Ibid.*, pp. 224 f.

was accorded to the member of the establishment. This was brought out by the Bishop of London.[19] The authorities, however, by insisting upon the limitation of the dissenting minister "to one meeting house or to the limits of one county"[20] laid themselves open to the criticism of Davies that the clergy of the establishment were not so limited. Owing to the immense size of the parishes, "twenty, forty and sometimes fifty miles long and proportionately broad,". chapels of ease had been erected to accommodate the scattered parishioners all served by one clergyman. Nevertheless, the minister who serves these various places does not incur "the odious epithet of itinerant preacher, a pluralist or nonresident. . . . Now I submit it to your lordship," continues Davies, "whether there be not at least equal reason that a plurality of meeting-houses should be licensed for the use of the dissenters here, since they are more dispersed and fewer in number? . . . I submit it also to your lordship whether there be not as little reason for representing me as an itinerant preacher, on account of my preaching at so many places for the convenience of one congregation, as that the minister of a large parish, where there are sundry churches or chapels of ease, should be so called for preaching at these sundry places, for the convenience of the parish?"[21]

It must be confessed that the logic neither of Davies nor of the champions of the establishment was consistent. At one point Davies could argue for the broad interpretation of the Act of Toleration in the English law of 1711, ignoring the fact that this interpretation meant one thing in the fixed traditional society of England and something quite different in a sparsely settled frontier social order of colonial Virginia. At another

[19] *Source Problems*, p. 218.
[20] "Dinwiddie to the Bishop of London," 1752, *ibid.*, p. 221.
[21] "Letter to the Bishop of London," 1752, *ibid.*, pp. 227 ff.

point he could argue from the irregularities incident to the large and sparsely settled parishes that the clergy were just as much itinerant preachers as the dissenting minister, thus identifying the practical non-conformity of colonial society with the inner logic and intent of the Act of Toleration. The authorities, on the other hand, in their determination to check the spread of dissent insisted upon a strict interpretation of the Act of Toleration in regard to dissenting ministers, ignoring the fact that this strict interpretation was contradicted in the practical workings of the Virginia establishment.

The real issue at stake between Davies and the colonial authorities seeking to protect the establishment was not primarily the meaning of the Act of Toleration nor the difference between the culture of England and the Old Dominion. The clash was between two different conceptions of religion, the external and institutional as opposed to the inner and personal. The logic of the expansive revivalistic faith of Davies was diametrically opposed to the conservative and externalized religion of the establishment. The one demanded freedom to create for itself congenial forms in a social order that was full of vast possibilities for change and development; the other was hopelessly identified with traditions and habits of life that were part of an aristocratic colonial culture destined speedily to disappear. The key to the whole situation was the matter of an itinerating ministry. Itineracy was for the establishment synonymous with chaos in the moral and religious life. Even Davies, thanks to his ingrained Presbyterianism, winced when dubbed an itinerating preacher. He did not have the insight nor the imagination to see that unrestricted itineracy was the logical outcome of the doctrine of the "new birth" and was necessitated by the exigencies of a frontier society. He professed obedience to the Act of Toleration while in his preaching and varied activities he presupposed a liberty incompatible with any acts of toleration, no matter how broad. It only remained for the more radical exponents of revivalism, the Separatist Baptists, to carry out the logical implications of Davies' position.

IV

The Virginia authorities continued to restrict the houses of worship and the number of those licensed to preach. What the dissenters were unable to gain by English interpretation of the law, by appeals to the higher law of nature, or by insistence upon equality before the law was achieved by other sterner agencies. The terrors of the French and Indian wars and especially of Braddock's defeat in 1755 furthered the cause of the dissenters more than argument and appeals to reason. For the Presbyterian dissenters who occupied the frontiers beyond the mountains were forced to bear the burden of war. While the Presbyterian leader Davies was arousing patriotism by eloquent sermons and the authorities were sending soldiers and supplies, the Presbyterians organized their churches very much as they pleased. New places of worship were opened and occupied unmolested. Matters of religion ceased to be of such transcendent importance when men were threatened by the tomahawk and the scalping knife.

The clergy themselves unwittingly played into the hands of the dissenters. The disorganized conditions of the colony due to the war and poor tobacco seasons made it difficult to pay the established clergy. A Reverend James Mauray of the establishment brought suit under certain acts of 1755 and 1758 to enforce the payment of the salaries of the clergy. The litigation came to a climax in 1764 when an unknown young man, Patrick Henry, sprang suddenly into fame by passionately championing the cause of the state and the people and denouncing a discredited and incompetent clergy. The effect was most disastrous for the parsons' cause. It served to accentuate the growing alienation between establishment and people, thus paving the way for the spread of dissent and the ultimate overthrow of the Anglican standing order. Much has been made of the influence of Presbyterian dissent upon Patrick Henry in this connection. His father was an Episcopalian and his mother a Presbyterian. Young Henry attended the Forks Presbyterian church with his mother where Davies preached. "She was in the habit of riding in a double gig taking with her young Patrick, who from the first showed a high appreciation of the preacher. Returning from the church she would make him give the text and recapitulate the discourse." [22] From these facts the inference has been drawn that Henry's oratorical style as well as his ideal of religious liberty, which made him a passionate defender of the persecuted Baptists, were very largely shaped by Davies.[23]

Many factors were concerned in the gradual attainment by Presbyterian dissent of a recognized position in the colony. There had been an increase in numbers and in ministers due to the revivals in religion from 1740. The restrictions in regard to itineracy were not strictly enforced. The patriotic attitude of the Presbyterians during the French and Indian War gained for them the respect of the colony. The fear of papal domination inspired by the war with France tended to make dissent and establishment forget their differences when face to face with a common enemy. The Presbyterian ministry were educated men and among them were outstanding and attractive individuals, such as Davies, who did much to win the respect of the upper classes. He was heard gladly in the Northern Neck, the

[22] Johnson, *op. cit.*, p. 45.
[23] W. W. Henry, *op. cit.*, Vol. I, pp. 15 f.

most aristocratic part of the Tidewater, where Presbyterianism flourished after Davies' visit in 1757. Accessions were constantly being made, even in the older settled regions,[24] thereby assuring to the dissenting Presbyterians a respectable and influential following. In the Valley the Presbyterians had been from the first the leading religious group. Finally, it must be remembered that the Presbyterians were not upstarts but came of a great church which had in the past far more in common with established religion than with dissent. Dissent was something superinduced by the logic of events upon the inner spirit and genius of the Presbyterian church.

By 1765 Presbyterian dissent had won for itself about all the freedom that could be expected under the Act of Toleration. We have no record that Presbyterian dissenters ever suffered violence as did the less fortunate Baptists. Whatever persecution they endured was limited almost entirely to the tongue or pen.[25] To be sure, the establishment still persisted. Dissenting ministers still had to seek licenses and legalized preaching places, but these were to be had for the asking. This was the achievement of the Presbyterians and it was gained peaceably. The legal recognition of the Presbyterians meant the admission of a group representing a church that stood for republicanism and the principles of representative democracy. This introduced a new note into the culture of Virginia. The old aristocratic cultural pattern was broken. The supremacy of the establishment had been effectively challenged. An opening had been made which a dissenting group more radical in spirit might use to overthrow the establishment and usher in complete religious liberty. It was in this sense that the Baptists supplemented the work of the Presbyterians.

[24] Gewehr, *op. cit.*, p. 93.   [25] Johnson, *op. cit.*, p. 59.

V

Just about the time that the Presbyterians had won for themselves a recognized status under the Act of Toleration all three groups of Baptists, the General, the Regular, and the Separatist, had found lodgment in Virginia. In the early eighteenth century the General Baptists had gained a tenuous foothold in southeast Virginia in the counties of Surry and Isle of Wight but remained a feeble folk. This group was Arminian in theology, lax in discipline, and lacking in evangelical fervor.[26] In 1751 the Regular Baptists founded the famous Ketocton church in Loudon County, northern Virginia. The present dignified old red-brick building dates only from 1854. But the magnificent grove of primeval oaks in front, together with the old graveyard in the rear, make it one of the historic spots in an historic state. The tide of modern life has swept past it into the swirl of the great cities, leaving it in melancholy isolation, but the descendants of those who once worshiped there still foregather among the lonely graves and under the shade of the ancient trees and bear silent testimony to the great rôle the pioneer church once played in the life of the American people.

From the Ketocton church as a center and in intimate contact with the Philadelphia Association the Regular Baptists spread throughout the Piedmont region north of the James River and reached the northern counties of the aristocratic Northern Neck. The Regular Baptists, thanks to their conservative theology (Calvinism) and their freedom from the emotional excesses of revivalism, never aroused the opposition of the estab-

---

[26] Newman, *History of the Baptist Churches in the United States*, pp. 289 f.

lishment as did the Separatists. The failure of the clergy to meet the religious needs of the middle and lower classes had created a spiritual need which made the Regular Baptists welcome, not only with the religiously disinherited classes but often also with individuals of the dominant group who were religiously inclined. Before the end of the eighteenth century the Ketocton church had grown into the Ketocton Association with thirty-six churches and some two thousand members. William Fristoe's *A Concise History of the Ketocton Baptist Association*, 1808, is particularly valuable for the light it throws upon the ideas as to democratic church organization, education for the ministry, church discipline, and theology of the Regular Baptists who, after the fusion of Regulars and Separatists in 1787, were destined to shape the theology, church polity, and discipline of the Baptist church.

The Separatists were the group who provided the Baptist communion with its revivalistic fervor. They owed their origin directly to the Great Awakening in New England and were called Separatists because of their intimate connection with the New England Separatist movement. Shubal Stearns was a Separatist preacher until 1751 when, like Isaac Backus, he became a Baptist and carried the revivalist enthusiasm of the Great Awakening into Virginia in 1754. Passing down the Valley of Virginia with his brother-in-law Daniel Marshall, likewise a Baptist preacher, he finally settled at Sandy Creek in Guilford County in the wilderness of North Carolina just over the Virginia line. This church became the center of the Separatist Baptist movement in the South.[27] The Separatist Baptists with their emphasis upon revivalism demanded a congenial setting. The revivalism that was stifled in New England flourished like the

---

[27] R. B. Semple, *History of the Rise and Progress of the Baptists in Virginia,* *1810,* pp. 2 ff.

proverbial green bay tree in the backwoods of North Carolina and Virginia. With their undisciplined emotional fervor, their disregard of learning, their itineracy and lay preaching the Separatist Baptists first realized the typical frontierized form of American Protestantism.

About 1760 the Baptist forces of dissent were mobilized for the conquest of Virginia for the revivalistic type of Protestantism with all its political and social implications.[28] In revivalistic waves the Regulars moved south from the historical Ketocton church in Loudon County. By 1770 the Regular Baptists were established in most of the counties north of Fredericksburg.[29] Contemporaneous with this expansion from the North the Separatists in the South had gained a foothold in Pittsylvania County and were spreading north towards the James River. In 1765 Samuel Harris, the first Separatist Baptist preacher to cross the James, was roughly handled in Culpeper County and took refuge in Orange County, which seems to have been more friendly to the Baptists.

The Regular and Separatist types of revivalism now first came in touch with each other and attempts were made in 1767 to unite them. These failed, due primarily to differences as to the importance of the "new birth." The Separatists, who drew their inspiration directly from the Great Awakening, insisted that the Regulars, who were not without their affiliations with the institutionalized type of piety, did not lay sufficient stress upon the vividness of religious experience in conversion and even admitted to baptism individuals who confessed that they had not been converted. The familiar narrow sectarian puritanism also emerged in the criticism that the Regulars made too much of dress.[30] Union of the two groups was not to take

28 The best account is in Gewehr, op. cit., Chap. 5.
29 Thom, op. cit., p. 11.
30 Gewehr, op. cit., p. 110.

place until twenty years later after success had made it necessary for the Separatists to iron out some of their crudities and to make a place for the cultural values represented by the Regulars. The happy fusion of these two groups, whose qualities supplemented each other admirably, is responsible, more than any other one thing perhaps, for the remarkable success of the Baptist church, especially in the South and West.

It was the Separatists that provided the spiritual dynamic for the unprecedented spread of the Baptist faith. With their religious enthusiasm and crude appeals to the emotions of the lower classes they made the Baptist faith distinctly the religion of the disinherited. Both Regulars and Separatists were revivalistic but the former were more restrained and tended to approximate the revivalism of Davies and the Presbyterians, of whom it was said, "Amidst the whole of the work there has been scarcely any tincture of enthusiasm." [31] The preaching of the Separatists, on the other hand, was accompanied by great excesses. According to the account of John Leland, a contemporary Baptist leader, the work of the Regulars was "regular and solemn," while that of the Separatists "was very noisy." [32] The Separatists had acquired from the New England Great Awakening a warm and passionate address accompanied by violent gestures. The preachers adopted a "holy whine" and, becoming deeply affected themselves, called out tears and tremblings and screams from their hearers, who would often "fall prostrate" or "lose the use of their limbs." Our pious eye-witness naïvely remarks, "Such heavenly confusion among the preachers and such a celestial discord among the people destroyed all articulation, so that the understanding is not edified but the awful echo sounding in the ears, and the objects in great distress, and great raptures before the eyes, raise great emotion in the heart.

---

[31] Gewehr, *op. cit.*, p. 111.   [32] Leland, *op. cit.*, p. 23.

Whether it be celestial or terrestrial or a complication of both, it is observed by the candid that more souls get first an awakening at such meetings, than at any meeting whatever." [33]

A familiar phase of these revivalistic phenomena was their utter lack of all moral orientation. Daniel Fristoe witnessed a meeting of some two thousand under the sway of powerful non-moral emotions, "some roaring on the ground, some wringing their hands, some in ecstasies, some praying, some weeping; and others so outrageous cursing and swearing that it was thought that they were really possessed of the devil." [34] The poverty-stricken conditions of a pioneer society and the almost complete lack of emotional discipline and restraint among the lower spiritually disinherited classes is the background which makes these curious religious phenomena intelligible. The religious leaders themselves, lacking the critical psychological knowledge of the present and led away by their own enthusiasm, were almost entirely devoid of sound judgment. This was true even of as powerful and scholarly an intellect as that of Jonathan Edwards. Revivalism saddled upon the religious life of American Protestantism a load of naïve primitive realism, effectively checked the sane and critical attitude of the eighteenth century, suffused superstition with an odor of sanctity, and gave to a crude supernaturalism a new lease on life. On the other hand, revivalism did provide a sort of raw emotional catharsis for the starved and neglected lower classes, harnessed their emotional life to higher loyalties, introduced the moral note into religion, and served to create a group consciousness and group ideals fraught with vast possibilities for social and political change. The excesses of these early revivals must be judged in

[33] *Ibid.*, p. 35. See also Semple, *op. cit.*, pp. 4 f.
[34] Quoted by Gewehr, *op. cit.*, p. 110.

terms of the age and not in terms of an enlightened, sophisticated, and scientifically nonreligious modern world.

VI

The reaction of the eighteenth-century Virginia society to the Baptists was varied. The Regulars were interrupted by occasional mobs or were reprimanded by magistrates but never suffered as did the Separatists. They had taken advantage of the results of the Presbyterian fight for toleration and secured licenses for preaching places. The presence of such leaders among them as Reverend David Thomas, "a learned man," won the respect of the upper classes.[35] Occasionally, however, even the Regular Baptists were roughly handled.[36] The effect of the orgiastic piety of the Separatists upon eighteenth-century Virginians is thus described by Leland: it "made the bystanders marvel." Some "thought they were deceitful." Others "thought they were bewitched." Still others would report that "God was with them of a truth."[37]

Perhaps the most common criticism of the Baptists was that they were poor and ignorant, a disinherited group. This criticism was not without its element of truth. It has been stated by a Baptist historian that throughout this period the Baptists of Virginia did not enjoy the services of a single college-bred man.[38] Writing in 1790, long after the triumph of the Baptists in the overthrow of the establishment, John Leland could say, "To this day there are not more than three or four Baptist

[35] Thom, *op. cit.*, p. 11.

[36] For data see *The Life of James Ireland, 1818,* by himself, Chap. 8, pp. 164 ff. Ireland was a Regular Baptist. See also William Fristoe, *op. cit.*, pp. 77 ff.

[37] Leland, *op. cit.*, pp. 23 ff.

[38] Newman, *op. cit.*, p. 303.

ministers in Virginia who have received the diploma of M.A.,
which is additional proof that the work has been of God and
not of man." [39] The Baptist preacher James Read, when he
began to preach, was unable to read or write. His wife became
his teacher and in time he was able to read the Scriptures. Read,
together with other Baptist evangelists of this type, was given
to vivid dreams which, like the prophets of the Old Testament,
he interpreted as factual revelations of the will of God.[40] Criticisms of the illiterate leaders were skillfully turned by the Baptists to their own advantage. "These reflections were of great
use to young converts and greatly confirmed them that they
were right—for in like manner the wicked ridiculed the Lord
Jesus and his followers in primitive times." [41] Thus did the
Baptist leaders cleverly identify their type of Christianity with
the class consciousness of the disinherited groups. The inevitable
result of a religion of the disinherited, such as that of the
eighteenth-century Baptists, was to encourage a clannish attitude within the group, the external correlative of which was
antagonism to the privileged groups and the intellectual refine-
ment and culture that they represented. This was later to prove
a deadly handicap to the Baptists.

This attitude of general disparagement was of course reflected in the frequent animadversions from the pulpits of the
establishment. "A certain parson," wrote Fristoe, "employed
his oratory on a certain occasion in defaming the Baptists; he
undertook to compare them with a number of things and those
of the meanest description; at length he made a full stop, as
though lost for comparison, or that the Baptists were beneath
all comparison—what shall I liken them to?—the diving ducks,
or rather to the herd of swine running violently down a steep

---

[39] Op. cit., p. 23.   [41] Fristoe, op. cit., p. 64.
[40] Semple, op. cit., pp. 5, 9.

place into the sea and perishing in the water." In reply to which humorous sally the protagonist of the despised Baptists remarks, not without a touch of naïve realism, "But the parson was mistaken in the figure, for among the many that have been baptized, none have been drowned." [42]

During the period from 1760 to 1768, when persecution was by the people rather than by the authorities, the meetings of the Baptists were often broken up by force and the worshipers severely handled. In one instance "a gun was brought by a person in a great rage and presented within the meeting house doors, supposed to shoot the preacher—at another instance, at the same place, a few being met at the meeting house to pray, sing praises and offer up their solemn devotion . . . a mob having collected, they immediately rushed upon them in the meeting house, and began to inflict blows upon the worshippers, and produce bruises and bloodshed, so that the floor shone with the sprinkled blood days following." Evidence of the state of public sentiment is shown in the fact that when a warrant was issued against the ringleaders and they were brought to trial "the disturbers of the peace could prove anything and everything they wanted . . . it was deemed a riot and all were discharged." [43] It was a favorite custom of young rowdies to ride their horses into the open-air meetings and even into the meeting-houses of the Baptists. Some of the indignities suffered are really unprintable in their coarseness. [44]

There is evidence, also, that in the popular imagination the very name Baptists inspired nameless forebodings amounting to downright terror, due to the age-long associations of the Bap-

[42] Fristoe, *op. cit.*, p. 79.
[43] *Ibid.*, pp. 77, 78.
[44] James Ireland, *op. cit.*, Chap. 8, for details. See also Gewehr, *op. cit.*, pp. 119 f.

tists with the Anabaptists and the excesses of Münster. By the
populace the Baptists were "charged with design . . . when
once they supposed themselves sufficiently strong, that they
would fall upon their fellow-subjects, massacre the inhabitants
and take possession of the country." As a result, "many of the
old bigots would feel their tempers inflamed, and their blood
run quick in their veins, and declare they would take up arms
and destroy the new-lights." [45] We have here a curious eighteenth-century parallel to the stories circulated with regard to
the Roman Catholics by the Apaists of the late decades of the
nineteenth century and the members of the modern Ku Klux
Klan.[46] The Baptists have long since lived down these ancient
prejudices but the anti-Catholic stereotypes are much more stubbornly persistent.

More serious charges of a civil and economic character were
brought against the Baptists. "At times when a congregation
was assembled for divine worship," we are told, "persons of a
persecuting disposition have taken the number of males at such
meeting, have stated the sum that the day's labor of each man
was worth, and then, by adding all together, have brought out
the sum total. Here they would expatiate; all this loss is sustained by the wretched new-lights, had it not been for them all
this might have been saved, and our country much enriched;
we fear times will grow worse and worse, without a stop be
made to the career, and some preventive devised that may
bring them to silence." In reply to this criticism the Baptists
asserted that "days could be spent in card playing, horse racing,
cock fighting, fish frying, barbacueing, and other fashionable
vices [!] without magisterial interference, and the perpetrators
go off with impunity—and often those who bore the civil sword,

[45] Fristoe, *op. cit.*, pp. 65 f.
[46] J. M. Mecklin, *The Ku Klux Klan*, Chaps. 4, 5.

were shamefully guilty of these enormities, and in some instances the ringleaders." [47]

This passage is a most striking illustration of the fundamental differences between the puritanical dissenting-revivalistic view of life and that of pleasure-loving aristocratic Virginia society. The clash between the two is all the more ominously significant in view of the fact that, through the former, the oppressed and disinherited groups of the Old Dominion found a philosophy of life which, aided by the great struggle for national independence and a crude pioneer democracy, was to triumph completely, wiping out the Anglican establishment which in many ways symbolized eighteenth-century Virginian culture. The crushing of that old culture with its tolerant and sane outlook upon life, its healthful love of play, its respect for decorum so disgustingly violated by the excesses of revivalism, its rational attitude towards religion, its sense of justice and love of liberty, at least for the ruling class, and the substitution for it of a narrow sectarian puritanism which saw in card playing, fish frying, and shooting matches shameful "enormities" was not an unmitigated blessing. It meant the ultimate triumph of a petty sectarian social ethics which strained at a gnat and swallowed a camel by condemning cards and dancing while later defending slavery. The sects at first were composed of propertyless disinherited groups bitterly opposed to slavery. As they became respectable property-holders their antislavery ideas disappeared.

VII

For the best part of a decade the authorities ignored the Baptists who suffered at the hands of mobs and rowdies. Popular persecution lasted approximately from 1760 to 1768 when there

[47] Fristoe, *op. cit.*, p. 72.

was a subtle shift of sentiment, especially among the lower classes, in favor of the Baptists. The disinherited were slowly beginning to realize that the despised Baptists were really fighting their battles. From 1768 to the beginning of the Revolution the persecution of the Baptists was more political than popular. The Baptists had been disturbers of the peace, more or less, for the best part of a decade and there must have been reasons for the government's suddenly taking note of this fact. The authorities were beginning to realize that the Baptist movement was a real menace to the old order of things.[48] Tirades against the establishment by Baptist preachers might be ignored but not increase in numbers and growing popularity with the masses. There was an instinctive feeling on the part of the authorities that the Baptists incarnated the spirit of social and political revolution.

The first instance of actual imprisonment of Baptists was in Spottsylvania, a county of the Northern Neck, where opposition to the Baptists had been most bitter. The fourth of June, 1768, John Waller, Lewis Craig, James Childs, and other Baptist leaders were seized by the sheriff and brought before the magistrates who bound them over under a penalty of a thousand pounds to appear at court.[49] It transpired at the trial of the Baptists that there was no law against preaching, not to mention the spread of heterodox theology. The men had to be arrested, therefore, upon a warrant that they were disturbing the peace. At the trial "they were vehemently accused by a certain lawyer, who said to the court, 'May it please your worships, these men are great disturbers of the peace, they can not meet a man upon the road, but they must ram a text of scripture down his throat.' "[50] This was obviously a mere pretext.

---

[48] Fristoe, *op. cit.*, pp. 76 f.   [50] *Ibid.*, p. 14.
[49] Semple, *op. cit.*, p. 15.

The real reasons· for the intervention of the authorities lay deeper and did not admit of concise formulation in legal terms. There were striking differences between the trials of the Baptists in eighteenth-century Virginia and in seventeenth-century Massachusetts. In Massachusetts the initiative came from the authorities, who were cruelly intolerant, while any expression of sympathy for Baptists and Quakers came from the common people. In Virginia the persecution was begun by the people and, when after a decade the people had begun to sympathize with the dissenters, the state reluctantly assumed the task of suppressing them. In Massachusetts we have no record that a single voice was raised by the leaders of the community, either in the seventeenth or eighteenth centuries, in behalf of the persecuted Baptists and the principles they represented. In Virginia the importance of the issues raised by the arrest of the Baptist leaders was at once recognized by no less a leader than Patrick Henry who, hearing of the confinement of the Baptist preachers in the Spottsylvania jail, journeyed fifty miles to volunteer his services in their aid. The old Presbyterian historian Foote has given us the following description of Henry's part in the trial:

"The king's attorney having made some remarks containing the indictment, Henry said—'May it please your worships, I think I heard read by the prosecutor, as I entered the house, the paper I now hold in my hand. If I have rightly understood, the king's attorney has framed an indictment for the purpose of arraigning, and punishing by imprisonment, these three inoffensive persons before the bar of this Court for a crime of great magnitude—as disturbers of the peace. May it please the Court, what did I hear read? Did I hear an expression, as of a crime, that these men, whom your worships are about to try for misdemeanor, are charged with,—with,—what?' Then in a low, solemn, heavy tone he continued—'preaching the gospel of the Son of God?' Pausing amid profound silence, he waved the paper three times around his head, then raising his eyes and hands to heaven, with peculiar and impressive energy, he exclaimed—'Great God!' A burst of feeling from the audience followed this exclamation." [51]

It is most significant that religious liberty was intimately associated in the minds of Henry and other leaders of that time with political liberty and the doctrine of natural and inalienable rights. "May it please your worships," continued Henry, "in a day like this,—when truth is about to burst her fetters—when mankind are about to be aroused to claim their natural and inalienable rights—when the yoke of oppression that has reached the wilderness of America, and the unnatural alliances of ecclesiastical and civil power, are about to be dissevered,—at such a period, when liberty,—liberty of conscience,—is about to wake from her slumberings, and inquire into the reason of such charges as I find exhibited here in this indictment . . . these men are accused of preaching the gospel of the Son of God." [52] To the sophisticated modern, enjoying religious liberty as one of the commonplaces of life, this language may sound amusingly melodramatic. For the men concerned it dealt with stern realities and voiced a lofty idealism foreign to a world mechanized by innumerable clever gadgets and prostituted to a pecuniary standard of values.

VIII

The persecution of the Baptists presented a serious problem to the authorities. History was repeating itself and they were realizing that "the blood of the martyrs is the seed of the church." The heroism of the Baptist preachers aroused the ad-

[51] Foote, *op. cit.*, pp. 316 f.   [52] *Ibid.*

miration of the crowd. When reviled they reviled not again. When struck they turned the other cheek. When imprisoned they continued to preach to the people through the bars of their jails. The nonplused authorities offered to release them if they would promise to be silent. This some refused to do. Others of their number with a curious disregard of the elementary principles of ethics "would give bonds not to preach and as soon as they were freed, they would immediately preach as before." [53] The mental attitude back of this apparently unethical conduct may be inferred from the language of the famous Separatist preacher, Samuel Harris, who after having been imprisoned and released rose in the congregation and said, "I partly promised the devil, a few days past, at the court house, that I would not preach in this county again in the term of a year. But the devil is a perfidious wretch, and covenants with him are not to be kept; and, therefore, I will preach." [54] The law and the constituted authorities were in league with the devil and hence had no moral claims to obedience. We have here an interesting illustration of the morally confusing effect of a highly emotional faith which finds in the intensity of its own feelings absolute ethical sanctions. The sense of honor which bound the godless gentleman of the upper classes to keep his word whenever given was foreign to such an atmosphere. This was a foretaste of the inherent lack of sanity which has always characterized the evangelical conscience when it deals with ethical issues suffused with powerful emotions. There is a sense in which the dissenting-revivalistic Protestantism has always been incompatible with a sane and trustworthy social ethics.

Meanwhile the problem was complicated for the authorities by the fact that the Baptists were increasing in numbers rapidly. In 1769 the Separatists had only two churches north and four

[53] Semple, *op. cit.*, p. 25.   [54] *Ibid.*, p. 282.

south of the James River. In 1774 they had thirty churches to the south and twenty-four to the north of the James and by the close of that year the Baptist historian Semple asserts that "they began to entertain serious hopes not only of obtaining liberty of conscience but of actually overturning the church establishment from which all their oppressions had arisen." [55] The Separatists outstripped the Regulars and after the union of the two in 1787 the Baptists became serious rivals of the Presbyterians, who had been the most numerous of the dissenting groups. A Baptist pioneer preacher asserted, "The Presbyterians read long sermons on dogmas of faith, fenced the table preparatory to the Lord's Supper by a tiresome exposition of the Ten Commandments after the old Scotch fashion, sung Rouse's version of David's psalms, were rigid in the enforcement of the observance of the Sabbath without due proportion of Christian morality on other days of the week, and were successful only in rendering themselves unpopular. They had the reputation of having been educated at college but were deficient in common sense." [56] If proper allowance be made for denominational jealousy and for exceptional leaders such as the Presbyterian Samuel Davies, these animadversions suggest very cogent reasons why the ignorant but earnest Baptist lay preacher was much better fitted to win the sympathy of the lower classes than the "high-brow" Presbyterian. The Presbyterians were severely handicapped by their inability to supply the demand for preachers. By the end of the war for independence the Baptists outnumbered the Presbyterians and had become the most numerous dissenting group in Virginia.

The persecution of the Baptists in Virginia was at best only half-hearted. "About thirty of the Baptist preachers were hon-

---

[55] *Ibid.*, pp. 24 ff.
[56] J. M. Peck, *The Christian Review*, October, 1852, pp. 494 ff.

ored with a dungeon," but never did the authorities go to the extremes of the colonies to the north, especially Massachusetts. The Baptist leader, John Leland, himself a native of New England, could say, "Virginia soil has never been stained with vital blood for conscience sake." [57] In 1790, not long after Isaac Backus had led a futile fight in Massachusetts for the dissenters,[58] John Leland wrote of the Baptists in Virginia, "We now sit under our own vine and figtree and there is none to make us afraid." [59]

The reasons for this failure of the authorities to suppress the Baptists are obvious. Their cause had powerful champions among the political leaders, such as Madison, Jefferson, Mason, and Patrick Henry. The masses were quick to detect the superiority of the piety and moral character of the ignorant but sincere Baptist lay preachers to that of the easy-going clergy. In an atmosphere already surcharged with the spirit of independence, just prior to the great struggle with England, the disinherited classes listened eagerly to men who proclaimed the infinite value of even the lowliest member of the community in the sight of God, the complete autonomy of the individual in all questions of religious loyalty, and a radical though negative democracy based upon the equality of all men before God in matters of sin and grace. The logic of the "new birth," preached in its most radical form by the Separatist Baptists, was thoroughly incompatible with the Anglican establishment and the aristocratic Virginia culture of which it was the expression. It made religion primarily a matter of the inner psychological series of reality and repudiated the establishment with all its trappings as a whited sepulcher full of dead men's bones.

---

[57] Leland, *op. cit.*, p. 25.

[58] Backus, *History of the Baptists*, Vol. II, Chap. 25. See also J. C. Meyer, *Church and State in Massachusetts*, Chap. 4.

[59] Leland, *op. cit.*

Among the Presbyterians the spiritual dynamite of the doctrine of the "new birth" was "cribbed, cabined and confined" by creed, ancient church forms, and an educated clergy. Among the Separatist Baptists these restrictions were lacking and the "new birth" became in their hands explosive, iconoclastic, and revolutionary, a mighty engine for social and political upheaval. Down to the bitter end, when the Baptists succeeded in stripping the establishment of its glebes, the last vestige of its privileged position, they manifested a singularly harsh and unsympathetic attitude towards the church. They never grasped the very real practical problems its overthrow entailed.

Chapter XI

Dissent and the Virginia Revolution

THE CALLING of the first continental congress in 1774 and the outbreak of the war in 1775 aided the cause of dissent in Virginia immeasurably. The radical Separatist wing of the Baptists now became active, sensing an opportunity doubtless to realize its hope for the abolition of the establishment and complete separation of church and state. At a joint meeting of the Separatist associations north and south of the James in August, 1775, it was determined to draft petitions, to be sent to the authorities and circulated throughout the colony for signatures, demanding that the church establishment be abolished, that religion be left to stand on its own merits and that all religious societies be given equal protection before the law.[1] It does not appear, however, that the Separatists presented their radical petition to the Convention of 1775; they confined themselves to the more immediate and practical matter of providing for the religious needs of Baptists who had enlisted as soldiers. It is significant that the radical wing of the Baptists had determined upon complete separation of church and state at least a year before Virginia had decided to separate from the mother country. It was not until political separation

[1] Semple, *History of the Rise and Progress of the Baptists in Virginia*, p. 62. C. F. James, *Documentary History of the Struggle for Religious Liberty in Virginia*, pp. 50 f.

had been determined upon that the Presbyterians championed religious separatism.

In their petition to the convention the Separatists, ignoring some of the older pacifist Baptist ideas, expressed themselves in complete harmony with the patriots struggling for national liberty and asserted "that they had considered what part it would be proper for them to take in the unhappy contest and had determined that in some cases it was lawful to go to war . . . that their brethren were left at discretion to enlist without incurring the censure of their religious community; and under these circumstances many of them had enlisted as soldiers, and many more were ready to do so, who had an earnest desire their ministers should preach to them during the campaign." The Baptists, therefore, requested of the authorities, "that they permit dissenting clergymen to celebrate divine worship, and to preach to the soldiers, or exhort, from time to time, as the various operations of the military service may permit, for the ease of such scrupulous consciences as may not choose to attend divine service as celebrated by the chaplain." [2] The Baptists were quick to realize the effect of the war upon the status of dissenters. They knew that the authorities were not in the position to antagonize a group as numerous and as united as the Baptists. The request was granted and thus the first long stride was taken towards the goal sought by the Separatists, namely, complete separation and the placing of all religious groups on an equal footing. This was the beginning of the Baptist war on the state-church, a war which continued long after the war of independence had been fought and won and ended in complete extermination of the hated establishment.

The Presbyterian historian, William Henry Foote, begins his

[2] W. T. Thom, *The Struggle for Religious Freedom in Virginia*, pp. 50 f. W. H. Foote, *Sketches of Virginia*, Vol. I, p. 321.

quaint and informing *Sketches of Virginia* with this observation: "There have lived men in Virginia whose names are worthy of everlasting remembrance. There have been events that should never be forgotten. There have been principles avowed, whose influence will be felt through all time." The convention that assembled May 6, 1776, in Williamsburg, goes far to corroborate Foote's statement, not only with regard to the men concerned, but also in the principles proclaimed. It was during this convention that Mason, Patrick Henry, Madison, and Jefferson succeeded with the support of the dissenters in making part of the organic law of Virginia the famous Bill of Rights, the sixteenth section of which contains this memorable language, drafted originally by Mason and slightly modified by Madison: "That religion, or the duty we owe to our Creator, and the manner of discharging it, can be directed only by reason and conviction, not by force or violence, and therefore all men are equally entitled to the free exercise of religion according to the dictates of conscience; and that it is the mutual duty of all to practise Christian forbearance, love and charity towards each other." [3]

This principle, later made more explicit in Jefferson's famous Act for the Establishment of Religious Freedom in 1785, is the basis of the claim that Virginia "is the first state in the history of the world to proclaim the decree of absolute divorce between church and state." [4] This claim has been disputed but not invalidated. [5] In the original draft of Article Sixteen by Mason,

[3] Foote, *op. cit.*, Vol. I, p. 322. *Source Problems in United States History*, edited by McLaughlin, Dodd, Jernegan, and Scott, p. 237.

[4] W. W. Henry, *The Part Taken by Virginia in Establishing Religious Liberty as a Foundation of the American Government*, Papers of the American Historical Association, Vol. II, p. 26.

[5] See Papers of the American Historical Association, Vol. III, pp. 205, 213, 457. H. J. Eckenrode, *The Separation of Church and State in Virginia*, pp. 44 ff.; Thom, *op. cit.*, p. 78; Humphrey, *Nationalism and Religion in America*, p. 375.

the word "toleration" had been used. "James Madison, the son of an Orange County planter, bred in the school of Presbyterian Dissenters, under Witherspoon, at Princeton, trained by his own studies, by meditative rural life in the Old Dominion, by an ingenuous indignation at the persecution of the Baptists, and by the innate principles of right, to uphold the sanctity of religious freedom," [6] rejected the word "toleration" on the ground that it implied an established religion which granted freedom to dissent. Subsequent events indicated that even the men who formulated this famous statement, not to mention the dissenters, were not clear in their own minds as to the practical implications of the freedom they championed.

On October 7, 1776, the assembly met as the representatives of an independent state. On October 11 a petition, asking that "all church establishment might be pulled down and every tax upon conscience and private judgment abolished" came up from Prince Edward County, whose inhabitants were largely Presbyterians. Petitions asking for the dissolution of the establishment came in thick and fast from all dissenting groups, particularly from counties in the Valley of Virginia, such as Augusta, Albemarle, Rockingham, Amherst, where the dissenting Scotch-Irish Presbyterians predominated.

All felt that the old establishment was doomed but there was great divergence of opinion as to what was to take its place. The problem of civil liberty had been discussed intensively for a long time by all groups and men were fairly unanimous as to its meaning. It was rendered fairly concrete through events in the political and economic spheres dealing with the relations of the colonies to the mother country. The famous Article Sixteen of the Bill of Rights on religious liberty breathed a fine spirit of liberalism that doubtless voiced the sentiments of the major-

[6] George Bancroft, *History of the United States*, 1861, Vol. IV, pp. 416 f.

ity of the people. The problem of religious liberty, however, was far more subtle and difficult than that of civil liberty. The question of civil liberty was one of definite issues between England and the colonies. The problem of religious liberty turned upon certain ill-defined notions of liberty of conscience and the separation of the political and religious spheres. Never before in the history of the world had a state been run on the basis of a complete divorcement between church and state. The nearest approach had been made in Rhode Island, but the little colony had been looked upon for a century and a half as a dangerous nest of radicals by the other New England commonwealths. There were few precedents suggesting how to give concrete formulation to the generous principles of Article Sixteen.

II

The period from 1776 to 1785, when disestablishment was completely achieved, was filled with tentative efforts of the dissenters to put into practice the implications of Article Sixteen. The Baptists petitioned in June, 1776, to be "married, buried and the like without paying the clergy of other denominations." [7] The effect of the passage of the Bill of Rights upon the conservative Presbyterians is seen in the memorial of the presbytery of Hanover, October 24, 1776, recounting in sober and dignified fashion the injustice of forcing the people of the frontier counties, where there were few Episcopalians, to pay taxes in support of an establishment. This was particularly obnoxious to the Scotch-Irish Presbyterians of the Valley of Virginia. The memorial contended that "there is no argument in favor of establishing the Christian religion but what may be pleaded with equal propriety for establishing the tenets of Mahomet." An

[7] *Source Problems*, p. 237.

establishment is "highly injurious to the temporal interests of any community" because it tends to retard population and hinder the progress of arts, sciences, and manufactures. Furthermore, the "gospel needs no such civil aid" because the founder of the church declares his kingdom is not of this world. The following anticipated what was to become orthodox American doctrine: "We would humbly represent, that the only proper objects of civil government are the happiness and protection of men in the present state of existence; the security of the life, liberty and property of the citizens; and to restrain the vicious and encourage the virtuous by wholesome laws, equally extending to every individual. . . . But that the duty which we owe to our Creator, and the manner of discharging it, can only be directed by reason and conviction; and is nowhere cognizable but at the tribunal of the universal Judge." [8]

This document, which on the whole seemed to champion the Baptist doctrine of complete separation of church and state and to follow out the logic of the famous sixteenth article, closed with the request, that dissenters of every denomination may be "exempted from all taxes for the support of any church whatsoever, *farther than what may be agreeable to their own private choice or voluntary obligation.*" [9] This statement was repeated in substantially the same language the following year in a memorial of June 3, 1777.[10] It is obvious that this language might be interpreted in support of the form of assessment sought by Pendleton and the conservatives. The Presbyterians, as subsequent events were to show, had not yet arrived at the clear-cut philosophy of separatism championed by the Baptists. At a

---

[8] T. C. Johnson, *Virginia Presbyterianism and Religious Liberty in Colonial and Revolutionary Times,* pp. 84, 85.
[9] James, *op. cit.,* p. 224.
[10] Johnson, *op. cit.,* p. 89. James, *op. cit.,* p. 90.

meeting, June 19, 1777, the Hanover Presbytery appointed a committee to come to "a final determination concerning church establishments." [11]

Men differed widely in their interpretation of Article Sixteen. The radical Baptist saw in it a sanction for complete separation of church and state. The Presbyterians wavered in 1784 but finally supported the radical Baptist position. The Anglicans thought it meant at best a more tolerant union of church and state. The establishment still existed and was most intimately associated with the institutions and way of life of the community. To abolish it in the swift and radical fashion demanded by the Baptists would be little short of a revolution. The cause of the conservatives was further aided by the inevitable reaction and demoralization that always accompany war. Men such as Pendleton, Nicholas, Harrison, and others, trained in the traditions of English liberalism represented by Burke, were sincerely convinced that the maintenance of some sort of an establishment for the teaching of religion was necessary to the preservation of public morals and good citizenship. To this end they sought "to see the reformed Christian religion supported and maintained by a general and equal contribution of the whole state upon the most equitable footing that it is possible to place it." [12] It was contended that so long as each supported the denomination of his choice and all sects were equal before the law, the intent of Article Sixteen was not defeated.

According to Jefferson "desperate contests" took place "almost daily" from 1776 to 1779 and certain laws were passed looking to the realization of the ideal of Article Sixteen and the removal of the disabilities of the dissenters, namely, "the laws

[11] James, *op. cit.*, p. 103.
[12] *Journal of House of Delegates*, October, 1783, p. 12; Eckenrode, *op. cit.*, p. 72.

which rendered criminal the maintenance of any religious opinions (other than those of the Episcopalians), the forbearance of repairing to (Episcopal) church or the exercise of any (other than Episcopal) mode of worship, to exempt dissenters from contributions to the support of the Established Church; and to suspend until the next session, levies on the members of that church for the salaries of their own incumbents." This last piece of legislation, passed in 1779, really destroyed the establishment, for it severed the economic nerve necessary to its continued life. The explanation of the stubborn nature of the struggle Jefferson found in the fact that "although the majority of the citizens were dissenters . . . a majority of the legislature were churchmen." This conservative and influential element secured the passage of a bill looking to some sort of religious assessment. The old establishment was abolished but its shadow still lingered in the form of proposed state support of religious teachers.[13]

The position of the conservatives took the form of a General Assessment Bill called the "Bill Establishing a Provision for Teachers of Religion" and complementary to the General Incorporation Bill. Its preamble indicates what it intended to do:

"Whereas the general diffusion of Christian knowledge hath a natural tendency to correct the morals of men, restrain their vices and preserve the peace of society, which can not be effected without a competent provision for learned teachers, who may be thereby enabled to devote their time and attention to the duty of instructing such citizens as from their circumstances and want of education can not otherwise attain such knowledge; and it is judged such provision may be made by the legislature, without counteracting the liberal principle heretofore adopted and intended to be preserved, by abolishing all distinctions of pre-

[13] *Works of Jefferson*, Ford Edition, Vol. I, pp. 53 ff.

eminence among the different societies or communities of Christians." [14]

This preamble very definitely recognizes that Christianity was basic in the pattern of American culture, especially at this early period, and that some sort of knowledge of it was necessary to the training and education of a citizenship alert to its duties and obligations. Over against this very real sense of the social responsibility involved was the radical and uncompromising spirit of liberty championed by the Baptists, preached more feebly by the Presbyterians and maintained by such leaders as Madison and Jefferson with their eighteenth-century philosophy of natural rights.

The position of the conservatives found sympathy with sections of the country outside the Tidewater. From Amelia County came a petition, November, 1784, typical of others, expressing fear at the declension of religion "chiefly by its not being duly aided and patronised by the civil power." If this continues it will be "fatal to the strength and stability of civil government," for, the petitioners assert, "were all sense of religion rooted out of the minds of men scarce anything would be left upon which human laws would take hold." They asked for a general assessment to support a broad and tolerant religious establishment in the interests of "public utility" and the "virtue and happiness of their constituents." They felt that this would be no encroachment upon religious liberty provided that everyone "is permitted to worship God according to the dictates of his conscience." [15] This was an attempt to combine two things, namely, some sort of training in religion because it was so intimately associated with public morals and citizenship and the right of

[14] Given in James, *op. cit.*, p. 129. Humphrey, *op. cit.*, p. 394.
[15] *Journal of the House of Delegates*, p. 11; Eckenrode, *op. cit.*, p. 84.

the individual to establish and support his own church freely
so long as this did not injure public morals. Religion was thus
placed very much in the same category with compulsory education or health legislation in present-day society.

III

The bill for assessment in the support of religion dragged
along until the end of the war and came up for serious consideration in 1784. Meanwhile, the country was suffering from
the demoralizing effects of the war which had left religion and
the church in a most deplorable condition. The idealistic enthusiasm of the days of the Declaration of Independence had
given place to a conservative reaction. Before and during the
war, liberal, not to say radical, ideas had spread all over the
country. Skepticism was rife in the colleges, from William and
Mary to Harvard. This gave to the assessment proposed for
the support of religion an importance which it would not otherwise have enjoyed. Most important of all, perhaps, was the
fact that two able leaders, hitherto identified more or less with
the forces making for liberty, Patrick Henry and Richard
Henry Lee, now gave their powerful support to the assessment
bill. The motives back of their position are thus expressed by
Lee: "Refiners may weave reason into as fine a web as they
please but the experience of all times shows religion to be the
guardian of morals and he must be a very inattentive observer
in our country who does not see that avarice is accomplishing
the destruction of religion for want of legal obligation to con-
tribute something to its support." [16]
Patrick Henry was the most powerful leader in the state. His
support of this bill seems a repudiation of all those fine ideals

[16] Semple, *op. cit.*, p. 56; Eckenrode, *op. cit.*, p. 75.

of liberty for which he had so bravely fought before and during the Revolution. Henry began life as an agitator. This fiery orator and master of the emotions of men was, however, really a conservative at heart. The lapse of the years had cooled the fiery enthusiasm of his youth and we find him, after the battle for national freedom had been won, striving to defend Virginia against two great evils, the undermining of morals and religion by French infidelity and the infringement of the rights of the state by the federal Constitution. Any cause championed by Henry became through that very fact important. His name was identified in the popular imagination with ideals dear to the hearts of the masses. Though nominally an Episcopalian, by training he belonged to the dissenting group. His mother was a Presbyterian and, as we have seen, he listened as a boy to the dissenting Presbyterian leader, Samuel Davies, whose sermons he afterwards discussed with his mother. His political supporters were found mainly among the dissenters who, Jefferson tells us, constituted two-thirds of the state at the Revolution. His chief following was in the Piedmont region.

It was at this critical juncture that Presbyterian dissent revealed the effects of its essential conservatism and its ancient affiliations with a church establishment. In May, 1784, the Hanover Presbytery presented a memorial, reiterating its objections to the assessment bill set forth in earlier memorials.[17] Apparently the Presbyterian attitude had not altered since 1777.[18] In October, 1784, however, the Presbytery presented another memorial departing radically from earlier positions and tentatively accepting the principle of assessments.

This memorial is most interesting as an attempt on the part of the ablest of the dissenting groups to come to terms with the exceedingly difficult problem of the rôle of religion in a free

[17] James, *op. cit.*, pp. 227 f.   [18] *Ibid.*, p. 89.

society. They insisted that religion is "a spiritual system" and hence should be free from molestation by the state. On the other hand, they likewise insisted that it "is absolutely necessary to the existence and welfare of every political combination of men in society to have the support of religion and its solemn institutions, as it affects the conduct of rational beings more than human laws can possibly do." It follows, therefore, that "it is wise policy in legislators to seek its alliance and solicit its aid in a civil view, because of its happy effect upon the morality of its citizens." In other words, religion and morals are indissolubly related. The state must further the morals of its citizens. To what extent may it make use of religion to this end without infringing upon religion as a "spiritual system" with its own laws, sanctions and free spontaneous life? This problem is still with us in spite of our great tradition of the complete separation of church and state.

Foote thus outlines the position which seems to have been tentatively assumed by the Presbyterians: "First, religion as a spiritual system is not to be considered as an object of human legislation, but may, in a civil view, as preserving the existence and promoting the happiness of society. Second, That public worship and public periodical instruction of the people, be maintained in this view by a general assessment for this purpose. Third, That every man, as a good citizen, be obliged to declare himself attached to some religious community, publicly known to profess the belief in one God, his righteous providence, our accountableness to him, and a future estate of rewards and punishments. Fourth, That every citizen should have liberty annually to direct his assessed proportion to such community as he chooses. Fifth, That twelve titheables, or more, to the amount of one hundred and fifty families, as near as local circumstances will admit, shall be incorporated, and exclusively direct the application of the money contributed for their support." [19]

This apparent desertion of the cause of the dissenters by the Presbyterians on the matter of assessment brought down upon them severe criticism. Madison in a letter to Monroe, April 12, 1785, had this to say: "The Episcopal people are generally for it (assessment) though I think the zeal of some of them has cooled. The laity of the other sects are generally unanimous on the other side. So are all the clergy, except the Presbyterians who seem as ready to set up an establishment which is to take them in as they were to pull down that which shut them out. I do not know a more shameful contrast than might be found between their memorials on the latter and former occasion." [20] Rayner, in his *Life of Jefferson*,[21] has this rather caustic remark on the Presbyterians: "The particular object of the dissenters being secured, they deserted the volunteer champion of their cause, and went over in troops to the advocates of a general assessment. This step, the natural proclivity of the sectarian mind, showed them incapable of religious liberty upon an expansive scale, or broader than their own interests, as schismatics."

Foote, the Presbyterian historian, offers the following apology for his church: "There was a strong impression that some kind of an assessment would be demanded by a majority of the citizens of the state and it appears that for a time there was a leaning that way in some, at least, of the members of the presbytery." In another connection he says, "When the bill for a general assessment was brought forward, with such an advocate as Patrick Henry and with the Episcopal Church to support it,

---

[19] Foote, *op. cit.*, Vol. I, p. 338. The memorial is given in James, *op. cit.*, pp. 231 f.
[20] James Madison, *Writings*, 1900-1902, Vol. II, p. 13, quoted by Eckenrode, *op. cit.*, pp. 90 ff.
[21] P. 141.

it was generally supposed that it would certainly become law." Without endorsing the principle of assessment but assuming that some sort of an assessment was inevitable the Presbyterians proposed "the least offensive form in which the assessment could be levied." [22] It was easy for a church springing originally from the state-church type to make this compromise. Complete separatism was never a matter of deep conviction with the Presbyterians as with the Baptists.

In connection with this temporary defection of the Presbyterians a somewhat unseemly controversy has been waged between Baptist and Presbyterian historians from the "filial piety" point of view as to the priority of the claims of Baptists and Presbyterians in the struggle for religious liberty in Virginia.[23] The two groups supplemented each other admirably. The Presbyterians had won toleration before the Baptists appeared and might have stopped there had not the Baptists with their radical separatism made the triumph of religious liberty complete. The Presbyterians brought intelligence and culture and statesmanship to the aid of dissent; the Baptists provided the religious enthusiasm and a radical position combined with numbers and a popular appeal. If the New England establishments had been forced to fight such a combination instead of insignificant handfuls of Baptists and Quakers, the story of New England dissent might have been quite different.

IV

In the fall of 1784 everything pointed to the passage of the assessment and incorporation bills, although it was generally

[22] Foote, op. cit., Vol. I, pp. 338, 455. See also Eckenrode, op. cit., pp. 89 f.
[23] For the Baptist claims see James, op. cit., pp. 41 ff., 241 ff. For the Presbyterian claims see Johnson, op. cit., and the Central Presbyterian of Richmond for May 16, 1888.

felt among the dissenting groups that this was an attempt to set up the establishment in a slightly different form. On November 17 Patrick Henry was elected governor, thus depriving the bill of the most influential leader in the state. The strength of the establishment was in the Tidewater counties and the counties to the south. The chief source of dissenting opposition was in the counties of the Valley and to the southwest. The midland counties where Patrick Henry's influence was especially strong were divided. Henry was able to unite the midland counties with the Tidewater region and hence the strength he brought to the support of the bills of the conservatives. The Valley counties of Rockingham and Rockbridge sent in petitions against the program of the conservatives, which Madison was inclined to interpret as protests of the Presbyterian laity. Doubtless they likewise expressed the traditional opposition of the Western frontiersmen to the policies of the conservative East. Deprived of the leadership of Patrick Henry the divided midland counties began to drift to the support of the democratic West. How greatly the conservative majority had shrunk was indicated by the vote of forty-seven to thirty-eight in favor of the incorporation bill, December 22, 1784.[24]

In the debate on the matter of incorporation and assessment in 1785 all classes were aroused. In 1776 the Methodists, being still a part of the establishment, had petitioned against disestablishment.[25] By 1785 they had become a separate church and cast in their lot with the dissenters, thereby weakening the forces of the establishment, especially in the crucial Piedmont section.[26] Though Methodism joined the forces of dissent too late to play an important part in the struggle it really belongs to

[24] Eckenrode, *op. cit.*, p. 101.
[25] James, *op. cit.*, p. 75.
[26] C. H. Ambler, *Sectionalism in Virginia, 1776-1861*, 1910, p. 40.

the dissenting tradition. Methodism was a neo-puritanical movement of moral dissent from the abuses of the time. Like the
dissenting-revivalistic groups it stressed a radical emotional
change, the "new birth," which manifested itself in a totally
altered life. This is the very essence of the dissenting-revivalistic tradition. The Methodists were originally and still remain
essentially moral dissenters. Says a critic, "The chief hinge on
which their whole scheme of religion turns is that no action
whatever is indifferent." [27] The quintessence of Methodism is
found in the following from a sermon by Wesley: "Here is a
short, a plain and infallible rule before you enter into particu-
lars. In whatever profession you engage you must be singular
or be damned! The way to hell has nothing singular in it; but
the way to heaven is singularity all over. If you move but one
step towards God, you are not as other men are." [28] This expresses the dissenting "come-outer" spirit of Methodism. Separation from the world, difference, uniqueness, moral singularity—these are the spirit of Methodism. This obviously harmo-
nizes with the dissenting tradition, developed in opposition to
the churchly tradition, of spiritual separation from the world
and a secularized church.

The Methodist church, however, was never able to rid itself
entirely of earlier affiliations with an establishment. More than
any of the other churches it is accustomed to intermeddle in
politics and morals, in this sense differing radically from Wesley and early Methodism. It has never taken the principle of
separatism as seriously nor applied it as consistently to the problems of religion as have the Baptists and Presbyterians. "Con-

[27] L. Tyerman, *Life and Times of the Reverend John Wesley*, 1890, Vol. I,
p. 85, cited by U. Lee, *The Historical Background of Early Methodist Enthusiasm*, 1931, p. 121.
[28] Lee, *op. cit.*, p. 122.

nectionalism" stressed by Wesley as the key to the corporate life of the Methodist church has tended to socialize Methodist moral ideals.[29] The result is that, whether intentionally or not, the Methodist church tends to assume a more or less magisterial moral attitude on matters of social ethics as though God had committed, if not to the Methodist church, at least to evangelical Protestantism the keeping of the social conscience of the nation. It is hardly an accident that it is the church which in its past has not been forced by persecution to stress the great American doctrine of separation of church and state that has erected an imposing building in Washington, facing the Capitol and hard by the new Supreme Court building, whence it keeps watch and ward over the morals of the American people.[30]

The passage of the bill incorporating the establishment alarmed the Presbyterians and stiffened the traditional opposition of the Baptists. The dissatisfaction among the Presbyterian laity, especially of the western counties, at the action of the Hanover Presbytery in October, 1784, when it seemed to have repudiated the dissenting position for that of the conservatives, now found expression in a vigorous memorial of August, 1785, against incorporation and assessment which a Presbyterian historian claims "expressed the mind and heart of the Presbyterians of the time." [31] The Baptists also took action August 13, 1785, against the bill for assessment, reiterating the Baptist separatist doctrine that "religion was a thing apart from the concerns of the state." [32] Madison, with characteristic astuteness, prepared his famous "Memorial and Remonstrance," one of the ablest

---

[29] J. J. Tigert, *A Constitutional History of Methodism*, 1894, pp. 58 f.

[30] Pezet, "The Temporal Power of Evangelism," *The Forum*, Vol. LXXVI, pp. 481 ff. For the Methodist point of view see Stanley High, *The Church in Politics*, 1930. Also, *The Forum*, Vol. LXXVI, pp. 668 f., 756 f.; Vol. LXXXIII, pp. 264 f.

[31] Johnson, *op. cit.*, p. 110.

[32] Eckenrode, *op. cit.*, p. 107.

politico-religious deliverances of the times, which his political lieutenants, George Nicholas and George Mason, broadcasted with such success that the tide was turned. Petitions piled up as they had never done before, even the Quakers and Methodists being represented.[33] Assessment was defeated, the act of incorporation repealed, and on December 17 Jefferson's famous "Act for the Establishment of Religious Freedom" was passed, the heart of which is contained in the following provision: "Be it enacted by the General Assembly, That no man shall be compelled to frequent or support any religious worship, place or ministry whatsoever, nor shall be enforced, restrained, molested or burthened in his body or goods, nor shall otherwise suffer on account of his religious opinions or belief; but that all men shall be free to profess, and, by argument, to maintain their opinions in matters of religion, and that the same shall in no wise diminish, enlarge or affect their civil capacities." [34]

This famous statement from the pen of Jefferson, which was but an enlarged reiteration of Article Sixteen of the Bill of Rights, was enthusiastically received in Europe and played its part in advancing the French Revolution.[35] The passage of this historic measure would hardly have been possible without the support of Baptist and Presbyterian dissenters.

It is to the everlasting credit of the Baptists that, during the critical period when it seemed inevitable that some form of assessment for the support of religion would become law, they never swerved from their loyalty to the dissenting doctrine of separatism. From the very beginning of the controversy they announced their determination "to oppose the law for a general assessment, and that for the incorporation of religious so-

[33] Eckenrode, *op. cit.*, p. 111.   [35] Humphrey, *op. cit.*, p. 404.
[34] Johnson, *op. cit.*, p. 118.

cieties, which were in Agitation." [36] From this position they never receded. To be sure, one misses among the overtures from the Baptists at this critical time the statesmanlike ability, found in the Presbyterian memorials, which led the biographer of Patrick Henry to say in regard to Jefferson's famous bill that "the Presbytery (Hanover), representing the Presbyterians of the state, had expressed with remarkable precision and force, the proper relations of church and state, before the great statesman had drafted his act defining those relations, and that the act was no advance on the position taken by the Presbytery." [37]

The Baptists did not as a rule belong to the cultured and influential classes. The Baptist historian Newman states that at this time they "possessed a number of highly gifted men, who had surmounted the disadvantages of lack of literary and theological culture by private study; but it does not appear that they had enjoyed the services of a single college-bred man." [38] Two things consistently characterized the Baptists during this struggle, love of liberty and hatred of the establishment. They championed freedom as does every persecuted and disinherited group. They hated the establishment as the embodiment of all the forces that hinder their rise. The Baptist church was recruited from the disinherited groups in the community who had little to lose and much to gain by the revolution. It meant freedom from oppression of the privileged classes, religiously, socially, politically, and economically. It offered unlimited possibilities for getting revenge upon the establishment which had persecuted and imprisoned their preachers and heaped abuse upon their heads as an ignorant and lawless rabble. After the

[36] James, *op. cit.*, p. 131.
[37] W. W. Henry, *Life, Correspondence and Speeches of Patrick Henry*, Vol. I, pp. 498 f.
[38] Newman, *History of the Baptist Churches*, p. 303.

real fight for freedom was won with the passage of Jefferson's bill in 1785 the Baptists, with a persistence almost vindictive, continued their opposition to the establishment until the incorporating act was repealed in 1787 and in 1799 the glebe or church lands reverted to the state. The establishment had occasion to rue its persecution of the Baptists.[39]

[39] Gewehr, *op. cit.*, pp. 213 f.

Chapter XII
Dissent and Rights of Conscience

THE GREAT struggle for religious liberty in Virginia will always be of interest to those who seek to trace the rise of typical American ideals or follow the grand march of Western civilization. It is particularly valuable for the light it throws upon the contribution of the dissenting groups to religious liberty in American life. At least four well-defined groups are distinguishable, the conservatives of the Tidewater, the Presbyterians, the Baptists, and the philosophical liberals such as Madison and Jefferson. The position represented by the conservatives, Pendleton, Nicholas, Harrison, and Richard Henry Lee, was merely an echo on American soil of the traditional English philosophy of society so eloquently defended by Burke in his *Reflections on the French Revolution.* The arguments advanced also remind us of those which the contemporary conservatives of Massachusetts put forward in defense of their establishment. Society for the Virginia conservatives as for Burke was an organic entity, consisting essentially of customs, laws, traditions, and ancient ways of life in which are embodied the tested social wisdom of the past. Pendleton and Nicholas and Lee would doubtless have accepted Burke's profoundly religious notion of "the divine tactic" by which society is organized and run. For them religion was as integral a part of society as the pattern is an integral part of the texture of an oriental rug. Religion was the natural guardian of morals, the principle that assured obedience to law and submission to constituted authorities, the source of the feeling of piety and reverence which knit past and present into a living whole. The group most closely affiliated with the conservatives were the Presbyterians. Neither Knox, the father of Scotch Presbyterians, nor his great mentor, John Calvin, would have sympathized greatly with any form of separatism. Calvin conceived of the church as a "holy community" which included the whole of society, as in the case of the Genevan church-state. A similar social ideal actuated John Cotton and Winthrop in the founding of their Bible commonwealth. Calvinism "never questioned the ideal of a unity which included Society and the State, natural life and worship, and the separation of a holy separate community from the ordinary life of humanity always remained a crime." [1] Obviously this early organic conception of society of John Calvin, realized more or less in the state-establishments of Geneva, Scotland, and New England, had little use for any philosophy of separatism.

But, long before the Scotch-Irish Presbyterians reached American soil, separatism in the form of opposition to the divine right of kings had become part of their philosophy of church and state. Andrew Melville in a famous sermon before King James VI said: "Therefore, Sir, as divers times I have told you, so now again I must tell you there are two kings and two kingdoms in Scotland; there is King James the head of the commonwealth, and there is Christ Jesus the King of the Church, whose subject King James VI is and of whose kingdom he is not a king, nor a lord, nor a head but a member." [2] The

---

[1] Ernst Troeltsch, *The Social Teachings of the Christian Churches*, Vol. II, p. 623.

[2] Quoted by J. N. Figgis, *The Divine Right of Kings*, 1914, p. 286.

famous fiction of the medieval imagination, "the divine right of kings," was evolved primarily to help the state to vindicate its rights threatened by the church. If both church and state exist by divine right they are at least coördinate in dignity. The separatism involved is *functional* as in the Middle Ages rather than absolute but it paved the way for the complete autonomy of the state after the Renaissance and the complete separatism first achieved in America.

The Scotch Presbyterians did not champion this doctrine until they suffered from the heavy hand of the Stuarts in Scotland and were forced into the ranks of the dissenters in England toward the end of the sixteenth century. Persecution makes strange bedfellows. In their plea for liberty based upon the divine sanction for the separation of church and state the Presbyterians were joined by the Catholics under the leadership of the astute Jesuit controversialist, Cardinal Bellarmine. Catholics were suffering even more than Presbyterians from Stuart intolerance. "Brought into conflict with the power of the secular governments that recognized no exemption from their oversight, the Jesuits, who had become the chief champions of the Catholic Church and the Papacy, were now forced as the Calvinists had already been to develop doctrines of a limitation of royal power in the interests of the people on the one hand, and on the other of a separation of the fields of ecclesiastical and secular jurisdiction." [3] There is something particularly intriguing in the spectacle of a Cardinal of the Catholic church talking the same language as dissenting Presbyterians in the interest of religious toleration.

Anabaptists and other dissenting groups, with more radical ideas of separatism, willingly supported the moderate separatism of the dissenting Catholics and the Presbyterians. The limited

[3] C. H. McIlwaine, *The Political Works of James I*, 1918, p. xxii.

separatism of the latter was at least a step towards the radical separatism of the former. Thus was popularized in the imaginations of dissenters of the seventeenth century the fiction of the two societies so basic for the thought of Roger Williams. It became for Presbyterian, Quaker, Baptist, as well as persecuted Catholic, an idea fraught with unlimited possibilities for maintaining the integrity and freedom of the spiritual life when threatened by the state. Men became habituated to the thought that in the church and the state we have to do with two different spheres of human interest, each with rights and duties of its own and each in a way self-sufficient. By the end of the seventeenth century the Presbyterians had become committed to this limited notion of separation of church and state based upon the great medieval fiction of divine rights.

But Presbyterians, no more than Catholics or Erastians, contemplated the possibility of a state with more than one religion. Separation in the form of a dualism of church and state did not necessarily ensure tolerance. It might make it all the easier for the church to be intolerant. *Separatism is meaningless and valueless as a means to freedom without a plurality of religions.* This plurality the Presbyterians at this stage were just as unwilling to admit as the Catholics or King James. The philosophy of Presbyterian and Catholic in this controversy did not go beyond the notion of a separation between a given church and a given state in a social order. It did not contemplate a separation between the state and a plurality of churches. The weakness both of Bellarmine and of the Presbyterians was their intolerance. Both appealed to divine right in defense of the rights of their own religious group as opposed to intolerant Stuart Erastianism; neither was willing to extend the aegis of divine right to include *both* Presbyterianism and Catholicism. "They were right in asserting that there were two kingdoms; they were wrong in denying that there might be twenty-two." [4] Such a separatism did not necessarily further the cause of tolerance. The difference between the Presbyterian separatist tradition as opposed to that of the Baptists and Quakers was that the Presbyterians contended only for a *dualistic* separatism while the Baptists and others contended for a *pluralistic* separatism. The Presbyterians had still to understand that the problem is not that of the differences between church and state solely but of differences between many groups, among which perhaps the state is the largest and most comprehensive.

When, therefore, the Synod of Philadelphia in 1729 denied "that the civil magistrate hath a controlling power over synods with respect to the exercise of their ministerial power; or power to persecute any for their religion," [5] it announced no new nor peculiarly American doctrine. It was merely repeating a principle of Presbyterianism as old as Andrew Melville and King James. It is hardly true to fact, therefore, to say of the Scotch-Irish Presbyterians, "To them we are indebted for the separation of church and state in our government." [6] They did not bring with them a radical notion of separatism as did the Baptists. They were familiar only with a *dualistic* separation. The *pluralistic* separatism of the Baptists was forced upon them by the exigencies of a pioneer society with its great diversity of sects, and they assimilated it only gradually. Not until May 28, 1787, did the Synods of New York and Philadelphia alter the Confession of Faith "so as to eliminate the principle of state-churchism and religious persecution and to proclaim the re-

---

[4] Figgis, *op. cit.*, p. 290.
[5] *Records of the Presbyterian Church*, pp. 94 f.
[6] R. D. W. Connor, *Race Elements in the Population of North Carolina*, 1920, p. 83.

ligious liberty and legal 'equality of all Christian denominations." [7]

A comparison of the proof texts cited when the Confession was adopted in 1647 and those cited to justify the changes made in 1788 when all traces of church-statism were eliminated is illuminating. The Confession of 1647 cites the Old Testament in support of the state-church ideal; the Confession as revised in 1788 cites the New Testament in justification of complete separation of church and state. An inspired and infallible Bible is quoted as authority in both cases and yet it is made to prove in 1788 exactly the opposite of what it was cited to establish in 1647. The dogma of an absolutely infallible Bible usually ends in self-stultification.

This background of historical facts must be borne in mind if we are to understand the conservative attitude of the Presbyterians in Virginia, their willingness at first to abide by the stipulations of the Act of Tolerance, and their refusal to come out unequivocally for disestablishment and the complete separation of church and state until political separation from England had been declared and the Bill of Rights with the famous sixteenth article of Mason and Madison had been adopted. It was then that the Hanover Presbytery drew up the memorial of October 24, 1777, repudiated to be sure in the memorial of October, 1784, but reasserted in that of August, 1785, taking the Bill of Rights "as the magna charta of our commonwealth" and joining hands with the Baptists in the struggle for disestablishment and complete separation of church and state. Of churches as of individuals, it may well be said that no man can escape from his past.

---

[7] Schaff, *Church and State in the United States*, papers of the American Historical Association, 1883, Vol. II, No. 4, 1888, p. 431.

II

The attempt is constantly being made by writers with ecclesiastical affiliations to prove that the ideas of leaders such as Madison, Patrick Henry, and Jefferson were derived from the dissenting groups, either Baptists or Presbyterians. We have alluded to the Presbyterian claims that Patrick Henry owed his ideas of religious liberty to the influence of the dissenting Presbyterian, Samuel Davies, and that Mason's and Madison's famous Article Sixteen of the Bill of Rights was anticipated in the memorial of the Hanover Presbytery. It has been claimed that Jefferson derived his ideas of democracy from watching a Baptist congregational meeting in his neighborhood.[8] Of Madison, to whom, even more than to Jefferson, goes the credit of having guided the liberal forces of Virginia to final victory, a Baptist writer asserts, "The great idea which he [Madison] put forth is identical with that which had always been devoutly cherished by our Baptist fathers, alike in the old world and the new, and which precisely a century and a half before had been perfectly expressed in the celebrated letter of Roger Williams to the people of his own settlement, and by him incorporated into the fundamental law of the colony of Rhode Island." Madison's philosophy, in other words, "is precisely the same with the 'soul liberty' so earnestly contended for by the Baptists of every age." [9] Even Catholic scholars, not to be outdone by Presbyterians and Baptists, claim that Jefferson and Madison owed their liberal ideas not to Locke and Sidney but to Cardinal Bellarmine.[10]

[8] Tracy, *The Great Awakening*, p. 419.
[9] C. F. James, *Documentary History of the Struggle for Religious Liberty in Virginia*, p. 135.
[10] See J. C. Rager, *Political Philosophy of Blessed Cardinal Bellarmine*,

For anyone conversant with the life and writings of Madison it is difficult to find any connection between his ideas as to church and state and the famous separatism and "soul liberty" of Roger Williams. That Madison was familiar with Williams' writing is doubtful and that he was familiar with Bellarmine is more than doubtful. Madison was a communicant of no church and does not seem to have been particularly religious. He was reared an Episcopalian and his most intimate friends, as an undergraduate at Princeton, were Caleb Wallace, Samuel Stanhope Smith, and John Blair Smith, Presbyterian clergymen who later played parts in the struggle for freedom in Virginia.[11] The man who perhaps influenced Madison most was President Witherspoon who took a special interest in him; after graduation Madison did a year of graduate work under Witherspoon's guidance.[12] It is at least possible that Madison was imbued with the idea of the separation of church and state by Witherspoon who brought to Princeton a strong antipathy to a state-controlled church as a result of his fight with the Moderates in Scotland.[13]

Madison in reality has very little in common with any of the dissenting sects. In regard to the assessment contest he said, "The Presbyterian clergy have at length espoused the cause of opposition, being moved either by fear of their laity or a jealousy of the Episcopalians. The mutual hatred of these sects

1926, pp. 34 ff.; James Brodrick, *Life and Work of Blessed Robert Francis Cardinal Bellarmine*, 1926, pp. 235 ff.; J. A. Ryan and M. F. X. Millar, *The State and the Church*, 1922, p. 118. The so-called "Bellarmine myth" has been subjected to a somewhat devastating analysis by Schaff, "The Bellarmine-Jefferson Legend and the Declaration of Independence," *American Society of Church History*, Vol. III, 1927.

[11] Gaillard Hunt, *James Madison and Religious Liberty*, Report of the American Historical Association, Vol. I, pp. 165 ff.

[12] W. C. Rives, *Life and Times of Madison, 1859-1868*, Vol. I, pp. 24 ff.

[13] V. L. Collins, *President Witherspoon*, 1925, Vol. I, Chap. 2; see also Vol. II, pp. 196 f.

has been much inflamed by the late act incorporating the latter. I am far from being sorry for it, as a coalition among them could alone endanger our religious rights, and a tendency to such an event has been suspected." [14] This is hardly the language of an admirer of the dissenting groups. He was fond of Voltaire's aphorism, "If one religion alone were allowed in England, the government would possibly become arbitrary; if there were two the people would cut each other's throats; but as there is such a multitude they all live happy and in peace." "In a free government," Madison added, "the security for civil rights must be the same as that for religious rights; it consists in the one case in a multiplicity of interests and in the other in the multiplicity of sects." [15]

Madison, Mason, and Jefferson had far more in common with the great traditions of freedom that go back to Sidney and Locke than with those of the leaders of the dissenters. Certainly one searches in vain for any influence of essentially dissenting ideas in Madison's great political broadside, *Memorial and Remonstrance*, which is perhaps the best statement of his position. This famous document starts with the phrase from Article Sixteen of the Virginia Bill of Rights, "Religion or the duty we owe our Creator, and the manner of discharging it, can be directed only by reason and conviction, not by force or violence." It follows that freedom of conscience is "in its nature an unalienable right." [16] In interpreting "unalienable" Madison invoked the familiar eighteenth-century philosophy of natural rights. "It is unalienable because the opinions of men, depending only on the evidence contemplated by their own minds,

[14] Madison, *Writings*, Vol. I, p. 175, quoted by James, *op. cit.*, p. 139.
[15] Quoted by Hunt, *op. cit.*, p. 170.
[16] The *Memorial and Remonstrance* is given by Rives, *op. cit.*, end of Volume I. See also James, *op. cit.*, pp. 256 ff. *Source Problems in United States History*, pp. 256 f.

can not follow the dictates of other men; it is unalienable also, because what is here a right towards men is a duty towards the Creator. . . . This duty is precedent, both in order of time and decree of obligation, to the claims of civil society. Before any man can be considered as a member of civil society, he must be considered as a subject of the Governor of the Universe; and if a member of a civil society, who enters into any subordinate association, must always do it with a reservation of his duty to the general authority, much more must every man who becomes a member of any particular civil society, do it with a saving of his allegiance to the Universal Sovereign. We maintain, therefore, that in matters of religion, no man's right is abridged by the institution of civil society, and that religion is wholly exempt from its cognizance."

On the basis of these fundamental assumptions, Madison proceeds to build up in clear-cut, logical fashion his argument against assessment. Since religion, from its very nature, lies outside the authority of society, it cannot be within the jurisdiction of any legislative body whose powers are derived and, hence, limited. Representatives of government, therefore, who presume to regulate religion transcend their powers and violate inalienable rights of the people, "and are tyrants."

The bills for the incorporation of an establishment and assessment for its support violate the principle of equality, "which ought to be the basis of every law," for, "if all men are by nature equally free and independent, all are to be considered as entering into society on equal conditions." Hence, all have "an equal title to the free exercise of religion according to the dictates of conscience." This freedom being a right that inheres in the individual primarily, we are not in the position to oppose by law the belief which another man arrives at in the exercise of this same individual right, although this belief may be diametrically opposed to our own. On all matters of religion a man is accountable only to his God.

Every bill in support of any religious establishment implies that the "civil magistrate is a competent judge of religious truth or that he may employ religion as an engine of civil policy. The first is an arrogant pretension, falsified by the contradictory opinion of rulers in all ages and throughout the world; the second, an unhallowed perversion of the means of salvation."

An establishment contradicts the nature of the Christian religion itself, "for every page of it disavows a dependence on the powers of this world." It originated and flourished without the support of human laws and even in spite of them. To demand political support for such a religion implies "that its friends are too conscious of its fallacies to trust it to its own merits."

The facts of history go to show that ecclesiastical establishments "instead of maintaining the purity and efficacy of religion, have had a contrary operation." This is due to the fact that rulers have prostituted holy religion in the interest of ends it was never designed to serve.

It is the boast of America that it offers an asylum for the oppressed of every nation. The bill proposing an establishment repudiates this claim and is, therefore, a violation of the American tradition. It is most unwise, for any state that supports an establishment will have a tendency to encourage men to seek other and more liberal communities and will prevent the immigration which is so much needed by pioneer communities.

Finally, an establishment is inimical to peace and harmony among rival sects. "Torrents of blood have been spilt in the old world by vain attempts of the secular arm to extinguish religious discord by proscribing all differences of religious opinion." The real solution is to be found in the opposite policy of complete religious liberty assured by equality of all sects before the law. An establishment dims the light of Christianity, enervates the laws and assumes the impossible task of settling issues of "singular magnitude and delicacy" by the crude method of a majority vote. This historic document was the first incisive statement of the ideal of religious liberty in this country.

In the light of our modern psychology and philosophy it is easy to pick flaws in this eighteenth-century philosophy of Madison. We now recognize that the so-called inalienable rights of life, liberty, pursuit of happiness, or the right to worship God according to the dictates of conscience, are really fictions of the imagination. A right is meaningless outside of a social situation. We may define a right as consisting of powers and capacities of the individual sanctioned and controlled by society. A right to worship God according to the dictates of our own conscience can no more exist outside of society than can the right to own property. It follows, therefore, that any attempt to base complete religious liberty on the assumption that we enjoy this liberty, or right, prior to the regulations of society and before a man enters into social relations involves us in psychological and sociological absurdities.

It is an interesting fact of history, however, that men do not live according to the principles of psychology or of science, but largely by the fictions of their own imaginations. When these great fictions, liberty, equality, fraternity, or freedom of conscience become suffused with intense emotion and render articulate the dearest loyalties of the masses of men, they take on a psychological reality, which is just as effective in influencing conduct and shaping the affairs of state as though they were objectively real. The immediate and incontrovertible reality of the emotional enthusiasm aroused by these fictions and voiced through them tends to overflow, as it were, and lend to them a spurious objective reality, which in the light of cold logic and the facts of psychology and history they do not possess. It is one of the paradoxes of life that the most valuable ideas are those which, from the standpoint of the prosaic realities of science and common sense, are pure illusions.

III

A perusal of the various petitions and memorials of the Baptists during this great struggle for religious liberty suggests that, so far as their philosophy of the relations of church and state is concerned, they had far more in common with the philosophical liberals than with the conservatives and Presbyterians. In an earlier chapter we have seen that in the radical separatism of Roger Williams and his Baptist predecessors, religion was completely divorced from the state and all social regulations upon the assumption of its essentially unique and spiritual character. For Roger Williams the state exists as an entity in and of itself with its own laws, systems of morals, judicial and legislative functions, entirely independent of religion. The state, owing to its inner logic and purpose, is not in the position to deal with religious problems. It follows, therefore, that in the radical separatist philosophy, the sanctions for religion are to be found solely in its spiritual and divine character. It belongs to a different sphere entirely from the state. It is spiritual; the state is secular. It is intimate, subjective, and personal; the state is public, objective, and social. The state is a creation of man and partakes of man's imperfection; religion reflects the finality and perfection of its divine Author.

This enables us to understand why the social note was conspicuously lacking in the petitions of the Baptists of Virginia. They were inclined to ignore entirely the fact that a church, from the nature of the case, must exist as a phase of a certain social order with all the social implications, rights, duties, and what not that this involves. We sense constantly a more or less tacit assumption that religion is essentially subjective, spiritual, and supernatural, involving only duties and obligations between the individual and his God. This intimate and spiritual note is to be traced back to the old dissenting doctrine of separatism with its notion of the sect composed of individuals who have had immediate personal experience of the saving grace of God, on the basis of which they have been baptized and voluntarily covenant with one another to live together separate from the world.

There is obviously a fundamental similarity between the doctrine of natural rights, as applied by the philosophical liberals to religion, and the spiritual separatism of the Baptists. In both cases we have a complete dualism. In the one case, it is a dualism between nature and nurture; in the other, it is a dualism between the spiritual and the secular. The Baptist separatist had but to substitute the fictions of the philosophy of natural rights for his theological fictions to find himself thoroughly at one with Madison and Jefferson. It is not surprising, therefore, to find John Leland, perhaps the ablest and most influential of all the Baptist leaders in Virginia at this time, writing an interesting tract, *Rights of Conscience and therefore Religious Opinions not cognizable by law, or, the High-Flying Churchman stript of his legal robes appears a Yaho,* 1791, naïvely identifying Baptist separatism with that of Jefferson. In it he makes this curious and for that age truly astonishing statement, "Government has no more to do with the religious opinions of men than it has with the principle of mathematics." [17] This at once suggests the ideas of Jefferson, of which the following is

[17] P. 13.

typical: "Our civil rights have no dependence on our religious opinions any more than our opinions in physics or geometry." [18]

There was, however, a fundamental difference between the dissenters and the philosophical liberals. For the latter there was but one dualism, that of nature and nurture; for the dissenters there were two, nature and nurture, and the church and the world. These were fused by the Baptists and, to a less extent, by the Presbyterians in the sense that the fictions of the theological imagination upon which they based their separatism were identified with the fictions of the philosophical imagination in terms of which Madison and Jefferson justified their separatism. The dualism of nature and nurture, natural rights and civil rights, upon which the thought of Madison turned, was not Christian. It went back through Locke, Grotius, Aquinas, Ambrose, Cicero, and the Roman Stoics to Panaetius and the Greeks. [19] The thought of the Baptist separatist was thus double-faced like Janus, the Roman god of the doorway, looking both towards the outer world of society and the inner spiritual world of the eternal verities of the Kingdom of God. The political and philosophical side of their thought was but the obverse of the theological. Madison and the philosophical liberals had no place for the fictions of the theological imagination. In this respect they followed the lead of Locke who had already begun to divorce the great doctrine of natural rights from all theological and ecclesiastical trappings.

IV

It is an interesting fact that all questions of freedom in the American colonies during the latter part of the eighteenth cen-

[18] *Common Place Book*, quoted by Gilbert Chinard, *Thomas Jefferson*, 1929, p. 102.
[19] Ritchie, *Natural Rights*.

tury turned upon the interpretation given to the great fictions of natural rights. If we ask why Massachusetts, after having fought a great war on the basis of the lofty doctrines of the Declaration of Independence, still stubbornly maintained her establishment and denied to her dissenting citizenship the freedom she demanded from England, the explanation is to be found in her interpretation of the doctrine of natural rights. Massachusetts and New England never accepted wholeheartedly the doctrine of natural rights, as did the great Virginians with their dissenting supporters. To be sure, there is in that jumble of confused and irreconcilable ideas, the Bill of Rights laid down in the Massachusetts constitution of 1780, a magnificent gesture of homage to "the right as well as the duty of all men . . . to worship the supreme Being" in their own way, but this is immediately followed by regulations for the maintenance of an establishment. The muddle-headedness of this famous document merely reflected the muddle-headedness of a state that never was able to include the dissenter within the charmed circle of the magical formulas of natural rights by which she justified her political independence.

Articles Two and Three of the Declaration of Rights reflect two factors in Massachusetts culture which had existed side by side, more or less, even from the seventeenth century but which had never been reconciled, namely, the philosophy of the establishment and the philosophy of natural rights which received spectacular dramatization in the American and French revolutions. The older and by far the more deeply ingrained in the culture of Massachusetts was the philosophy of the establishment. It needs only a cursory examination of articles Two and Three to convince one that in the minds of the men who drafted them and of the voters who adopted them the habits of thought and conduct gained through the stern discipline of the theocracy of the seventeenth century and the modified establishment of the eighteenth century, were final and authoritative. Loyalty to inalienable rights of conscience was at best merely superficial and sentimental. It may well be doubted whether there was a single Massachusetts leader, outside the ranks of the dissenters, who really grasped the full implications of the phrase "inalienable rights of conscience."

To be sure, much has been made of the educative work of the Massachusetts clergy in thundering from their pulpits the unalterable and inalienable rights of the colonists to revolt from England.[20] A member of the "filial piety" school of historians has even claimed that when John Wise of Ipswich published his *Vindication of the Government of the New England Churches* in 1717 he "laid down the everlasting principles of democracy" and anticipated Jefferson by half a century or more in his championship of natural rights.[21] But a perusal of Wise's *Vindication* brings out the fact that his thought moved entirely within the circle of the philosophy of the establishment. Wise merely made use of the doctrine of natural rights to justify the more democratic Congregational party in their opposition to the Presbyterianizing party led by the Mathers. One looks in vain for any evidence that Wise ever applied these magical formulas to the rights of the dissenters at his door. For Wise, reason, nature, and divine revelation were ultimately one, for "each is equally an emanation of God's wisdom."[22] The New England establishment was sanctioned for Wise by divine revelation, by right reason and nature. How was it possible for the dissenters ever to enjoy the benefits of the great doctrines of natural rights in the thought of man thus circum-

[20] Baldwin, *The New England Clergy in the American Revolution.*
[21] H. M. Dexter, *Address on John Wise.*
[22] Wise, *op. cit.*, p. 22.

scribed? The clergy maintained this position down to the end
of the century.

The problem of the rights of the dissenters really struck the
"blind spot" in the social imagination of the New England
authorities. Even in the thought of as liberal a statesman as Sam
Adams the great fictions of natural rights did not include the
rights of conscience of lowly dissenters. This seems all the more
remarkable since Sam Adams had much in common with Jefferson and was on the committee with Jefferson to draft the
Declaration. On two occasions he had an opportunity to apply
his radical democratic ideals to the problem of the dissenters,
namely, when he was present at the famous conference with
the representatives of the Massachusetts dissenters in Philadelphia in 1774 and when he presided over the meeting of the
freeholders of Boston in 1780 to discuss the famous articles Two
and Three of the Massachusetts constitution on religion.[23] Yet
we have no evidence that Massachusetts' great protagonist of
freedom ever sympathized with Madison, Jefferson, and the
leaders of dissent in their comprehensive application of the
great fictions of natural rights to the problem of the dissenting
minorities.

V

The place that inalienable rights played in the thought of the
clergy was not essentially different from the place they occupied
in the philosophy of the powerful group of merchants and
lawyers from which sprang the "Essex Junto," the original
germ of the Federalism destined to dominate Massachusetts
for a generation. The position of this group was stated in an
able pamphlet, *The Essex Result,* probably by Theophilus

[23] *Boston Gazette,* May 12, 1780.

Parsons of Newburyport, published in 1778.[24] It epitomized
the political and economic philosophy of the Federalist group
in the form of a searching criticism of the constitution drafted
by the assembly in 1778 and probably had much to do with its
rejection.[25] This closely reasoned broadside, like the deliverances of all groups at this time, paid due homage to the magical
formulas of natural rights. "All men are born equally free" [26]
with certain natural rights. Some of these rights are alienable
and some inalienable and among the latter are "the rights of
conscience." These inalienable rights are "determinable by right
reason, which may be and is called a well informed conscience." [27] On entering into social relations a man surrenders
rights that are essentially unalienable in character for an adequate equivalent. "This equivalent consists principally in the
security of his person and property." [28] The function of the
state is to protect the civil rights which a man accepts in lieu of
his natural rights, surrendered when he becomes a member of
society.

After paying lip homage to inalienable rights of conscience,
the author proceeds to draft the plan of a social order in which
power is placed in the hands of the propertied and cultured
classes. The writer of this pamphlet was apparently unaware of
the absurdity of trying to reconcile the fiction of inalienable
rights of conscience with rights of property in any social order
where the latter are really paramount. For obviously the pure
fiction of "unalienable rights of conscience" cannot compete
with the brute fact of the predominance of rights of property.
Any attempt on the part of the dissenter to take seriously the

[24] Theophilus Parsons, Jr., *Memoir of Theophilus Parsons*, 1859, pp. 358 ff.
[25] A. E. Morse, *The Federalist Party in Massachusetts*, 1909, p. 18.
[26] T. Parsons, *op. cit.*, p. 365.
[27] *Ibid.*, p. 365.
[28] *Ibid.*, p. 367.

much-vaunted "unalienable right" to worship God according
to the dictates of conscience involves necessarily immunity
from ministers' rates and the right to own church property and
to dispose of money and property freely in all religious matters.
To tax a dissenter's property to support a religious establishment not sanctioned by his conscience is merely to subordinate
rights of persons and the much eulogized "unalienable rights
of conscience" to rights of property. The political leaders of
Massachusetts never were able to draw this distinction and make
it valid in law. This explains the muddle-headedness of articles
Two and Three in the constitution of 1780. This pamphlet
suggests the position that natural rights occupied in Federalism
and explains also the economic basis of the vitality of the establishment and the continued persecution of the dissenters. During
the glorious period of the Revolution it was property rather
than rights of conscience that spoke the last word in Massachusetts as to the status of dissent.

VI

It was unfortunate that dissent in New England lacked the
numbers and the leadership that would have enabled it to capitalize the liberalism that accompanied the Revolution. The dissenting leaders were unable to utilize the great slogans of
natural rights. They were forced to argue the matter from the
utilitarian and mercenary point of view of the ruling propertied
classes. Backus, the ablest of the dissenting leaders, was a sincere but unlearned man and was hardly equal to the tasks that
faced him. In *The Independent Chronicle*, December 2, 1779,
he accepted the opening statement of the much-debated Article
Three of the constitution of 1780 that the happiness and good
order of society "essentially depend upon piety, religion and

morality" and that to this end public instruction in piety and religion are necessary. Backus even claimed that "to teach piety, religion and morality without Jesus Christ is the depth of pagan darkness." A critic asserted that in making these concessions Backus surrendered the case of the Baptists with their insistence upon separation of church and state.[29] What Backus objected to, of course, was the teaching of piety and morals through an established church. The supporters of the establishment contended that Backus could not concede that good morals and the highest type of citizenship depend upon Christian piety and deny the right of the state to provide effective instruction in matters of such transcendent importance without being inconsistent.

Backus cluttered up his public statements on behalf of the dissenters with lengthy citations from the more spiritual utterances of Jesus and the writers of the New Testament in favor of liberty of conscience and the separation of church and state. The clergy could easily offset these with citations from the Old Testament in favor of a state religion and, as both were quoting from a presumably infallible Book, the result was that the argument became all the more confused. When Backus praised "the perfect spiritual nature of Christ's kingdom," he suggested the radical separation of Roger Williams and the seventeenth-century Baptists. But when he conceded to his opponents their central contention and said, "To teach piety, religion and morals without Jesus Christ is the depth of pagan darkness," he repudiated radical separation and assumed responsibility for the solution of a problem for which in reality he had no solution, namely, the training of a citizenship in which the sanctions of public morals are drawn from the teachings of Protestant Christianity. The position of Backus is still held, in theory

[29] William Gordon, *The Independent Chronicle*, May 18, 1780.

at least, by the great dissenting-revivalistic churches and they are still as far from a solution of the problem as he was.[30]

By far the most enlightened and penetrating of all the discussions of the famous Article Three of the constitution was from the pen of "Philanthropos," [31] presumably a Baptist,[32] who went directly to the heart of the matter in his opening statement, "For if by piety we are to understand real goodness of heart or 'true heart religion' it is not true that 'preservation of civil government essentially depends upon it.' " Piety in the strictly religious sense is not essential either to morals or good government. Civil government in fact does exist without piety. The majority of the inhabitants of even Christian commonwealths are devoid of piety. Past history is replete with the records of great states with admirable laws in which Christian piety was utterly unknown. Here we detect an echo of Roger Williams. Furthermore, insists delightfully clear-headed "Philanthropos," if "the preservation of civil government *essentially depends upon piety*, it follows that it is *essentially necessary* that the Governor, the Council and the Representatives of the people should be *men of piety*." [33] This would necessitate "an inquisition" in the case of all public officials and politicians to see whether the root of the matter, Christian piety, is in them. The suggestion is intriguing and at the same time preposterous. Such a test of citizenship wipes out the lines of demarcation between church and state. In particular, it destroys the integrity and authority of the state. Here again we are reminded of Roger Williams.

Morality, as opposed to piety, "Philanthropos" defines as "an upright conduct of the citizens of this commonwealth to-

[30] See J. M. Mecklin, *An Introduction to Social Ethics*, Chap. 15.
[31] *The Independent Chronicle*, March 2, 16, 23, and April 6, 13, 1780.
[32] Backus, *History of the Baptists*, Vol. II, p. 227.
[33] *The Independent Chronicle*, March 2, 1780.

wards each other." The necessity of moral conduct in this sense is basic for "the preservation and good order of the state." The good magistrate punishes the evil-doers "not because they sin against God but because they sin against the state." Morality of this sort "has nothing of Christianity in it." It is a universal trait found wherever there is a well-ordered state, whether that state be Christian or pagan. This sort of morality does not need Christian teachers for its propagation. "Philanthropos" did not go into the delicate and difficult question as to whether such a secularized morality existed in Massachusetts in 1780. Neither did he raise the question as to whether in communities such as New England, where religion and morals were inextricably blended, any appeal to moral sentiment would be forced to reckon with institutionalized religion. It was a great interpreter of the Constitution who wrote, "Things which, estimated by the prevailing community standards, are profane and blasphemous, are properly punished as crimes against society since . . . they have a direct tendency to undermine the moral support of the laws and to corrupt the community." [34] Obviously "Philanthropos" had far more in common with the radical separatism of Roger Williams than with the nondescript attitude of Isaac Backus.

VII

It should be evident from this and foregoing chapters that the greatest single obstacle to complete religious liberty in Massachusetts in 1780 and earlier was the confusion of leaders of church and state as to the real meaning of rights of conscience. This confusion is to be traced directly to the insidiously educative effect upon the minds of men of the selfish and sin-

[34] T. M. Cooley, *A Treatise on Constitutional Limitations*, 1890, Chap. 13, p. 676.

ister partnership between religion and vested interests. "A member of the convention" in his reply to Backus said, "A man might lawfully support a worship which he could not in conscience attend: For such a worship, however erroneous he might judge it to be, with regard to the terms of salvation, might still inculcate such precepts of morality as might be the means of securing to and protecting him in the quiet possession of his just rights and *it is certainly proper that a man should pay for his protection.*" [35] The minister's rate was a good business investment in the eyes of the tax-paying propertied group because it enabled the state to hire approved teachers of a conservative ethics that safeguarded their rights of property and their privileged position. Against such a philosophy of society, voicing as it did the selfish interests of powerful conservative groups, the dissenting-revivalistic piety made little headway with its idealistic appeal for the separation of church and state. The most unlovely phase of the long struggle between dissent and the Massachusetts establishment during the eighteenth and the first quarter of the nineteenth century was undoubtedly this constant emphasis of the purely mercenary motive. In the debates, the legislative acts, and the public utterances of political and even of religious leaders there is an utter absence of any note of idealism or any recognition of the lofty moral and spiritual values at stake. Along with Yankee "simplicity and frugality" which impressed the founder of American Methodism, Bishop Asbury,[36] went other traits which led Washington to remark, "Notwithstanding all the public virtue which is ascribed (to New Englanders) there is no nation under the sun (that I ever came across) pay greater adoration to money than

---

[35] *The Independent Chronicle,* February 10, 1780.
[36] Francis Asbury, *Journal,* Vol. II, p. 381.

they do." [37] Washington's generalization finds interesting corroboration in the comment of William Ellery Channing during his sojourn in Virginia, 1798-1800: "I blush for my own people when I compare the selfish prudence of a Yankee with the generous confidence of a Virginian. Here I find great vices but greater virtues than I left behind me. There is one single trait that attaches me to the people I live with more than all the virtues of New England. They *love money less* than we do. They are more disinterested. Their patriotism is not tied to their purse strings." [38] Purely mercenary motives had long taken precedence over any regard for conscientious scruples of the dissenter. As we shall soon see, it was only after the famous Dedham decision of 1820 had made it possible to tax orthodox Trinitarian Congregationalists to support established churches served by Unitarian ministers and the question of religious liberty had become tied to the purse strings that the way was paved for the complete deliverance of the long-suffering dissenter.

[37] Cited by J. T. Adams, *Revolutionary New England*, p. 436.
[38] *Memoir of William Ellery Channing*, 1851, Vol. I, pp. 82 f.

Chapter XIII: The Passing of the Old Firm of Moses and Aaron

B Y THE end of the eighteenth century forces were at work in Massachusetts and Connecticut destined in time to destroy the unholy alliance between the church and the selfish vested interests voiced in Federalism that blocked the way to freedom for the dissenters. These forces were partly religious, partly political and economic. The rapid increase of the dissenters was a constant and growing menace to the establishment. By 1795 the Baptists had 136 churches, 110 ministers and 8,667 members in Massachusetts. Their total membership in New England was 21,922. The Baptists, to be sure, were never as numerous and as influential in New England as in the South. In Virginia, for example, they boasted in 1790 an enrollment of 22,500 members or more than in the whole of New England.[1] They were, however, a force constantly to be reckoned with and they were increasing.

In the convention called for the adoption of the Federal Constitution the Baptists were the strongest dissenting group, having twenty representatives. Backus favored adoption but the bulk of the Baptist delegates voted against it, primarily because it contained no express guarantee of individual rights of conscience. The Baptists in Virginia, headed by the veteran

[1] John Asplund, *The Annual Register of the Baptist Denomination in North America to November 1, 1790*, p. 82.

John Leland, opposed ratification for the same reason. The liberals Randolph and Madison, with deeper insight into the problem, supported ratification on the ground that the Constitution placed all sects upon the same basis. They saw in the free competition among a multiplicity of sects the best guarantee of liberty. At the last moment Leland, who was sure of election from Orange County, withdrew in favor of Madison, a proof of Baptist confidence in the latter's political wisdom.[2] Madison had much to do with Virginia's ratification of the Constitution.

It was Baptist votes that sent Madison to the first congress in 1789, and it would appear that the Baptists were the only religious group that came out strongly in support of Madison's famous first amendment. A committee of Baptists headed by John Leland sought to unite the Baptists of Virginia and the South with those of New England in support of Madison's amendment. It has even been suggested that Madison's reference in his speech in support of his amendments to "a great number of our constituents who are dissatisfied with it [the Constitution], among whom are many respectable for their talents and patriotism, and respectable for the jealousy they have for their liberty" applied to the Baptists who had opposed the Constitution because of its lack of adequate guarantees of religious liberty.[3] It is probably claiming too much to say, "To the Baptists beyond a doubt belongs the glory of engrafting its best article on the noblest Constitution ever framed for the government of mankind." [4] But there can be no doubt that

---

[2] Humphrey, *Nationalism and Religion in America*, pp. 470 ff.

[3] C. F. James, *Documentary History of the Struggle for Religious Liberty in Virginia*, pp. 159 ff. The letter of the Baptist committee to President Washington seeking assurance of religious liberty in the Constitution was penned by Leland and is given by James, *op. cit.*, pp. 171 f.

[4] James, *op. cit.*, p. 168.

the first amendment states, though in restricted fashion, the great Baptist principle of complete separation of church and state. The first amendment may be truly called the Magna Charta of our religious liberties, for the embodiment in the Constitution of the Baptist doctrine of separatism was bound to exercise a steady pressure upon all the states so that by the end of the fourth decade of the nineteenth century complete separation of church and state had been embodied in all the state constitutions.[5]

II

During the last decade of the century the Methodists were spreading rapidly in New England. They had found it necessary to break with the parent church and draw up in 1784 "A Form of Discipline," repudiating "a national establishment which we cordially abhor as the bane of truth and holiness, the greatest impediment in the world to the progress of vital Christianity." [6] From this time on the Methodists made common cause with the dissenters.

The Methodist Discipline begins with the query, "What may we reasonably believe to be God's design in raising up the preachers called Methodists?" To this the answer is, "To reform the continent and spread Scripture holiness over these lands." It is not surprising, therefore, that a religious movement seeking moral reform combined with a revivalistic piety, the goal of which was perfect holiness in the individual, did not find in New England particularly congenial soil. This is shown in the pungent comments in the *Journal* of the patron saint of American Methodism, Bishop Asbury. His first reaction to

[5] Humphrey, *op. cit.*, pp. 487 ff.
[6] *Methodist Form of Discipline*, 1787, pp. 1 ff.

New England was, "I do feel as if there had been religion in this country once; and I apprehend there is little in form and theory left." [7] As he preached, "some smiled, some laughed, some swore, some talked, some prayed, some wept." [8] The preacher was uncomfortable and his impression of the people "unfavorable." "Never have I seen any people who would talk so long, so correctly and so seriously about trifles." [9] The Yale students came "like other *very genteel* people to mock and deride; but God struck some of the vilest of them." [10] Boston, especially, seems to have aroused his evangelical scorn. He characterized it as a town of "theaters, sinners, blind priests and backsliding formal people and multitudes who are gospel hardened." Quite fittingly, God punished this perverse town at the time of his visit with a most malignant fever so that many were "buried in the night, without any tolling of bells or funeral solemnity, thrown into a coarse coffin or tar sheet." [11] A visit of Asbury should have filled the people of Boston with panic fear. Characteristic of the practical piety of the Methodist was his remark, "The great wants of Boston are good religion and good water." [12]

Two things in Massachusetts society offended Asbury in particular, its respectability and its priests. "Out of fifteen United States, thirteen are free, but two are fettered with ecclesiastical chains. . . . My simple prophecy is that this must come to an end with the present century. The Rhode Islanders began in time and are free; hail sons of liberty! Who first began the war? Was it not Connecticut and Massachusetts and priests are now saddled upon them. O what a happy people these would

[7] Francis Asbury, *Journal*, Vol. II, p. 102, June 4, 1791.
[8] *Ibid.*, p. 103.   [11] *Ibid.*, p. 323, August 5, 1798.
[9] *Ibid.*, p. 112.   [12] *Ibid.*, Vol. III, p. 105.
[10] *Ibid.*, p. 86.

be if they were not thus priest-ridden." [13] In another connection he remarks, "How can this city [Boston] and Massachusetts be in any other than a melancholy state; worse perhaps for true piety than any other parts of the Union: What! reading priests, and alive? . . . I could tell of a congregation that sold their priest to another congregation in Boston for the sum of one thousand dollars; and hired out the money at the unlawful interest of twenty-five or thirty per cent. Lord have mercy upon the priest and people that can think of buying the kingdom of heaven with money! How would it tell to the South, that priests were among the notions of Yankee traffic?" [14]

The "respectability" by which Asbury characterized the more or less smug self-sufficiency that marked the privileged classes in New England society at this time was especially offensive to this champion of the religion of the disinherited. The Yale students were offensive because they were "very genteel." The worst criticism he could make of the Quakers, with whom he fell into controversy, was that they were "respectable." "Ah! there is death in that word," says the ascetic Methodist leader. "I fear what is properly the reproach of Christ has long been wiped away from this *respectable people*." [15] It was indeed a curious turn of the wheel of fortune that transformed the erstwhile despised and rejected Quakers, who once gloried in the fact, into the respectable and esteemed citizens, while the position they once occupied was taken by the Methodists. Typical of the "respectable" status of many Quakers was the position of William Northey in Salem, sketched by William Bentley in his *Diary*.[16]

Doubtless no other passage in holy writ has given the despised and disinherited dissenter more comfort than this:

13 *Ibid.*, Vol. II, p. 199.   15 *Ibid.*, p. 265.
14 *Ibid.*, Vol. III, pp. 105, 106.   16 Vol. III, pp. 93 f. See also pp. 419 f.

"Blessed are ye when men shall revile you and persecute you and shall say all manner of evil against you falsely for my sake." This was the sign manual of divine favor and there is practically no limit to the auto-suggestive power of the man who feels that he is a martyr. Men do not despise and persecute the "respectable" man; hence the very easy inference that respectability and spiritual worth are incompatible terms. The church which Asbury labored in sickness and health to found has flourished mightily. Today the Methodist church with its far-flung organization, its institutions of learning, its mission enterprises and millions of property is not only respectable but is feared and flattered and its leaders, sitting close to the seats of the mighty, have sought to shape the laws of the nation. If, as Asbury imagined, power and respectability and the praise of men are indications of loss of spiritual worth, then the Methodist church of today would prove a bitter disappointment to its founder.

The road to respectability which the dissenting Methodist was destined to travel was very similar to that already traveled by the "respectable" Quaker and the near-respectable Baptist. In fact, the treatment of the Methodists in New England suggests the treatment of the Baptists forty years earlier in Virginia. They were forced to preach in barns, taverns, court rooms, kitchens, though they were sometimes tendered the use of Sandemanian, Separatist, or Baptist churches. Asbury complained constantly of the lack of hospitality as opposed to the treatment accorded him in the South. The preachers were often hustled by the mob. In Lancaster, New Hampshire, the crowd carried off a Methodist preacher "and ducked him in the river with shouts." [17] As a rule, this persecution was more or less

[17] A. Stevens, *Memorials of the Introduction of Methodism into the Eastern States*, 2nd series, 1852, p. 144.

harmless, such as casting stones and snowballs, setting the dogs on them or frightening their horses,[18] though not always.[19] Occasionally there were fines, seizures of goods, and imprisonment. The clergy found the Methodists especially obnoxious because of their unorthodox theology and from their pulpits "kept up a weekly cannonading" against them. The aristocratic, class-conscious, and bigoted clergy were the embodiment of many qualities the Methodists opposed as incompatible with true religion.

On the whole, this latest addition to the dissenting groups found hard sledding in New England. "They were denounced from pulpits, maltreated in the courts, interrupted in the course of their sermons with charges of heresy, and assailed in the streets by the rabble. Washburn was hooted through the villages; Hedding cursed with outcries on the highway; Dow's nose was publicly wrung; Sabin was knocked down and struck on the head to the peril of his life with the butt of a gun; Wood was horse-whipped; Christie summoned out of bed to answer a charge of violating the laws by marrying a couple of his people; Willard wounded in the eye by a blow, the effects of which he still shows; Mudge denied the rights of a clergyman and arraigned before the magistrate for assuming them; Kibby stoned while preaching and Taylor drummed out of town." [20] These persecutions were at their worst from 1795 to 1805 when they began to die out. This was doubtless due in part to increase in numbers. By the end of 1805 the Methodists numbered over ten thousand in New England and were increasing rapidly. Even the struggling Boston society showed a gain.[21] The greatest gains were in the pioneer states of Maine (then

[18] *Ibid.*, p. 151.   [20] *Ibid.*, p. 206.
[19] *Ibid.*, p. 76.   [21] *Ibid.*, p. 207.

part of Massachusetts), New Hampshire, Vermont, and western Massachusetts.

Church rates were demanded of Methodists as in the case of other dissenters. Asbury asserts that in 1793 in Needham, Massachusetts, "the majority of the people prefer the Methodist preachers; and want to pay them by a tax on the people, but brothers Smith and Hill absolutely refused this plan; for which I commend them." [22] Church rates were subsequently taken from the Needham Methodists to the amount of over a hundred dollars.[23] The Methodists refused to fit into the establishment even when it was to their advantage. Their societies became incorporated, as in the case of the Lynn society, "to prevent the Methodists from being obliged by law to pay Congregational tax." [24]

Towards the close of the eighteenth century it is possible to detect a subtle change in the treatment of the dissenters in Massachusetts. In 1794 a Baptist of Medford was seized for church tax and imprisoned in Boston. "But it caused such an alarm in Boston and the news from thence which reached Medford the next Saturday caused such an alarm there that two men were sent twenty miles on the Lord's day, who released the prisoner, without paying the tax or any cost about it. And very few now in our country will dare make distress upon any for ministerial taxes." [25] This was quite a change from the treatment of the Baptist exhorter in Hingham in 1782. By 1805 persecution of Methodists had practically ceased and by 1810 the Methodists in Pittsfield, Massachusetts, were holding prayer-meetings in the house of the Congregationalists.[26] The stigma

---

[22] Op. cit., Vol. II, p. 172.
[23] Ibid., Vol. III, p. 70, 1802.
[24] Ibid., Vol. II, p. 198.
[25] Backus, History of the Baptists, Vol. II, p. 379.
[26] Asbury, op. cit., Vol. III, p. 289.

of Methodism, to be sure, still lingered. Asbury found it expedient to preach in the evening for "at the stated hours people ought to attend their own places of worship"—the New Englander was still in John Adams' phrase "a meeting-going animal." Furthermore, Asbury preferred to preach under cover of night "because I knew there were not a few who were ashamed to be seen going to a Methodist meeting." [27] Open persecution, however, had practically disappeared. Powerful national forces were beginning to make themselves felt, even in intransigent Massachusetts, to the advantage of dissent.

III

Most important for the cause of dissent in Massachusetts was the spread of a healthful diversity of opinions in politics in the bitter controversy engendered by the impact of Jeffersonianism upon the arrogant and intolerant Federalism.

It was the conservative poet Aristophanes who called Socrates "the gadfly of Athens." From 1800 Jefferson with his liberal ideas became the political and religious "gadfly" of the provincial and self-centered New England establishments. For reasons that are perfectly obvious, his ideas never penetrated New England thought and life. They presupposed an agrarian and pioneer society and New England was just making the transition from a farming and seafaring to a manufacturing community. As a rule, radical political or social ideologies spring up in the attempt to rationalize unconscious needs and frustrated wishes caused by deep-seated maladjustments. This was true of the great ideologies of the American and French revolutions. In New England the normal process of history was reversed and the ideas of Jefferson were superinduced upon New

[27] *Ibid.*, p. 290.

England society as a result of movements of a national and international character lying outside New England. The New Englander was forced to discuss Jefferson's ideas, to vote on them and to undergo the very uncomfortable experience of seeing them made the basis of national policies. These ideas did not cause a revolution but they did arouse in groups and individuals a sense of inequalities and injustices which before had been taken as part of the eternal order of things. Jeffersonianism became the philosophy of the politically and religiously disinherited.

Jeffersonianism was not able to supplant Federalism, for the latter was singularly well adapted to the pattern of New England culture, especially in the states of Connecticut and Massachusetts with their establishments. The merchants and bankers held the purse-strings in the closed corporation of Federalism; the lawyers provided the brains and technical skill necessary for the proper manipulation of law and government in the interest of the aristocracy; the office-holders looked after the votes during elections; the clergy provided the sanctions of good morals and holy religion which, "like the precious ointment upon the head, that ran down upon the beard, even Aaron's beard," lent to the whole selfish combination a certain odor of sanctity. "The old firm of Moses and Aaron" had become almost indispensable to the New Englander's philosophy of life.

Now for the first time in two hundred years effective opposition had arisen to the entrenched and privileged groups, necessitating the give and take of ideas and the development of a healthful public sentiment. It was an uncomfortable because a wholly unwonted experience for the old Bay state. Lack of experience and tested traditions of free speech explain the crude

and abusive nature of this clash of ideas. Before Massachusetts
could develop a national point of view she had to learn to discuss national issues intelligently and tolerantly. How very difficult it was for the Bay state to accept a national point of view
that failed to coincide with her own is shown by an incident in
Salem in 1804. When the fourth of July was celebrated in the
church of the Republican Bentley, the Federalists could not
stomach the sight of the front of the pulpit of an established
church decorated with an "elegant engraving of Jefferson who
was also displayed on the front gallery on glass of gold," but
got up a procession of their own with "oration, entertainment,
etc." [28] Thus did a petty provincialism assert its essentially anti-
nationalistic point of view.

IV

A brilliant champion of Jeffersonianism and the cause of dissent in New England was Abraham Bishop, who was something
of a radical. Was restraint to be expected in Republican leaders
in a thoroughly hostile environment where they were constantly
exposed to thrusts such as that from the exquisite snob, Fisher
Ames, who said à propos of a proposed Federalist paper, *The
Palladium*, "It should whip Jacobins [Republicans] as a gentleman would a chimney-sweep, at arm's length, keeping aloof
from his soot"? [29] A lady of Boston society said, "I should as
soon have expected to see a cow in a drawing room as a
Jacobin." [30] It was against this snobbishness that Bishop revolted
and the very impudent abandon of his language is especially
illuminating as giving the reactions of a man thoroughly im-

[28] *Diary of William Bentley*, Vol. III, p. 97.
[29] Cited by Morse, *The Federalist Party in Massachusetts*, p. 199, footnote.
[30] J. W. Chadwick, *William Ellery Channing*, 1903, p. 67.

bued with the great ideas of Jefferson and the French Revolution.[31]

With unerring instinct Bishop recognized that the archenemy of the ideas of Jefferson and the citadel of intolerance and obscurantism in New England was the old firm of Moses and Aaron, or the establishments, and against them, therefore, he directed the brunt of all his attacks. "Moses and Aaron find it profitable to walk hand in hand. The clergyman preaches politics, the civilian prates of orthodoxy, and if any man refuses to join the coalition they endeavor to hunt him down to the tune, 'The church is in danger.'" Such a situation inevitably warps the characters of men. "When a foreigner enquired of one of our citizens what was the most characteristic trait of New England, the frank answer was this, *We are taught hypocrisy from our cradles;* and such an answer will always be true, till Moses and Aaron shall be content to labor separately in their vocations. The character of those who join this coalition from motives of convenience may be well imagined. They are hypocrits and *having no righteousness of their own they affect to trade on the old stock, and are always exclaiming about the piety of our forefathers.*" [32]

To the Jeffersonian liberal the much praised moral asset of "steady habits" associated with the establishment was often a delusion and a snare. For just as "the sailor nailed the needle of his compass on the cardinal point and swore that it should

[31] For Bishop's life see Professor W. A. Robinson's sketch in the *Dictionary of American Biography*. Bishop's ideas are found in his Phi Beta Kappa oration at Yale, 1800, on "The Extent and Power of Political Illusion," which the college authorities would not let him deliver; his "Wallingford Oration," March 11, 1801, in celebration of Jefferson's election; his "Proofs of a Conspiracy," 1802, a slashing arraignment of the New England establishments; and his "Oration in Honor of the Election of Jefferson and the Acquisition of Louisiana," 1804. The most important for our purposes is the "Wallingford Oration."

[32] "Oration in Wallingford, Connecticut," 1801, p. 13.

not be always traversing, so does the New England friend of order: but he cautiously conceals the oppression and imposture which sustain these habits." This slogan of "steady habits" exerts "a talismanic effect upon the minds of our people" so as to blind them to all new truth and block the way to progress. "Paul was a setter-up of strange gods: but the handwriting of ordinances, that sacred palladium of steady habits, was nailed to the cross and by virtue of this very innovation you, the people of New England, claim to be the heirs of the new covenant." Are the "steady habits" of New England "so very sacred as to arrest the progress of truth? Are the men who profit by these habits so very learned as to be able to pronounce our state of society the best possible? Surely the world before has produced their equals." [33]

More important still is the effect of "steady habits" on the higher values of life. "Let us now see whether our steady habits have not calmly assumed dominion over the rights of conscience and suffrage. Certainly the Trinitarian doctrine is established by law and the denial of it is placed in the rank of felonies. Though we have ceased to transport from town to town Quakers, New Lights and Baptists; yet the dissenters from our prevailing denomination are even at this moment praying for the repeal of those laws which abridge the rights of conscience. By virtue of steady habits obsequiousness to the clergy is accepted in lieu of respect for religion." The catholic and humanizing spirit of Jeffersonianism prompts finally a vigorous protest against the ingrained provincialism seen in "the *clannish* character of New England, the consequence of our almost general derivation from one country, the family alliances, producing patriarchs in opinion and the too general habit of whole towns committing to a few individuals the power to dictate to. them

[33] *Ibid.*, pp. 14 f.

opinions on all subjects." The situation is not a new one, "for the same union of church and state, the same proud boast of pure morals, superior science and the same national pride throughout characterized the Jews, Catholics and all the tyrannies of the earth." [34] This was strong medicine for the stomachs of "the unspotted lambs of the Lord" but it was needed.

V

Jeffersonianism and dissent showed their spiritual kinship in that both tended to take root and flourish in the same sections, such as the frontier religions of Vermont, New Hampshire, and Maine. [35] The democratic Republican ideas also found congenial soil in those parts of Massachusetts where dissenters were numerous, such as the rural population of the Old Colony counties of Plymouth, Bristol, and Barnstable, the fisherfolk of the Cape, the farmers of Essex and Middlesex, and portions of the Berkshires where Baptists and Methodists were increasing rapidly. [36] The loyalty of Berkshire dissenters to Jefferson is illustrated by the following incident. Reverend John Leland, a native of Worcester County, who had served the Baptist cause in Virginia until the separation of church and state in 1786, returned to his native state in 1791. In 1808 "while he was settled in Cheshire (in the Berkshires) the farmers around him made a mammoth cheese, weighing thirteen hundred pounds, and sent it by him as a present to President Jefferson. Mr. Leland made the journey a grand preaching tour of four months, in which he preached seventy-four times. . . . Curi-

[34] "Oration in Wallingford, Connecticut," 1801, pp. 16 ff.
[35] Stevens, op. cit., Chaps. 20, 27.
[36] A. B. Darling, Political Changes in Massachusetts, 1824-1848, 1925, p. 36.

osity to see the mammoth cheese and to hear the 'mammoth priest' drew together immense congregations." [37] Upon his arrival in Washington Leland was invited to preach before Congress. Manasseh Cutler, who heard his sermon, called him "the cheese-monger, a poor, ignorant, illiterate, clownish preacher." [38] This was the reaction of the representative of the Massachusetts aristocracy to a man who has every claim to be called a patriot and who was one of the founders of the most democratic of all the dissenting-revivalistic churches.

Leland's association with Jefferson in Virginia had been close and his debt to Jefferson appears on every page of his *Rights of Conscience Inalienable*, 1791. "Let every man speak freely without fear," said Leland, "maintaining the principles that he believes, worship according to his own faith either one god, three gods or no god or twenty gods, and let government protect him in so doing." [39] This suggests at once Jefferson's language in his *Notes on Virginia*, "But it does me no injury for my neighbor to say there are twenty gods or no god." [40] Leland wrote, "But is uniformity attainable? Millions of men, women and children have been tortured to death to produce uniformity and yet the world has not advanced one inch towards it." [41] This is almost a verbal reproduction of Jefferson's language, "Is uniformity attainable? Millions of innocent men, women and children, since the introduction of Christianity, have been burnt, tortured, fined and imprisoned, yet we have not advanced one inch towards uniformity." [42] The ideas of Leland's *Rights of Conscience* are so completely dependent upon those of Jefferson that entire passages read as though they were little more than paraphrases of the pages of Jefferson.

[37] Backus, *op. cit.*, Vol. II, p. 473.
[38] Robinson, *loc. cit.*, p. 146.
[39] Leland, *op. cit.*, p. 13.
[40] Jefferson, *op. cit.*, p. 292.
[41] Leland, *op. cit.*, p. 12.
[42] Jefferson, *op. cit.*, p. 293.

The Baptist leaders had completely appropriated the ideas of the great Virginian on religious liberty in spite of the charge of atheism constantly hurled at him by the "friends of order." In 1807 the Chowan Baptist Association of North Carolina sent Jefferson an address of appreciation for his championship of religious liberty.[43]

The Methodists, while subjected to the same disabilities as the Baptists, do not seem to have taken the militant and radical attitude on the matter of religious liberty, characteristic of the Baptists. In 1803 that tireless champion of religious liberty, John Leland, speaking for some forty-two Baptist clergymen and exhorters, four thousand communicants and possibly twenty thousand attendants, presented a plea to the Connecticut authorities for disestablishment.[44] The Baptists sought the coöperation of the Methodists. Asbury has this comment in his *Journal:* "The Baptists of Connecticut have sent their petition from the Assembly to the Legislature of Connecticut to the bishops of the Methodist church, that they may have their aid in obtaining toleration: what can we do and how is it our business? We are neither popes nor politicians: let our brethren assert their own liberties. Besides who may now be trusted with power? The Baptists are avowed enemies to Episcopacy, be the form of church government as mild as it may; now it seems popes, as they would otherwise term us, may be useful to them, nor are they too proud to ask for help; but our people will not be pushed into their measures; their bishops have no coercive power of this sort: if the Baptists know not what to do we can not tell them."[45] This is a curious combination of petty

[43] D. H. Gilpatrick, *Jeffersonian Democracy in North Carolina, 1789-1816,* 1931, p. 122.
[44] Greene, *The Development of Religious Liberty in Connecticut,* p. 429.
[45] *Op. cit.,* Vol. III, p. 104.

denominational jealousy and the political shrewdness frequently characteristic of the leaders of the Methodist church. One misses in this utterance the forthright and courageous championship of the inalienable rights of conscience and the complete separation of church and state that always marked the Baptists.

VI

By 1793 the dissenters were beginning to show political strength. In fact, the Baptists and Methodists with a few radicals formed the bulk of the Republican party in Connecticut until after the war of 1812 when large Republican gains in the land of "steady habits" encouraged the dissenters to hope for the complete religious liberty that came with disestablishment in 1818.[46] It was not until 1807, when the Republicans elected James Sullivan governor and his friend, the staunch Republican, Reverend Bentley of Salem, preached the election sermon, that the dissenting groups may be said to have won for the first time something like political supremacy in Massachusetts. The greatest variety of groups composed the Republican vote and they were lacking in any comprehensive unifying bonds, either economic, social or religious, such as the ties that lent to the Federalist group its singular vitality; all groups, however, were united in their opposition to the establishment. It was natural, therefore, that among the first measures championed by the Republicans was a Public Worship Bill, the object of which was to relieve the disabilities of the dissenters. This was the first serious menace to the establishment. "The fury of the opposition was great" and they did not hesitate to play politics by an appeal to religious prejudices and characterized it as "the

[46] Greene, *op. cit.*, pp. 393, 405.

Infidel Bill." [47] The affiliations of Jefferson with the deism championed by Paine in his famous *Age of Reason*, published in 1794, were skillfully capitalized by the clergy to keep the orthodox loyal to Federalism.[48] The theology of the chief dissenting groups, such as Baptist and Methodist, was orthodox. It was not surprising, therefore, that in spite of Republican control the bill was defeated by a vote of 127 to 102.

The Federalists speedily regained control and their return to power registered itself at once in the courts. The rates due Reverend Kendall, serving Baptist churches in Middleborough and Kingston, were denied him on the ground that the Baptists of Kingston were not incorporated, and in 1810 in the case of Reverend Barnes versus the first parish of Falmouth the court actually ruled that ministers' rates could only be paid to incorporated societies. This stultified the legal precedents valid for thirty years that "religious societies" included corporate and incorporate societies. Incidentally, it illustrated the indeterminate status of dissent which emerged again and again in the contradictory decisions of the courts. This decision was a last attempt to stem the rising tide of dissent and immediately aroused widespread opposition. It bore especially hard upon Baptists and Methodists whose religious organizations were more or less informal in character.

Again in 1811 the Republicans were in power and passed, amidst great excitement, the Religious Freedom Act which freed the dissenter, provided with a certificate, from paying taxes to the established church whether or no his religious society was incorporated. This was a long step towards religious liberty and doubtless outran the mature public sentiment of the

---

[47] *Diary of William Bentley*, Vol. III, pp. 345 ff.
[48] For the furore aroused by Paine's book, see Morse, *op. cit.*, Appendix, Vol. I.

commonwealth. It would probably have been nullified when the Federalists came into power again in 1812 but for the pressure of other forces within the establishment itself, aiding the cause of the dissenter.[49]

VII

The strength of the New England establishments had always rested upon homogeneity of religious beliefs among the masses. In spite of the rise and spread of the various forms of dissent there was no serious break in this homogeneity until the first decade of the nineteenth century when Unitarianism began to spread in and around Boston. Matters came to a head in connection with the squabble over the filling of the Hollis chair of Divinity in Harvard in 1803, founded, strange to say, by a Baptist. The election of a Unitarian to this professorship and the capture of Harvard by the Unitarians led to the founding of a theological school at Andover by the Trinitarians in 1807. A terrific theological battle ensued, in which the Trinitarians were led by Morse and the Unitarians by Channing. Actual schism came with the preaching of the famous ordination sermon of Jared Sparks in Baltimore in 1819 by Channing, generally considered the Unitarian manifesto of independence.

This schism brought to the front a most important issue, namely, the ownership of the church property. In 1811 a decision of the courts upheld the right of the parish of Sandwich to choose and dismiss ministers and to retain the church property, but it was in the famous Dedham case of 1820 that the issue between Trinitarians and Unitarians came to a head. The minister of Dedham just outside Boston resigned in 1818. The

---

[49] J. C. Meyer, *Church and State in Massachusetts*, pp. 154 f. J. F. Thorning, *Religious Liberty in Transition*, pp. 59 f.

Trinitarian and Unitarian factions each had a candidate, the first being acceptable to the church and the second to the town. The town outvoted the church and the Unitarian candidate was chosen. The Trinitarians withdrew, organized a church of their own and went to law to get possession of the church property. In 1820 the court decided that the church held the church property as a trustee of the parish and when the Trinitarians seceded the property still remained the possession of the parish. This decision caused much hard feeling, for the Trinitarians looked upon it as "plundering" them of their property, and in fact it did cause within a few years the loss of eighty churches valued at hundreds of thousands of dollars. The Unitarians were very much in the minority but owed their triumph to the parish voters who were not church members.[50]

It is impossible for one familiar with the treatment of the dissenters in the past by these orthodox Trinitarian Congregationalists to feel much sympathy for them. They represented an establishment which for two hundred years had an unbroken record of religious oppression and intolerance. The orthodox Trinitarians were very much "at ease in Zion" so long as it was only Quakers, Baptists, and Methodists who were being taxed against their religious scruples to support the establishment. When the tables were turned by the Dedham decision and they found themselves in the same status with the dissenters and were taxed in their turn to support Unitarian ministers chosen by the majority votes of the parishes, they cried to high heaven of the injustice done them. So long as taxes were levied for their benefit they were smugly content; when taxes were levied on them to support the hated Unitarians they suddenly began to see that the dissenters had a case. So long as it was a matter of conscience they were unmoved; when it became a matter of

[50] Meyer, *op. cit.*, Chap. 6. Thorning, *op. cit.*, pp. 63 ff.

the pocket-book they began to talk of religious liberty. The
spectacle is not inspiring but it was merely the logical outcome
of the economic realism that had dictated the religious policies
of the Bay state for generations. The New England establishment was at best a gnarled and unlovely growth, the sap of
which had long been poisoned by habitual intolerance and
greed. Its passing was no more sordid than the long and weary
years of its outworn existence. The Unitarians with their so-
called liberalism now became the chief supporters of the establishment. Their loyalty never wavered until its downfall in
1833.

That the radical implications of the Dedham decision were
not at first felt even by those immediately concerned is shown
by the fact that Trinitarians and Unitarians united to maintain
the establishment in the convention of 1820. This merely veri-
fies what Bishop had said nineteen years before, namely, that
where "impostures have been of long standing they have gained
strength by age and no single exertion can compass the emancipation of the minds of our people from the tyranny of the
'friends of order'; it will require time and much patient exertion to effect it." [51] That Bishop was correct is shown by the
results of the constitutional convention of 1820. It was called
primarily to keep Massachusetts "a snug little Federalist state"
by separation from Maine which was becoming too democratic.[52]
In the debates, however, the religious issue soon took precedence over all others. The level of debate was not high.
Hardly an argument was advanced for or against the establishment that had not been touched upon forty years before in
the convention of 1780. The idealism of the revolutionary era
was lacking. Inalienable rights of conscience were seldom alluded to. The debate turned upon two things, religion as a

[51] "Wallingford Oration," p. 29.   [52] Meyer, *op. cit.*, p. 184.

"public utility" [53] and methods of taxation to support it. The strength of the sentiment in favor of disestablishment was measured by the vote on the resolution of Childs of Pittsfield designed to put all denominations on the same footing. This was defeated 136 to 246.[54] The Bay state was still in the grip of "steady habits."

VIII

Several things impress the reader of these debates. The first is the colossal self-satisfaction of the conservatives with themselves and the establishment. Reverend Tuckerman of Boston said, "Our religion is a perfect system of reciprocal rights and duties extending to every relation and circumstance of life." [55] Blake of Boston said that he had traveled along the Atlantic coast "and except in our cities had frequently found nothing to remind him that he was in a Christian country. Massachusetts in this respect stood on an eminence." [56] Rhode Island and New York occupy a lower moral plane than Massachusetts because they have no establishments.[57] Freeman of Boston was "tired of appeals to other states"—Massachusetts was the only state with an establishment. "He knew not what right they had to dictate to us; we ought rather to give an example to them." [58] Dutton made the perfectly astonishing statement that under the existing constitution "no case of persecution for conscience sake ever did or ever can arise." [59]

The speeches of the conservatives are characterized by an uncritical and naïve ancestor-worship. Almost every speaker begins by insisting that the constitution is a masterpiece of political

---

[53] *Journal of the Convention*, p. 370.
[54] *Ibid.*, pp. 347, 559.
[55] *Ibid.*, p. 360.
[56] *Ibid.*, p. 364.
[57] *Ibid.*, pp. 358, 359.
[58] *Ibid.*, p. 367.
[59] *Ibid.*, p. 371.

wisdom bequeathed to them by their ancestors and must be touched with "trembling hands." One can almost hear the awe-struck tone of the voice of Saltonstall when he said at the close of a lengthy standpat speech. "I stand as in the presence of our ancestors; they conjure us not to destroy what they have planted with so much care and under the influence of which we have so long flourished; but to transmit to posterity what is only a *trust-estate* in us." [60] An intelligent respect for an-cestors is of course thoroughly admirable, as Burke has shown us. But when we consider that all this bathos was inspired by the determination to preserve the muddle-headed Article Three of the constitution dealing with the establishment, we fail to feel any enthusiasm either for the wisdom of the ancestors who framed it or for the intelligence of the filial piety that refused to alter it. The liberal Baldwin found some other use for an-cestors than to "perch ourselves on their tombstones and sing a requiem to their ashes." [61] Ancestor-worship is of course a subtle form of self-flattery and enables us to understand why the Massachusetts leaders found their unreasoned conservatism so thoroughly delightful.

The reactions of Webster, the ablest mind in the convention, are exceedingly illuminating. He seemed to have felt that the effect of the "steady habits" of the past and the determination to treat religion as a "public utility" would decide the issue. He was aware that "there were those in this hall who con-sidered religion as something that concerns only the individual who receives it. He did not so view the matter. He considered it the only security of the good order of society, as the basis of the moral character of the community, as the only protection of a free government." [62] Whether this really expressed Web-

[60] *Ibid.*, p. 390.   [62] *Journal*, p. 449.
[61] *Ibid.*, p. 366.

ster's personal convictions as to the wisdom and necessity of an establishment or whether he made this profession because he saw that this was "the sentiment of this convention" is a question. That Webster could be quite convinced of the desirability of an establishment and in another connection could "entreat the gentlemen to consider that if their debates were to go abroad literally reported, the impression would be that religious liberty did not exist among us" [63] would suggest that the "god-like" Webster was singularly lacking in a sense of humor.

Webster does not seem to have had strong convictions one way or another but viewed the matter from the point of view of the practical politician. He took no part in the general debate on Article Three, doubtless because he anticipated the ultimate decision. He saw that the real problem was one of securing taxes to support an establishment that was already in process of dissolution. This came out in particular in the debate on the resolution offered by Williams of Beverley,[64] making every religious society autonomous in the matter of raising funds and choosing teachers, leaving each individual free to join the society of his choice and taxing persons who fail to unite with any society, such taxes presumably going to the support of the Congregational church. This resolution sought to assure support of religion as a "public utility" while at the same time giving freedom to religious groups and individuals. Webster saw that this took the taxing power and the control of funds out of the hands of the state and struck a death-blow at the establishment. He contended that the law of 1811 enacted by the Republicans had placed incorporated and unincorporated societies on the same basis and allowed a man to go from one society to another. Webster, therefore, proposed as a substitute for Williams' resolution the following: "That it is not expedient to make any further alteration in the third article of the declaration of rights, except to provide that all monies paid by the subject for the support of public worship and of the public teachers of piety, religion and morality [it would be interesting to know what Webster meant by this threefold distinction] if he shall request it, be applied to the public teacher or teachers, if any, on whose instruction he attends, whether of the same or of a different sect or denomination from that in which the money is raised." [65] This made it possible to keep the taxing power in the hands of the state.

Webster insisted again and again that the convention could not lay down the broad proposition that the state has a right to compel every taxpayer to support religion as a "public utility" on a par with schools or courts of justice while permitting men to join every sort of society varying widely in their expenditures. "It was too clear to be argued," said Webster, "that there could be no equality, unless there was a security that one man, of a given amount of property, should pay as much as his neighbor of the same amount of property." [66] So long as it was possible for "half a dozen rich men in a parish to form one of these new created societies, and pay a dollar a year, while all the expense of maintaining public worship and religious instruction should, in effect, be thrown on the others" the establishment was little more than a farce. When faced with the alternatives of an establishment of this sort and disestablishment proposed by Childs, Webster preferred "the proposition of the gentleman from Pittsfield." [67]

To realize how accurately Webster grasped the situation one has but to remember that in 1820 the religious societies of Massachusetts were divided as follows: Congregationalist, 373;

[65] *Ibid.*, p. 444.
[66] *Ibid.*, p. 460.
[67] *Ibid.*, p. 448.

Baptist, 153; Methodist, 67; Friends, 39; Episcopalian, 22; Universalist, 21; and the rest, 23.[68] That is to say, the religious societies of the establishment only outnumbered the other societies by forty-eight. The implications of this situation are at once obvious. The establishment, already split by the Unitarian schism, had a bare majority. To tax the other three hundred and twenty-five religious societies in support of the Congregationalists was patently unjust. On the simple principle that the taxpayer has a right to say what is done with his money Webster's idea of absolute equality of taxation, while economically just, was obviously impracticable. Furthermore, with several hundred religious societies teaching different brands of religion it was foolish to talk of religion as a "public utility" such as the mails or the public schools. The hard reality of the religious situation in 1820 had reduced the argument for an establishment to an absurdity. The old firm of Moses and Aaron was doomed and it was only the sentimental loyalties and the unenlightened conservatism of the leaders that prevented them from grasping the situation. The three proposed amendments affecting the establishment were submitted to the people and rejected by a vote of 19,547 to 11,065.[69] The people were no wiser than their leaders.[70]

Powerful forces were active, however, favoring the cause of the dissenters. The old tie-wig Federalism of Fisher Ames and John Adams was rapidly passing. A new Federalism built around merchants and manufacturers and bankers was in process of formation. The old Federalism was narrowly provincial; the new Federalism was national in outlook. The old Federal-

[68] Meyer, op. cit., p. 187.
[69] Meyer, op. cit., p. 200. Thorning, op. cit., p. 77.
[70] Meyer, op. cit., p. 198, thinks that the conservative politicians had intentionally confused the issues so as to ensure the defeat of disestablishment.

ism wanted free trade and sought to imitate England; the new Federalism wanted protection of industries and a national tariff barrier. A place had to be found for the religion of the Irish Catholic immigrant whose labor was needed by industry. Thus did the economic realism, always the most powerful force in the life of the Bay state, educate the people, largely through an appeal to selfish economic interests, to cultivate the tolerant point of view. Curiously enough, this selfish economic realism was destined to lay the material bases for a literary and spiritual renaissance that gave to New England, for a short time at least, the commanding position in American life.[71] All these forces combined to break down the "steady habits" which had prolonged the life of the firm of Moses and Aaron. In 1832, as a result of a growing demand, the legislature enacted a measure that annulled the famous Article Three and the bill became law in 1833 by a popular vote of ten to one.

IX

A distinguished Massachusetts historian has said, "Massachusetts, as colony and Commonwealth, by every known test of eminence, has produced more distinguished men and women in proportion to her population than any other state in the Union." [72] Uncritical generalizations in the nebulous field of social values are always dangerous. Another Massachusetts historian, for example, suggests a "test of eminence" when he said that Boston "was the only place in America where they

[71] Darling, *op. cit.*, *1824-1848*, Chap. 1, 5. L. Parrington, *Main Currents in American Thought*, 1927, Vol. II, pp. 296 ff.

[72] Morison, *Builders of the Bay Colony*, p. 53. This statement is probably based upon an article by Henry Cabot Lodge in the *Century Magazine*, September, 1891, and reprinted in his *Historical and Political Essays*, 1892, pp. 138 ff.

hanged men for their religion" [73] but this doubtless is not the "test of eminence" intended. If it be true that religious liberty is "the greatest distinctive contribution of America to the sum of Western Christianized Civilization," [74] which statement seems to have the support of the scholars of Europe,[75] it would seem that according to the highest "test of eminence" provided by American culture, namely, the furtherance of re-.ligious liberty, Massachusetts, both in men and measures, must be content to take her place well down towards the bottom of the list of the thirteen colonies. The old Bay state during the first two centuries of her history simply did not "carry that line of goods." With characteristic Yankee thrift she only added this commodity when it became profitable.

If the query be raised as to why a state that has made such invaluable contributions to national life remained the last stronghold of intolerance, the answer must be sought in the intensive provincial-mindedness which race, religion, politics, and geographic isolation conspired to induce. This provincialism has proven both an asset and a liability to the Bay state. It prepared the soil for distinct and valuable cultural traits such as civic pride, an intensive cultivation of institutional life in school, church and state, early maturity of culture, and a shrewd regard for sectional interests not found in any other state. This local pride still lingers and it is doubtful whether there is any other civilized community that can rival Massachusetts in the meticulously pious and scholarly industry with which forgotten worthies of the past, family-trees, town and county histories, furniture, dress, manners, and relatively insignificant documents,

---

[73] Backus, *op. cit.*, Vol. II, p. viii.
[74] W. T. Thom, *The Struggle for Religious Freedom in Virginia*, p. 554.
[75] Ernst Troeltsch, *The Social Teachings of the Christian Churches*, Vol. II, p. 672. M. Freund, *Die Idee der Toleranz*, pp. 242 ff.

such as a seventeenth-century ship's list of passengers, are preserved and studied. One of the surest ways to keep the respect of one's fellows is to maintain one's self-respect and to do this it often becomes necessary to defend the good name of one's ancestors. This is perhaps a praiseworthy weakness but one may be permitted the remark that while *de mortuis nihil nisi bonum* is doubtless an admirable superscription for a family cemetery it ill becomes the historian.

This narrow provincialism, likewise, had its serious weaknesses. It bred a complacent self-assurance and a cock-sure attitude upon the exceedingly difficult question of religious liberty that find few parallels in history. John Cotton thus haughtily repudiated the criticisms of English liberals of his treatment of the Baptists Clarke and Holmes, "We believe there is a vast difference between man's inventions and God's institutions . . . we compel none to man's inventions"; in 1681, Increase Mather said that he had never known the state to molest men because of their opinions; Cotton Mather in his *Magnalia* dilated upon the divinely ordained excellencies of the establishment with a swelling satisfaction that was grotesquely naïve; the liberal John Wise thought the "New England way" was the embodiment of nature and divine revelation; Reverend Amos Adams in an election sermon on 1770 said, "We dwell in a land of light, a region of liberty"; Reverend Andrew Eliot of Boston wrote a friend in England in 1771 in regard to the treatment of the Baptists, "There is nothing in the present complexion of this country that looks like persecution. Both the magistrates and ministers are as free from it as they ever were in any age or country"; John Adams at the Philadelphia conference in 1774 claimed that the Massachusetts establishment was "the mildest and most equitable that was known in the world"; William Ellery Channing made the amazing statement in his election sermon, 1830, "The government of the Commonwealth has uniformly distinguished itself by the spirit of religious freedom. Intolerance, however rife abroad, has found no shelter in our halls of legislation." All these men were obviously sincere. Whence this singular obtuseness as to the meaning of religious liberty, this utter inability to exercise intelligent self-criticism?

The explanation is to be sought in the texture of Massachusetts society. The spirit of liberty may be, as in the case of Rhode Island, the birthright of a people; it may be, as in the case of Pennsylvania, the creation of a wise and tolerant founder under whose benign policies men of diverse race and creed are taught to dwell together in amity; it may be purchased, as in the case of Virginia, through the give and take of diverse geographic, religious, and economic interests directed and interpreted by wise leaders and constantly illuminated by intimate contacts with the more advanced culture of the mother country. None of these conditions were present in Massachusetts. Fate made her from the very beginning the land of the "Everlasting YEA" and the "Everlasting NAY." Her leaders from John Cotton down to Garrison and Sumner were educated by a cultural environment to believe that they were everlastingly right and their opponents everlastingly wrong.

Tolerance for the Greek was born of magnanimity or greatness of soul that rises above the petty and sordid level of passion and prejudice and the provincial mind and views life steadily and views it whole. Magnanimity ($\mu\varepsilon\gamma\alpha\lambda o\psi v\chi i\alpha$) was for Aristotle "the crown of the virtues." [76] Massachusetts lacked the poise and insight characteristic of the rich and varied Greek life that produced Aristotle's great-hearted men. Consequently, one searches in vain among the Massachusetts wor-

[76] See his classical description in *Nicomachean Ethics*, Bk. IV, Chap. 7.

thies for the spirit of magnanimity and large-heartedness necessary to tolerance. This virtue did not flourish in the narrowly circumscribed provincial atmosphere of the Puritan.

Tolerance for the Christian may be due to the tender compassion born of a deep sense of the pathos of life, as in the case of the Sermon on the Mount and the thirteenth chapter of First Corinthians. It may be due to a profound insight into the mystery and tragedy of existence, as when Roger Williams wrote to the obdurate John Endicott, "I beseech you to remember it is a dangerous thing to put this to the may be. . . . It is possible, you may well say . . . that I have fought against God." [77] But these choice flowers of the Christian life did not flourish in the poisoned atmosphere of the theocracy. The harsh and strait-laced world of the Puritans had no place for sweet charity while mystery and tragedy took on the superficial veneer of their theology and became as ghastly unreal as the witches, the devils and the hell-fire that haunted their dreams.

In the soil of this provincial and unreal world the founding fathers sowed the dragon's teeth of an unenlightened and vindictive intolerance, from which sprang a gruesome harvest of banishments, bloody beatings and hangings. Even after these had disappeared, the original planting continued to bear its crop of gnarled and bitter and poisonous weeds in the form of petty persecution and haughty disregard of the rights of the weak while a spirit of infinite self-sufficiency turned the arrows of outside criticism like a target of steel. Intolerance thus became an institution in the Bay state. It grew to maturity like some giant of the forest whose twisted limbs and unsightly trunk throw a sinister shadow all around it. It did not go down in the storm of revolution. It died a slow and lingering death.

[77] *Letters of Roger Williams: Publications of the Narragansett Club*, Vol. VI, p. 225.

Its branches, gaunt and broken and hideous, marred the land-scape long after the sap of life had run low. Men went their ways in a new day and tolerated this melancholy relic of an unlovely bygone age largely because a naïvely sentimental re-gard for their ancestors prevented them from giving it even a decent burial.

Chapter XIV
The Legacy of Dissent

MADISON's hope that his country might be blessed with a multiplicity of sects as a safeguard of religious liberty has been fulfilled. There are today 212 different denominations in this country, comprising 55 per cent of the adult population with 232,000 churches, only 24,000 less than the total number of public school buildings.[1] Of the forty-four and more millions of adult church members, thirteen millions are Catholics, almost eight millions are Methodists, over seven millions are Baptists, and two and a half millions belong to the Presbyterian communions. That is to say, the great dissenting-revivalistic denominations today include over forty per cent of the total of adult church members and two-thirds of the total of all Protestants.[2]

These churches were split by the Civil War. The bulk of the northern Baptists, Methodists, and Presbyterians is found in the great centers of population that lie west of the Hudson, east of the Mississippi, and north of the Ohio rivers. The southern sections of these three churches are almost entirely confined to the former confederate states, the Baptists being strongest in the southern Appalachians and the Southwest, the

[1] C. L. Fry, *The United States Looks at Its Churches*, 1930, pp. 3 f. The more bizarre among these sects are described by C. W. Ferguson, *The New Book of Revelations*, 1930. For a selected bibliography, see pp. 461 f.
[2] Fry, *op. cit.*, pp. 26 f.

Methodists and Presbyterians in the Piedmont regions of Virginia and the Carolinas.[3] During the great period of expansion, the first half of the nineteenth century, these three churches alone kept pace with the swelling tide of population. From 1820 to 1860 the Methodists grew from 65,000 to 1,250,000, the Baptists from 100,000 to 800,000, and the Presbyterians from 40,000 to 500,000.[4] The first two of these especially were frontier churches. They grew to their present positions of power and influence in most intimate connection with the material and spiritual development of the nation. The "frontierized Christianity" which they embodied became the typical form of American Protestantism. We have, then, to ask how far the traits of the dissenting tradition which they inherited from the past have become through them integral elements in American culture.

I

The conception of the church that prevails in American democracy is derived primarily from two great streams of thought within the dissenting tradition, the one associated with Locke and the political liberals Madison and Jefferson, the other deriving from Leonard Busher and Roger Williams and faithfully preserved by the Baptists. Locke defines a church as follows: "A church then I take to be a voluntary society of men, joining themselves together of their own accord in order to the public worship of God, in such a manner as they judge acceptable to him, and effectual to the salvation of their souls." [5] Locke was deeply influenced by the dissenters. He entered

---

[3] Fry, *op. cit.*, pp. 34 f. for maps.

[4] Edward Channing, *History of the United States*, 1927-1930, Vol. V, p. 221.

[5] John Locke, "A Letter Concerning Toleration," *Works*, Vol. V, p. 9.

Christ Church College, Oxford, in 1652, when the great dissenting leader and scholar John Owen was dean and vice-chancellor of the university. In 1682 Locke wrote, but never published, a defense of the Independents for organizing churches on a voluntary basis.[6] The dissenting idea of the church as a voluntary organization was presupposed in Locke's theory of toleration [7] and was taken for granted in the thought of the American revolutionary liberals who followed Locke.

The church which Locke defined from the point of view of social organization and function was visualized by Busher, Williams, and the Baptists more from the point of view of the contrast between spiritual and secular, and the necessity for spiritual autonomy. Locke stressed the social and objective, Williams the spiritual and subjective phases of the church. Williams asserted, "Civil peace will never be proved to be the peace of all subjects or citizens of a city in spiritual things: the civil state may bring in orders, make orders, preserve in civil order all her members: but who ordained that either the spiritual estate should bring in and force the civil state to keep civil order, or that the civil state should fit, judge and force any of her subjects to keep spiritual order?" [8] This passage implies the familiar ideal of American democracy, namely, that the state deals with all organizations in their social and secular relations only; that the function of the state is to maintain peace and justice through the equal application of the laws to all organizations religious or otherwise; that civil peace can be maintained only in civil matters and by secular means while spiritual peace must be maintained by spiritual authorities; that

[6] Extracts of this *Defence of Nonconformity* are given in H. R. F. Bourne's *Life of John Locke*, 1876, Vol. I, pp. 457 f.

[7] Seaton, *The Theory of Toleration Under the Later Stuarts*, p. 237.

[8] *Publications of the Narragansett Club*, Vol. IV, p. 80.

where disputes of a purely religious nature endanger the civil peace the state may intervene, but solely in the interests of society and not of religion. The essence of the church with Williams and the Baptists was the spiritual autonomy of a voluntary religious organization.

The definitions of the church found in the decisions of the American courts are strikingly suggestive of the dissenting idea. In a Massachusetts decision the court stated, "The church consists of an indefinite number of persons of one or both sexes who have made a public profession of religion and who are associated together by a covenant of church fellowship for the purpose of celebrating the sacraments and watching over the spiritual welfare of each other." [9] In another decision in a court of the far South we find similar language. "The church is a voluntary association of its members united together by a covenant or agreement for the public worship of God." [10] Other decisions could be cited to show that the dissenting notion of a voluntary organization or covenant primarily for religious needs has become widely embodied in American law as constituting the essence of the church. What are the implications of this notion of the church?

II

The greatest single contribution of the dissenting tradition to American life is the separation of church and state, which follows naturally from the sectarian notion of the church. To be sure, many other factors were concerned. The differences and jealous rivalries between the thirteen colonies in matters

[9] Stebbins *vs.* Jennings, 27 Massachusetts 172, cited by Brown, *The Canonical Juristic Personality*, p. 122.
[10] Hundly *vs.* Collins, 131 Alabama 234.

of religion, the fact that all the growing colonies were competing for immigrants, and finally a loosely organized pioneer society with its encouragement of freedom and spontaneity in religion as in other things—all these and other factors combined to make separation of church and state natural and necessary. While these factors assured a setting congenial to separatism "the American form of separatism is essentially the result of the sectarian phase of Protestantism." [11]

The influence of radical sectarian separatism is seen in the fact that the existence of the church proper as an organized body is not recognized in American law. A church is a spiritual entity and differs from a religious corporation which is a "body politic, created by law, composed of several individuals, whose principal object is to establish and regulate the congregation or religious denomination, acting under a common name and endowed with perpetual succession, and vested with the capacity of acting in many respects, however numerous the association may be, as a person." [12] From the point of view of the law the church as a spiritual entity is thus ignored. The church is treated as merely one of a variety of corporate bodies.

A religious group has, therefore, two aspects. "It has a body, the society, with which courts can deal, and a soul, the church, with which courts can not deal. The church is the spiritual entity with spiritual sanctions and spiritual bonds of union. The society is the temporal body with spiritual understandings and temporal articles of association. The church is subject to spiritual censure, the society is subject to the temporal powers that be. The object of the church is preaching of the gospel; the object of the society is the management of property. The members of the society are not necessarily members of the church and the

---

[11] Rothenbücher, *Die Trennung von Staat und Kirche*, p. 171.
[12] R. H. Tyler, *American Ecclesiastical Law*, 1867, p. 55.

members of the church are not necessarily members of the society. The church may exist and be recognized by the courts of the land though there is no church, and the church may exist and be recognized by its spiritual superiors though there is no society." [13]

Just as in the more radical forms of dissent so in the American society of today there is a dualism between the sphere of religion and that of the state. What the state does through legal enactments does not, and from the nature of the case cannot, affect the purely religious sphere. What takes place in the purely religious sphere cannot be recognized by the state so long as it keeps its purely religious aspect. "Since the church is thus entirely removed from temporal control it follows that incorporation will not affect it in the least. The spiritual entity created by spiritual means can neither be swallowed up nor affected by a temporal corporation created under temporal statutes. The corporation can exist without the church and the church without the corporation. The corporation created by the state may continue though the church is dissolved, while the church may continue though its charter has expired or has been cancelled by the state. Each is derived from a different source, has different powers and is absolutely independent of the other." [14]

We have, then, this rather anomalous situation in American society; two centers of rights and obligations are set up, the secular and the religious. The laws, rights, and privileges that hold within the given church communion do not depend for their validity upon the laws of the state. The notion of separatism in American law is singularly suggestive of the great ideas of Roger Williams. The state recognizes in the sphere of

[13] C. Zollmann, *American Civil Church Law*, 1917, p. 74.
[14] *Ibid.*, p. 75.

religion a set of laws over which it has no control. The state tacitly recognizes the independence and self-sufficiency of this body of regulations. When an unorthodox minister is tried for heresy and un-frocked by his church he cannot appeal to state law. The state recognizes the decision of the church court as final. In 1871 the Supreme Court in the case of Watson vs. Jones, concerning a disputed Presbyterian church property in Louisville, Kentucky, had the following to say: "In such cases where the right of property in the civil court is dependent on the question of doctrine, discipline, ecclesiastical law, rule, or custom, or church government, and that has been decided by the highest tribunal within the organization to which it has been carried, *the civil court will accept that decision as conclusive, and be governed by it in its application to the case' before it.*" [15]

When the state does interfere in the sphere of the rights of a religious group, it is usually in the interest of the common law rights which a man enjoys as a citizen of the community. The results of church trials have been reviewed by courts where property interests were concerned or where the given church organization did not follow out faithfully the requirements of its own laws. The very fact that the laws and regulations within a given religious group are not valid for the whole community and therefore are not in a position to dominate public sentiment, the final arbiter of all law, makes it possible for the state to work in closer harmony with the church in America than in any other nation in the world.

It would be a mistake to imagine from the foregoing that religion, even in American democracy, is without any restrictions whatsoever. Religious activity is restricted in at least two ways. The Constitution lays down certain negative limitations,

[15] *United States Reports*, 13 Wallace, p. 680.

namely, that no one shall be discriminated against on religious grounds in the holding of any federal office and that no national establishment of religion shall ever be erected. It leaves the states free to solve their own religious problems, even to the extent of establishing a state religion if that can be done without conflicting with Constitutional rights. These are only *negative* restrictions looking to the equalization of the status of every religion so far as the Constitution is concerned.

Religion is restricted, in the second place, in that any exercise of religion injurious to public order or good morals is subject to legal control.[16] This intimate relationship between religion and public morals, growing out of the fact that religion and particularly dissenting-revivalistic Protestantism is not something superinduced upon American life but is an organic part of our cultural heritage, has raised a question as to whether, after all, church and state are really separated in the thoroughgoing fashion which the law would seem to indicate. It is claimed, for example, that this is "a Christian nation" and that Christianity is a part of the common law of the land. The question may very well be asked, then, as to whether there is not a fundamental contradiction between the position of the Constitution in which church and state are separated and the actual facts of our cultural history according to which Protestantism of the dissenting-revivalistic type has become the basis for ethical sanctions that give the law validity. The nature of the problem here involved will be clearer in the light of the historic position that the dissenting-revivalistic type of Protestantism has come to occupy in national sentiment.

[16] See Zollman, *op. cit.*, Chap. 1, and Schaff, *Church and State in the United States*, Papers of the American Historical Association, Vol. II, pp. 435 ff.

III

National sentiment has much in common with what has been called the "self-sentiment." [17] The "self-sentiment" centers around those ideas which are most intimate and personal and to which the individual constantly refers for guidance on issues of paramount importance. Similarly, national sentiment is composed of loyalties, usually associated with struggle and sacrifice in the past, to which the nation unconsciously appeals when matters involving its vital interests are at stake.[18] Just before and subsequent to the war of independence two sets of loyalties struggled with each other for supremacy in the formative period of the national sentiment of the American people. One set of loyalties centered around the great fictions of natural rights, bandied about on the tongues of preachers and politicians prior to the war, embodied by Jefferson in the Declaration, baptized by the blood and tears of the struggle for independence, and exemplified in most spectacular fashion in the French revolution.[19] The other was the unpremeditated arousal of something like a common body of sentiments in the sphere of religion when Whitefield preached the dissenting-revivalistic type of Protestantism from Maine to Georgia and first made the thirteen colonies aware of a common tradition. We have seen how these powerful religious sentiments became intimately connected with class and sectional interests and sometimes resulted in revolution, as in Virginia.

It was a pioneer society that provided the dramatic setting

[17] William McDougall, *Introduction to Social Psychology*, 1909, pp. 191 f. See also A. F. Shand, *The Foundations of Character*, 1920, Chaps. 4, 5.

[18] Muir, *Nationalism and Internationalism*, 1917, pp. 48 f.

[19] G. A. Koch, *Republican Religion: The American Revolution and the Cult of Reason*, 1933. This book came to the writer's attention after the above was in press.

within which these two great traditions, one political and natural, the other religious and supernatural, competed with each other for the favored position in the loyalties of the American people. There were phases of both traditions that seemed to fit the exigencies of a pioneer society. The primitivism of the dissenting-revivalistic piety with its emphasis upon undisciplined emotions, its anti-intellectualism, its crude Hebraistic ethics and radical individualism was admirably adapted to the loosely organized and unlettered frontier culture. Similarly, the highly abstract ideology of Jeffersonian democracy, with its emphasis upon natural rights, the contractual theory of society and its demand of the utmost freedom for individual initiative, suited the life of the backwoodsman. The farmers and frontiersmen were able to take over the lofty ideas of the Declaration of Independence without ever being made aware of the practical difficulties incident to the application of such a philosophy to a mature social order. It was their support that enabled Jeffersonianism to win in the contest with Federalism.

The liberal political and religious ideas of the French revolution spread rapidly in America because of the gratitude of a warm-hearted but uncritical people towards France for the aid rendered during the war of independence.[20] We have seen that in the case of dissenting leaders, such as the Baptist John Leland, the political liberalism of France and Jefferson was naïvely fused with dissenting ideals of religious liberty. What is perhaps even more remarkable, these liberal ideas, usually in the form of deism, penetrated the wilderness and cropped up on the frontier. The Baptist missionary J. M. Peck remarked that in 1794 in the far Northwest along the shores of the Ohio

[20] B. Faÿ, *The Revolutionary Spirit in France and America*, 1927, pp. 206 f. See also H. M. Jones, *America and French Culture, 1750-1848*, 1927. Koch, *op. cit.*

and Mississippi the great tide of immigration brought with it "French infidelity that threatened for a time to sweep away every vestige of Christianity." [21] This French deism was blended with Jeffersonian democracy, for "in the mysteries of divine providence infidelity and liberalism were combined." *The Age of Reason* was a popular book and the Bible was read "only in religious families." [22]

This widespread irreligious liberalism was of a superficial and flamboyant type and was confined to the upper classes, especially in the South. The middle and lower classes were not so much skeptical and irreligious as they were indifferent to all religious interests.[23] There was, however, a possibility that a democratic national tradition might arise akin to the anticlerical Voltairian ideals that inspired the democratic bourgeoisie of France during the ultramontane reaction against the excesses of the French revolution, for, as we have seen, Jeffersonian democracy took shape in conscious opposition to the establishments of New England and Virginia. Jefferson and Madison really had just as little love for the sects as for the establishments. How are we to explain the fact that the religiously indifferent democracy of Jefferson was transformed into the Jacksonian democracy of the fourth decade, by no means hostile to the deeply ingrained stereotypes of dissenting-revivalistic Protestantism?

About the end of the last decade of the eighteenth century friction began to arise, partly political and accidental and partly inherent and inevitable, between the peculiarly American dissenting-revivalistic Protestantism and the liberal and unortho-

---

[21] "The Baptists of the Mississippi Valley," *The Christian Review*, October, 1852, p. 498.

[22] *Ibid.*, p. 500.

[23] J. S. Bassett, *The Popular Churches After the Revolution*, Massachusetts Historical Society, February, 1915, pp. 259 f.

dox ideas of the French revolution.[24] This conflict is important, for in it we find the beginnings of the crystallization of a young and inchoate national sentiment in conscious opposition to continental influences. It was the triumph over deism that enabled the dissenting-revivalistic type of Protestantism to become not only the typical form of American religion but to secure for itself a central place in the pattern of national sentiment slowly taking shape. Abundant evidence of this conflict will be found by any student who takes the pains to read the biographies and journals of the itinerant preachers of the dissenting-revivalistic churches who fought and vanquished deism and irreligion in their great backwoods revivals.[25]

How serious this conflict was is indicated by the fact that about 1797 in the remote backwoods of North Carolina a debating society was formed among the Scotch-Irish "and furnished with a circulating library, replete with infidel philosophy and infidel sentiments on religion and morality." The issue was "what should govern, conscience, philosophy or the Bible? The authority of the Bible underwent a sifting discussion such as Carolina has never seen and may never see again." [26] The champions of the dissenting-revivalistic tradition took up the cudgels for orthodoxy. The Presbyterian Reverend McCorkle in 1798 published four discourses on *The General First Principle of Deism and Revelation Contrasted*. The pamphlet was not profound but merely repeated the arguments of Paley, Watson, and others. What really decided the argument was not the reasoning of the preachers but the pressure of a pioneer environ-

[24] Jones, *op. cit.*, pp. 388 ff.

[25] Peter Cartwright, *Autobiography*, 1857. Jacob Bower, *Autobiography*. John Firth, *The Experience and Gospel Labors of Reverend Benjamin Abbott*, 1820. Jacob Young, *Autobiography of a Pioneer*, 1858. N. Bangs, *The Life of Freeborn Garrettson*, 1838. For further source material see W. W. Sweet, *Religion on the American Frontier*, 1931.

[26] W. H. Foote, *Sketches of North Carolina*, p. 248.

ment. Deism could not flourish outside of a mature and sophisticated culture. It was no creed for Scotch-Irish pioneers. It could not be preached effectively. Its cold and oversimplified rationalizations could not compete with the vivid theology of the dissenting-revivalistic piety with its dramatic picture of the Lamb of God slain for the sins of the world, its personal devil, its judgment bar, its real heaven, and its physical hell fire that burns forever. Long years had to intervene and a far more refined and scientifically trained generation had to arise before men could be made aware of the crudities and inadequacies of this creed. The revivals that swept the country about 1802 and periodically thereafter ironed out the last vestiges of deism. It disappeared in the melting pot of the backwoods revival.

Even at this early period we can detect the genesis of the religious stereotypes that were to persist as parts of this fusion of revivalistic Christianity and one hundred per cent Americanism. "I do not know a single deist," wrote McCorkle in 1798, "that has the character of a man of plain good sense and unaffected goodness of heart. They are all, that I know, either men who have not thought much about religion or vain self-conceited men, or drunkards, or gamblers, or whoremongers. I do not know a deist that does not fall under some, but I know some who fall under two of the above descriptions." [27] The reason for this is that they lack the type of character based upon dissenting-revivalistic piety which assures correct thought and moral conduct. "There is a moral quality necessary to the study of revelation . . . into a sensual soul wisdom can not enter." [28] Forces were at work tending to make dissenting-revivalistic piety the ideal of character that was destined to become an essential part of traditional one hundred per cent Americanism in wide areas of this country. Volumes might be written upon

[27] *Op. cit.*, p. 51.   [28] *Ibid.*, p. 38.

the abusive epithets heaped high upon the heads of deists and the traditional heretics whose ideas threatened this piety, such as Voltaire, Rousseau, Paine, Renan, Ingersoll and, later, Darwin and Huxley. These are damned as un-American and dangerous to the faith and morals of the young. The stereotypes of the sectarian revivalistic piety became almost national in scope and influence. They were a phase of approved Americanism. Here we are to seek the cultural background that made possible the anti-evolution laws and the Scopes trial of 1925.

Just how intimately dissenting-revivalistic Protestantism was associated with Americanism is illustrated by the rise of Nativism, a movement of protest on the part of the old American stock against the immigrant tide, that began about the middle of the nineteenth century. In Know-Nothingism of the middle and Apaism of the end of the nineteenth century the call was always for a defense of "Americanism and Protestantism," where Protestantism was identical with the dissenting-revivalistic type. The post-war recrudescence of Nativism in the form of the Ku Klux Klan in 1915 again made Protestantism an integral part of one hundred per cent Americanism.[29] It is not surprising, therefore, that Lord Bryce could say that Christianity, "though not the legally accepted established religion," is in actual fact "the national religion" of America. Justice Brewer of the Supreme Court in a famous *obiter dictum* that created a great stir, asserted in 1892 that this is "a Christian nation." [30] The extent to which these statements are true to historical fact is due mainly to the influence of the dissenting-revivalistic tradition. Psychologically speaking, that is, from the point of view

[29] J. M. Mecklin, *The Ku Klux Klan*, Chap. 5.

[30] J. D. Brewer, *The United States a Christian Nation*, 1905. For additional literature, see Mecklin, "Religion and the Social Conscience," *Proceedings of the Northwestern University Conference*, edited by Betts, Eiselin, and Coe, November 15, 1929, pp. 130 f.

of the deeply ingrained religious stereotypes of American public sentiment, the dissenting-revivalistic Protestantism had become the "established" religion of the large majority of Americans. This is a fact of vast importance for the problem of religious tolerance.

IV

In spite of the famous achievements of the American nation
in the realm of legal tolerance through the technical separation
of church and state it is still the most intolerant among all the
civilized nations of the world. One has but to read the history
of such movements as abolition, prohibition, Comstockery, anti-
evolution, anti-Catholicism, and the struggle for academic freedom in church and state colleges to be amply convinced of this
fact.[31] This intolerance is spiritual rather than legal. It occurs
in that nebulous realm which the law cannot reach, where
thought and conduct are shaped by beliefs, loyalties, intangible
stereotypes in religion, morals, or otherwise. Here issues must
necessarily be decided in terms of what Burke has called "wise
prejudices." The unwise prejudices embodied in the public sentiment of large areas of this country, thanks to the prevalence of
an "established" religion created by the fusion between the dissenting-revivalistic type of Protestantism and the ideals of
patriotism and good citizenship, are responsible more than anything else for this widespread spiritual intolerance among the
American people.

Two types of tolerance have been bequeathed to American

[31] The literature on the subject is large. The following deal with more
recent phases: Maynard Shipley, *War on Modern Science*, 1927; Peter Odegard, *Pressure Politics*, 1928; *The World's Most Famous Court Trial: The
Tennessee Evolution Case*, 1926; S. G. Cole, *History of Fundamentalism*,
1931; L. Whipple, *The Story of Civil Liberties in the United States*, 1927,
is an excellent compendium of facts; Mecklin, *The Ku Klux Klan*, 1924.

democracy by the dissenting tradition, the one represented by the strict sect type such as the Baptists, the other by the mystical individualistic type of piety of the Quakers. Tolerance in the first case is formal and institutional, being based upon legal guarantees of absolute equality among all religious groups; tolerance in the case of the Quakers is, in theory at least, spiritual in that the group assumes no power to coerce the individual in matters purely religious. The latter form of tolerance is the more modern and places the greater strain upon a social order or a group who seek to realize it. The slow loss of influence by the Quakers during the eighteenth century and the remarkable spread of the dissenting-revivalistic denominations has had the effect of emphasizing the more restricted form of tolerance. Tolerance in American life is essentially institutional and legal rather than spiritual and moral.

Legal tolerance is the direct outgrowth of the triumph of separatism which is entirely negative and was sought by the sects in the interest of spiritual autonomy. Legal tolerance in the sense of assuring complete equality before the law for all sects merely follows out the logical implications of separatism. Legal tolerance, however, being merely negative, does not assure genuine tolerance which is a much subtler notion than mere equality before the law. True tolerance, in fact, cannot be enforced by law. It is psychological and spiritual and arises in advanced societies. Men find it necessary to adjust themselves to each other on delicate matters, as in religious beliefs, where it is impossible to lay down hard and fast laws. Tolerance in this higher sense presupposes education, insight, and a measure of mature social wisdom. It is in many ways the supreme test of a civilized society.

In the days of their weakness the dissenting-revivalistic groups were interested primarily in legal tolerance. With the complete separation of church and state and the attainment of their goal, legal tolerance, these churches lost their spirit of dissent and ceased to champion tolerance. Dissent and tolerance were preached primarily as a means through which to secure the spiritual autonomy that would make it possible to cultivate a particular type of piety. In granting this spiritual autonomy the state of course grants the right of men to organize in the interest of religion. Along with the right to organize goes the right to control the beliefs of the members of an organization and, where necessary, to cast out the conscientious objector. Thus we have the curious paradox that legal tolerance may become and has become the sanction for spiritual intolerance. The zeal of the emancipated dissenting-revivalistic churches in the spread of their particular types of piety leads inevitably to acts and policies of spiritual intolerance. They take advantage of legal tolerance to practice spiritual intolerance.

The dissenting-revivalistic churches, thanks to their earlier sectarian background, have no place for spiritual tolerance. Tolerance in the subtler and more spiritual sense is essentially *social*. It is born of a keen sense of the mutual honest divergences of belief among men trying to live together peaceably in society. Its very essence is a spirit of charity and compromise born of a deep insight into the mysteries of the universe and the infinite complexities of human life. The sects at first necessarily encouraged an individualistic view of life. They sought within the group the same unity of belief and rectitude of conduct achieved by the saint. This of course became more and more impractical as the sect grew in numbers. The narrow, intolerant, sectarian piety still stressed by the dissenting-revivalistic churches has thus become a colossal anachronism. It has blinded the eyes of these churches to their duty to cultivate a measure of spiritual tolerance within their own borders. It explains the fact that the real support of spiritual tolerance, and this must be said to their shame, now lies outside the churches in a thoroughly secularized and enlightened public opinion, a fact observable in any heresy trial. We have, then, this anomaly that the most precious phase of freedom and perhaps the severest test of a just society, namely spiritual tolerance, does not depend upon the official forms of religion for its support but upon a secularized irreligious public sentiment.[32]

It is no exaggeration to say that the failure of the powerful and privileged dissenting-revivalistic churches to solve the problem of spiritual tolerance within their own groups or even to appreciate its value has proven a deadly handicap to the spiritual life of the nation. The very loyalty of Americans to traditional legal tolerance has made it possible to capitalize this legal tolerance in the interest of a spiritual intolerance that amazes and amuses our European critics. These great churches have never awakened to a true sense of their responsibilities. The past still grips them. Once adjust the whole vast machinery of a church organization with its cultus, creed, polity, Sabbath schools, and colleges to the task of inculcating and faithfully preserving a stereotyped emotional attitude known as the dissenting-revivalistic piety and the door is closed forever to the cultivation of the spiritual tolerance or the attainment of the ideal of the thirteenth chapter of First Corinthians. Reason with its powers of criticism and science with its regard for the facts are subordinated to the predetermined logical scheme of a pattern of piety, an emotional attitude. If the findings of science threaten this piety, they are damned; if innocent modern amusements compete with this piety, they are banned; if vast systems of secularized education are indifferent to or undermine

[32] Jacks, "The Church and the World," *Hibbert Journal*, Vol. V, pp. 1 f. J. M. Mecklin, *Introduction to Social Ethics*, Chap. 15.

this traditional piety, they are viewed with suspicion and referred to in the pulpits as "godless"; theological watchdogs sniff the air of the classrooms of the theological seminaries and at the first scent of doctrines inimical to this piety the cry is set up and the pack give chase, often resulting in a spectacular theological auto-da-fé; colleges under church control advertise that they give a liberal arts degree the equal of that of any institution of the land plus a "religious atmosphere," but if hapless professors are caught instilling mental attitudes hostile to this sacrosanct piety they are pried loose from their positions by dubious methods often calling for investigation by the American Association of University Professors. The American people have never been able to forego the exquisite pleasure of prostituting their intellects to their feelings. It is so much easier to feel good than to think straight.

The typical form of dissent among the dissenting-revivalistic churches is the heresy trial. But this form of dissent is petty and often marked by a thoroughly unlovely sectarian animosity. In every heresy trial the sect concerned merely advertises its own limitations. For the public a heresy trial is more or less of a tempest in a teapot. The nation is well aware that its religious liberties are guaranteed by forces outside of and independent of the churches. By crushing the dissenter in their own midst the great dissenting-revivalistic churches emphatically demonstrate their incapacity to voice dissent in the larger social sense. If they do not have the tact, the charity, and intelligent leadership adequate to the task of utilizing dissent within their own group, how can they be trusted to guide the spirit of dissent when it affects the life of the nation as a whole? Our great dissenting-revivalistic churches would do well to study the policies of the church of the Middle Ages when it retained and turned back into the great stream of its own life the dissenting spirits, such as Saint Francis or Bernard of Clairvaux, by creating institutional forms through which they might serve the church.

It should now be clear why the attempts of the dissenting-revivalistic churches to solve great social issues such as slavery and prohibition fail to arouse admiration. The record of these churches in the recent unhappy prohibition fiasco is characterized by lack of social wisdom and marred by an unchristian intolerance and bigotry, the baneful effects of which are still with us.[33] Similar instances of thoroughly antisocial intolerance and dangerous obscurantism mark the story of the Fundamentalist movement.[34] Until these churches have rid themselves of their traditional sectarian lack of spiritual elasticity and have proven that they can deal with dissent within their own organizations wisely and sanely, the intelligent public will always distrust them as leaders on comprehensive and delicate social questions demanding for their solution the spirit of wisdom and tolerance. It is not without reason that the American people fear the hand of the church in politics or social reform.

V

The sectarian ethics was designed at first to meet the exigencies of a small and close-knit brotherhood drawn for the most part from the propertyless and disinherited classes. Its moral rubrics were determined by this fact. It stressed meekness, simplicity, thrift, opposition to all forms of luxury. Even in the case of Bishop Asbury, if we may trust his *Journal*, "respectability" was viewed as dangerous to the integrity of the Christian charac-

[33] Odegard, *op. cit.*, pp. 24 f.
[34] Cole, *op. cit.* J. M. Mecklin, *The Survival Value of Christianity*, 1926, Chap. 1.

ter. There was the most intimate and often meddlesome interference in the private affairs of the brethren in the interest of
their spiritual welfare. These ethical traits, which may not have
been without their justification where the sects were small, became highly objectionable in a later and more cultured age
when these same sects had developed into vast churches numbering millions. Here we are to seek the explanation of the intense antipathy of the modern liberals to the policies of dissenting-revivalistic leaders, such as Bishop Cannon in the fight
over prohibition. The puritanical reforming zeal, inherited from
the circumscribed life of the small and struggling sect, when
expanded into a nation-wide program was certain to be felt as
an unwarranted restriction of individual freedom. It aroused
the bitterest antagonism, and that not without justification.
Large sections of the dissenting-revivalistic churches seem never
to have outgrown their primitive sectarian swaddling clothes.

Reference has constantly been made in earlier chapters to
the tendency of the sects to raise the vices of the privileged
classes to the dignity of sins. This tendency we have noted in
Bishop Asbury's reactions to the habits of the privileged and
"respectable" classes.[35] The Baptists of Virginia elevated the
cock-fighting, dram-drinking, card-playing, dancing, horse-
racing, and theater-going of the aristocracy to the rank of sins,
which position they still occupy in large areas of the South and
Southwest where the Baptists prevail.

The introduction of this petty sectarian puritanism into the
life of a people just emerging into national consciousness was
not an unmixed good. In 1737 when Whitefield toured North
Carolina he found "a dancing master in every town." Billiards,
cards, backgammon, and diverse forms of gambling were prevalent. At the horse races all classes gathered from plantation

[35] See his *Journal, passim.*

owner to slave and the bets ranged "from a drink to a plantation." Gaming was doubtless congenial to the rough and venturesome life of the pioneer. In denouncing the excesses of a
pioneer society the backwoods preachers of the dissenting-revivalistic Protestantism, now coming into power, doubtless furthered the moral life of the people. But then as now their
moral crusades lacked social sanity. As early as 1800 strolling
players wandered through the uplands of the Carolinas from
Charleston theaters and young people in the towns and coun-
tryside organized amateur theatrical troupes. Towns such as
Newbern and Raleigh boasted theatrical societies. Here were
the crude beginnings of what might have developed into an art
of the people. But in the early decades of the nineteenth century
the dissenting-revivalistic preachers began to launch their tirades
against the theater. It was damned in the interest of the precious
dissenting-revivalistic piety. Slowly but surely the minds of
the masses were poisoned against this great art. A narrow
sectarian puritanism had begun to dry up the wellsprings of
natural esthetic and human interest and to usher in a deadly
moralism devoid of every touch of beauty or imaginative appeal.[36]

It should be obvious from the foregoing that the cultural
origins of the puritanism of New England and that of the
South and the Southwest are by no means identical. New England puritanism was the result of the habituation of the New
Englanders for the best part of two centuries to the discipline
of a theocratic society modeled after the pattern of the Geneva
of Calvin. Sectarian puritanism had little or nothing to do with
the molding of New England character. The puritanism of

---

[36] These data are taken from an unpublished doctor's thesis by G. G.
Johnson, *Social Conditions in North Carolina, 1800-1860*, Chapel Hill, North
Carolina, 1927.

the South and Southwest and to a large extent of the Middle West is sectarian, due to the dominance in these regions of the dissenting-revivalistic type of Protestantism. A critical comparison of these two types of puritanism would doubtless bring out many interesting differences. The New England puritanism, in spite of its many forbidding qualities, is inclined to be social and idealistic in its outlook. New England puritanism inspired the Anti-Saloon League, the abolition movement, and later Comstockery. The puritanism of the South is little concerned over great social issues but occupies itself with the violations of a petty sectarian ethics, such as Sabbath breaking, dancing, card playing, dram-drinking, or theater-going. The puritanism of New England felt the impact of centers of culture and a growing industrial and urban life. The puritanism of the South always suffered from the handicaps of an unprogressive agrarian culture, semi-pioneer in character and cursed by slavery. The South today is more puritan than New England and its puritanism is measured by the prevalence of the dissenting-revivalistic Protestantism.

The time has come when every thoughtful student of social ethics must ask himself the question whether the type of character encouraged by the dissenting-revivalistic Protestantism is any longer adequate to the ethical demands of modern society. Character is shaped by prevailing ways of life. Deeply imbedded in the pattern of the communal psychology of an age or a society lie certain fundamental attitudes that find rationalization in the form of an ideology. The scope and authority of a given ideology depend upon the extent of the way of life in which it is embodied rather than upon its logical consistency or scientific truth. Today many conflicting ideologies are finding expression in the Adullam's Cave of modern American society. There is the ideology of democracy with its em-

phasis of freedom and equality, the supremacy of public sentiment, the inherent goodness of human nature and the right of
all to happiness and a just share of this world's goods; there is
the ideology of science with its appeal to fact and experiment,
its strict subordination of emotion to reason, its deterministic
and naturalistic outlook on life; there is, finally, the ideology
of business with its selfish hedonistic philosophy of profits, its
radical laissez-faire individualism, its worship of material
wealth, its pecuniary measure of values, and its short-sighted
and complete surrender to a materialistic this-worldly view of
life. Opposed to these is the ideology of dissenting-revivalistic
Protestantism with its notion of sin, its emphasis of the depravity of human nature, the insistence that only a small part
of the human race is entitled to happiness and that in another
world, that disasters are visitations of divine wrath upon men
for their sins, that the human intellect cannot be trusted to
solve the ultimate problems of life, that the good life is not the
rational life but the pious life, and that the real goal and
meaning of life is to be found in an existence beyond the grave.

The clash in the field of morals between the ideologies of
democracy and science and the ideology of the dissenting-
revivalistic Protestantism is most evident. The dissenting-revivalistic idea of sin, reflected in our vindictive penal codes with
their utter lack of a sense of social responsibility for the criminal, is diametrically opposed to the idea of democracy that men
are not inherently sinful and that we are all "members one of
another" and hence responsible for each other's shortcomings.
Race prejudice, social habits inherited from slavery and recon-
struction, together with other factors, are doubtless concerned
in that most vindictive and dangerously antisocial form of punishment, namely lynching. It is hardly a mere historical coin-
cidence, however, that lynching has been most prevalent in

those regions where dissenting-revivalistic Protestantism with its vindictive individualistic attitude towards the sinner has been long dominant. The contention of dissenting-revivalistic piety that disasters which overtake individuals and nations are visitations of divine wrath in punishment for sin is rejected by science as superstitious and is condemned by the teaching of modern democracy that all men are entitled to their share of happiness and protection from misfortune so far as that is possible. The doctrines of revivalistic Protestantism that the human heart is depraved and that the highest type of character can only be purchased through a vicarious atonement is rejected both by science and democracy as psychologically absurd and immoral.

Strange as it may sound, there are many similarities between the ideology of the dissenting-revivalistic Protestantism and that of big business. Both are the outgrowths of a pioneer society and show the lineaments of a common parentage. The laissez-faire individualism of business finds its counterpart in the narrow individualism of sectarian piety. The captain of big business can afford to pay the popular revivalist to concentrate the attention of the workers upon the salvation of their individual souls in heaven, for any attempt at the salvation of society might lead to unpleasant economic complications. The orthodox doctrine that the ills of men are brought upon them largely by the hand of God for their sins falls in easily with the doctrine of traditional economics that economic ills, such as unemployment and wage-reductions, are the result of the working of nonmoral and inexorable economic laws. In view of this common cultural background it is not at all surprising to find that during the great steel strike of 1919 in Pittsburgh, where the dissenting-revivalistic type of Protestantism is deeply entrenched, not a note of protest on behalf of the workers was raised by the rich and influential churches. It was left for an obscure Slavic Catholic priest to appeal to the teachings of Jesus on behalf of the economically and socially disinherited in this stronghold of American industrialism.[37]

VI

Perhaps the most important and yet the most intangible of all the various elements entering into the legacy of dissent is a pervasive mental atmosphere which, for lack of a more exact term, we shall call primitivism. Christianity was primarily a religion of the disinherited. Its appeal has always been not to the wealthy or powerful or learned but to the poor in purse and spirit who bring to the consideration of the ultimate problems of life the simple openmindedness of the child. The world of the child as well as that of simple and disinherited groups such as the early Quakers is an oversimplified world. The child and the Quaker, by virtue of this very oversimplification of life, are often in the position to grasp elemental truths and to state them with convincing power and appealing charm. But the naïve primitive realism of the child and the Quaker has the defects of its qualities. It naïvely projects into the world of men and things the immediate convincing verities of the inner series of reality. It tends to discredit the intellect. It prefers a simple and sincere but utterly unsophisticated goodness of soul to a type of character won through wide experience of the world and a critical weighing of that experience. The primary source of this primitivism for the sects was the Bible, to which they went directly for all truth and which they revered as the savage does his fetich.

It is of course a familiar fact that there is in the sacred

[37] W. Z. Foster, *The Great Steel Strike*, pp. 177 f.

records, to which the sects are ever appealing, a naïve primitive realism which is the secret of the perennial appeal and the indescribable beauty of the gospel narratives. There is every reason to believe that the sacraments of Baptism and the Lord's Supper were not thought of by the primitive Christians as symbolic rites in which the symbolic elements and the divine factors symbolized were differentiated. The baptismal rite *was* an actual experience of the Holy Spirit; the eucharist *was* an actual partaking of the living Christ.[38] The sects felt and absorbed this primitive realism. It was particularly in evidence in the element of the supernatural in the gospels. The author of John's Gospel did not distinguish in his narrative of the raising of Lazarus between the poetic fictions of his pious imagination and the actual historic realities. Dreams, voices, visions might be and often were considered to be direct communications from the deity.

This atmosphere of primitive realism was taken over uncritically by the sects. It appears in the experiences of the early Quakers who found in the New Testament ample justification for the guidance of their "Inner Light." It is constantly in evidence in the biographies of the early dissenting-revivalistic preachers, such as Cartwright, James, Abbott, and Garrettson. If even the brilliant Edwards looked upon the violent physical experiences of those converted under his preaching as evidences of the supernatural, what are we to think of far less critical minds? This naïve primitive supernaturalism has become deeply ingrained in the habits and beliefs of Americans born and reared under the influence of the dissenting-revivalistic piety. It constitutes the deadliest handicap of American Protestantism in its strenuous efforts to adjust itself to a society that bases its values upon democracy and looks to science for intellectual guidance.

[38] Alfred Loisy, *The Gospel and the Church*, 1904, p. 232.

It is this fact that renders the history of the Fundamentalist movement of such importance for the understanding of American culture. Fundamentalism insists that if this naïve primitive supernaturalism be rejected it means the death of the dissenting-revivalistic type of piety and the utter collapse of traditional historical Christianity.[39]

What has given singular vitality and longevity to this primitivism ingrained in the dissenting-revivalistic type of Protestantism is undoubtedly the persistence of the frontier in American life down to the closing decades of the nineteenth century. The primitive traits of the dissenting-revivalistic piety, such as its naïve supernaturalism, its crass emotionalism, its lay preaching, its anti-intellectualism, its deeply implanted antagonism to the "respectable" and cultured classes, its crude psychology of sin, and its ferociously harsh Hebraistic ethics, cropped out in the Great Awakening. It failed to conquer the older, more cultured New England society and found its most fertile soil in the frontier. Its typical manifestation is found in the tremendous emotional upheavals of the backwoods revivals.[40] During the long period of growth, when trapper and explorer gave place to the early pioneer, the lone settler's cabin to the village and the town which, in turn, fell under the predacious rule of speculator and captain of big business, the revivalistic frontierized Protestantism remained supreme. We still have it with us in a sort of *fin de siècle* form as represented by Reverend W. A. Sunday. But in a world now aware of the insidious dangers growing out of a rampant capitalism, disillusioned and broken-hearted by the cataclysm of a world war and made cynical by racketeers and gangsters in high places as well as low, we have suddenly grown old and world-weary so

[39] J. G. Machen, *Christianity and Liberalism*, 1923.
[40] F. M. Davenport, *Primitive Traits in Religious Revivals*, 1905.

that the crude backwoods revivals seem pitifully inadequate to the alleviation of our spiritual ills.

The limits of this chapter do not permit of an adequate evaluation of the rôle of revivalistic primitivism in American culture. Starbuck in his epoch-making study of conversion suggests that conversion, occurring as it does around the period of adolescence, shortens the process of passing from the narrow world of the immature child to the wider horizon of the adolescent. That is to say, it speeds up the process by which the individual lives himself into his cultural heritage.[41] In a well-ordered society, family, school, church, and other means of social discipline assure to the immature individual an orderly and sane development of his spiritual nature without the stress and strain of conversion. In an immature pioneer society, however, in which we find that revivalism has flourished, it may very well be that conversion or the sudden and cataclysmic method of attaining the higher levels of personality was unavoidable, perhaps justifiable. In a mature and disciplined society conversion tends to become an anachronism. It was rejected by the more intensive and cultured society of New England and achieved its greatest triumphs on the frontier or in those remote communities where semi-pioneer conditions still prevailed. Revivalism has appealed primarily to primitive-minded disinherited groups such as the colliers of the English coal-fields, the suppressed classes of colonial Massachusetts and Virginia, and the backwoodsmen of a pioneer democracy.

It is of course quite possible for the cultural determinist to affirm that the revivalism of our "frontierized" American Protestantism with its speedy but cataclysmic induction of the immature individual into the higher values of life through con-

[41] Edwin D. Starbuck, *The Psychology of Religion*, 1904, pp. 224, 262. See also W. James, *Varieties of Religious Experience*, 1902, pp. 189 f.

version, its crude but morally vigorous Hebraistic ethics, its repudiation of the trappings of learning as inadequate to the demands of the frontier, and its capitalization of a harsh medieval theology in the interest both of religion and morals, was very largely predetermined by the conditions of a pioneer society. For the Edwardean revivalism was born on the frontier, marched with the frontier-line as it moved swiftly westward and steadily lost its hold upon the affections of the American people as they threw off the stereotypes of a pioneer society. Subtly and silently a revolution has taken place within the great churches of dissenting-revivalistic background manifested in the fact that now no longer, as was the case a century ago, is the primitive Christian tradition naïvely identified with the gospel preached by Edwards, Whitefield, Peter Cartwright, and the backwoods revivalists.

The complacent historical determinist can hardly deny, however, that along with this alleged cultural fitness of the revivalistic type of piety went very real handicaps. It perpetuated an outworn and impossible supernaturalism that still lingers to plague the religious leader and educator, making possible in backward communities foolish anti-evolution laws; it imposed upon a people devoid of any other means of satisfying the religious impulse a gross and crudely anthropomorphic other-worldliness with its heaven of winged angels sitting on cloud-banks, harps in hand, satirized in Mark Twain's *Captain Stormfield*; it seared the minds of the youth with the notion of a vindictive and cruel god gloating over a smoking hell in which we have the engaging spectacle of sinners roasting throughout all eternity; it popularized a hectic and flabby emotionalism which has made the heart rather than the .head the test of the truth of our highest loyalties, not only in religion and morals but also in politics; it ingrained into the moral sanctions of the average middle class American a childish ethics which placed dancing and card-playing on the same level with theft and lying and thus dulled the moral sensibilities of the masses of our citizens to the appreciation of the subtle ethical issues in our modern capitalistic social order; it foisted upon the nation as a whole a reforming sectarian spirit which made it possible to place the vast machinery of the churches and the religious loyalties of millions of Americans at the mercy of "bone dry" enforcement fanatics with their Quixotic scheme for legislating a nation of one hundred and twenty millions into teetotalers by means of a constitutional amendment; finally, when the outworn theology and the crude Hebraistic ethics were invalidated, as was inevitable with the spread of enlightenment, they left large masses of our fellow-Americans within the dissenting churches moral and spiritual bankrupts. These churches present today the tragic spectacle of great organizations with wealth and numbers and responsibilities but without great living traditions, without any real insight into modern life and no great consuming enthusiasms. They are like vast temples whose walls are embellished with the pious votive offerings of other days but on whose altars the fires of a pristine spiritual fervor have burned to ashes.

Index

Index